Voices of African Immigrants in Kentucky

Voices of African Immigrants in Kentucky

Migration, Identity, and Transnationality

Francis Musoni, Iddah Otieno, Angene Wilson, and Jack Wilson

UNIVERSITY PRESS OF KENTUCKY

Scholarly publisher for the Commonwealth,
serving Bellarmine University, Berea College, Centre
College of Kentucky, Eastern Kentucky University,
The Filson Historical Society, Georgetown College,
Kentucky Historical Society, Kentucky State University,
Morehead State University, Murray State University,
Northern Kentucky University, Transylvania University,
University of Kentucky, University of Louisville,
and Western Kentucky University.

Editorial and Sales Offices: The University Press of Kentucky
663 South Limestone Street, Lexington, Kentucky 40508-4008
www.kentuckypress.com

Library of Congress Cataloging-in-Publication Data

Names: Musoni, Francis, author. | Otieno, Iddah Aoko, author. | Wilson, Angene Hopkins, author. | Wilson, Jack (Jack A.), author.
Title: Voices of African immigrants in Kentucky : migration, identity, and transnationality / Francis Musoni, Iddah Otieno, Angene Wilson, and Jack Wilson.
Description: Lexington, Kentucky : University Press of Kentucky, [2019] | Series: Kentucky remembered: an oral history series | Includes bibliographical references and index.
Identifiers: LCCN 2019023529 | ISBN 9780813178608 (hardcover) | ISBN 9780813178615 (pdf) | ISBN 9780813178622 (epub)
Subjects: LCSH: Africans--Kentucky--Interviews. |Immigrants—Kentucky—Interviews. | Refugees—Kentucky—Interviews. |Africa—Emigration and immigration. | Kentucky—Emigration and immigration. | Transnationalism. | Oral history—Kentucky.
Classification: LCC F460.A24 M87 2019 | DDC 305.8009769—dc23

LC record available at https://lccn.loc.gov/2019023529

This book is printed on acid-free paper meeting
the requirements of the American National Standard
for Permanence in Paper for Printed Library Materials.

Manufactured in the United States of America

Member of the Association
of University Presses

Contents

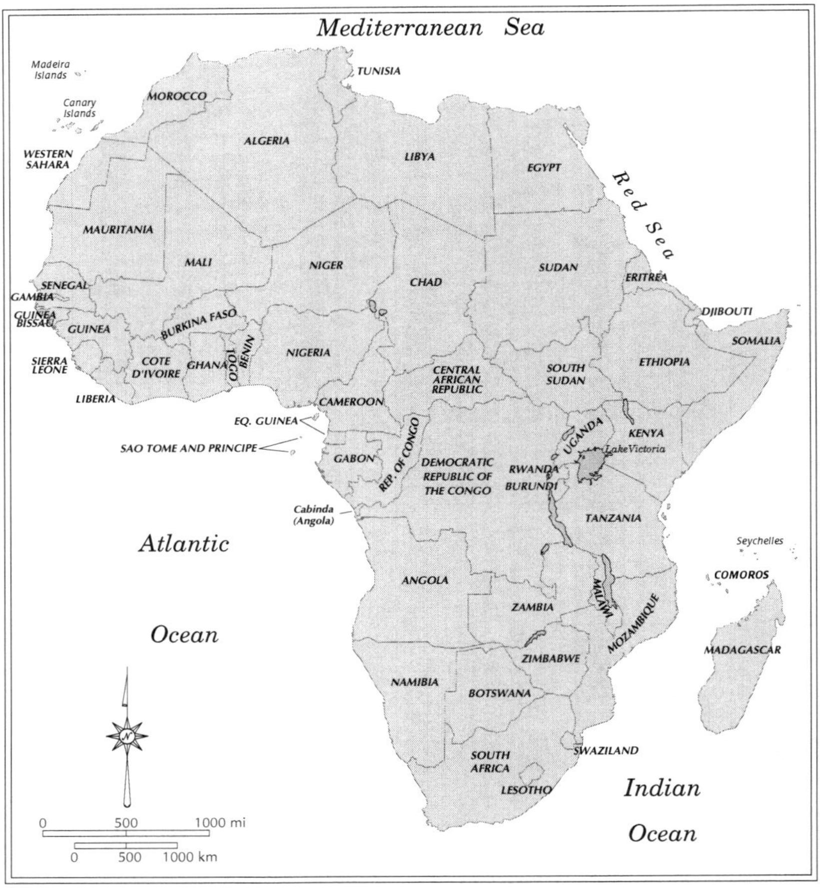

Map of Africa. (Map provided by Dick Gilbreath.)

Nations Represented by African Immigrants in This Book

Algeria
Botswana
Burundi
Cameroon
Côte d'Ivoire/Ivory Coast
Democratic Republic of Congo
Egypt
Ethiopia
The Gambia
Ghana
Guinea
Kenya
Liberia
Libya
Malawi
Namibia
Nigeria
Republic of Congo
Rwanda
Senegal
Sierra Leone
Somalia
South Africa
South Sudan
Tanzania
Uganda
Zambia
Zimbabwe

Series Foreword

Kentucky is an international leader in the field of oral history. Over the past several decades, thousands of its citizens have been interviewed. While oral history is, of course, only one type of source material, the very personal nature of recollection often discloses hidden aspects of history. Oral sources thus provide a vital thread in the rich fabric that is Kentucky history. Kentucky Remembered: An Oral History Series brings into print the most important of the state's collections of its citizens' oral history, with each volume focusing on a particular subject.

Voices of African Immigrants in Kentucky: Migration, Identity, and Transnationality is the thirteenth volume in the Kentucky Remembered series, which explores ways in which oral history connects the individual story to tradition and to the historical record. Nationally, there is an increasing number of oral history projects documenting the immigrant experience in the United States. This book draws from forty-seven oral history interviews conducted by the authors over a five-year period. As the subtitle suggests, this is not simply an account of migration stories but an exploration of the intersection of the complex issues of culture, community, and identity. *Voices of African Immigrants in Kentucky: Migration, Identity, and Transnationality* weaves together compelling narratives that demonstrate the sometimes far-reaching impact of oral history and archives in the exploration and interpretation of immigrant experiences.

Douglas A. Boyd
Terry L. Birdwhistell
James C. Klotter

Preface

> It is a human being that counts. I call gold, it does not answer. I call cloth, it does not answer. It is a human being that counts.
>
> —Akan/Ghanaian proverb

Voices of African Immigrants in Kentucky: Migration, Identity, and Transnationality is about particular human beings, individuals for whom the continent of Africa was their original home. Based for the most part on almost fifty oral history interviews with first-generation African immigrants in Kentucky, this book tells stories of their African pasts, of migration to the United States, specifically Kentucky, of dealing with struggles and successes, and of becoming individuals who are often simultaneously American citizens, "borderlanders," and transnationals who connect and contribute to two continents. One aim is not only to tap the richness of the oral history interviews in the book's narrative but also to suggest at certain points with endnotes marked with an asterisk that the reader listen to the actual voices themselves, easily available online in the African Immigrants in the Bluegrass Oral History Project at the University of Kentucky's Louie B. Nunn Center for Oral History. The majority of the participants in this oral history project were born and raised in Africa during the past seven decades, a period of history that coincides with independence in most African nations, which had almost all endured more than eighty years of colonial rule following European partition in the 1880s. Their interviews illustrate the political, cultural, and religious diversity in postcolonial Africa, the opportunities and challenges of life on the continent, the connections between modern Africa and the US, and the opportunities and challenges facing differently positioned immigrants in the US as well as the various forms and levels of contact that Kentucky-based immigrants have with the continent. Although the oral history interviews focus on individual experiences, there are common themes, events, and processes that migrants from the same country or region, regardless of differences in social, economic, or political standing, commonly refer to when they talk about why and how they made decisions to temporarily or permanently move to other countries or regions of the world. Being aware of developments that push migrants out of their countries of origin will help illuminate immigrants' accounts and experiences of relocation. Similarly, an appreciation of historical and contemporary events unfolding in the host country, in this case the United States, will increase understanding of immigrants' experiences.

Voices of African Immigrants in Kentucky is not a book *about* African immigrants as the strange "others" in Kentucky. We know stereotypes about Africa and Africans have been and remain rampant, even instilled, whether in talking about a continent of "developing countries" or using abhorrent ape references for black people.[1] Instead, this book takes seriously eminent African historian Ali Mazrui's rhetorical question to African and American educators at a 1994 conference in Nairobi, Kenya, when he asked whether Africa and Africans could be taught about in schools as "subject instead of object, as active rather than passive, as cause rather than effect, as center rather than periphery, as maker of history rather than incidental to history."[2] In this book African immigrants in Kentucky are active subjects: the cause, the center, and the makers of history. They speak. They have agency. They do the absorbing rather than being absorbed.[3] We believe oral histories of African immigrants are uniquely able to be vehicles for changing perspectives, for "moving the centre," to quote the title of one of many books by Kenyan Ngugi wa Thiong'o, who chose to write his 2006 novel *Wizard of the Crow* first in Kikuyu and then to translate it into English.[4] The renowned Nigerian author Chinua Achebe titled one of his many essays "Africa Is People."[5] We agree, and we invite the reader to meet some fascinating people, African immigrants in Kentucky, and to learn about their stories both before they came to the United States and after they arrived. They are now part of America as well as often still quite connected to their countries of origin.

Although this is a book based on oral histories, it is not organized as one individual story after another.[6] Rather, we are looking at the complicated process of becoming someone who could be called a transnational person, with illustrative examples from the interviews. We realize that our interviews, plus knowledge of and interaction with many other African immigrants, only scratch the surface of the stories of the almost 22,300 Africa-born individuals in Kentucky, not to mention the more than 2 million in other parts of the United States.[7] This book also does not offer a comprehensive look at immigrants in the entire state of Kentucky. Contacts for the oral history interviews began with individuals Angene and Jack Wilson knew over many years and radiated out from

Lexington and central Kentucky, where the four authors live. As well, not all the stories in this book take place in Kentucky. African immigrants have migrated within the United States as well as on the African continent. In a number of cases, the people we interviewed came to somewhere other than Kentucky first, including Alabama, Colorado, Florida, Georgia, Idaho, Indiana, Maine, Maryland, Michigan, Ohio, and Texas. Occasionally they began their American lives in New York City or in Washington, DC, and quickly understood that those cities were expensive places to live. Immigrants came to Kentucky for education, for jobs, because they were assigned to Lexington or Louisville as a refugee, or because they learned about these smaller Kentucky cities from family or friends. In several cases, the immigrants interviewed have moved recently to other states, and one to the Bahamas. Twenty-three of the continent's fifty-five countries are represented by interviewees: Algeria, Burundi, Cameroon, Côte d'Ivoire, Democratic Republic of Congo (called Zaire from 1971 to 1997 during Mobutu's rule), Ethiopia, The Gambia, Ghana, Guinea, Kenya, Liberia, Libya, Malawi, Nigeria, Republic of Congo, Rwanda, Senegal, Sierra Leone, Somalia, South Africa, South Sudan, Zambia, and Zimbabwe. Examples of migration within Africa include an interviewee who was actually Rwandan but born and brought up in Uganda before returning to Rwanda, and Ghanaians who taught in Nigeria and Botswana. Those who arrived in the United States as refugees came from camps in Tanzania and Namibia, as well as from Ethiopia, Kenya, and Uganda, having fled other countries such as Democratic Republic of Congo, Somalia, and South Sudan. One immigrant came to the United States from Cameroon via first Germany and then France, and another from Democratic Republic of Congo via Russia.

Although the African immigrant oral histories are the heart of this book, we have drawn examples and inspiration from people beyond those interviewed, including African immigrants we know very well and some we have met only briefly. In several cases African immigrants in Kentucky have written a book or chapters in a book. In other cases local magazines and newspapers have written about African immigrants. Kentucky Refugee Ministries in Lexington has hosted a program that interviews refugees on the community radio station. We reference other books that are collections of the stories of individual immigrants to Kentucky from a variety of countries, including Aimee Zaring's *Flavors from Home: Refugees in Kentucky Share Their Stories and Comfort Foods*, which features five African immigrants out of twenty-three stories, and Keith Gilbertson's *Slowly Is the Journey: Stories from Bluegrass*

Community and Technical College ESL Students, which includes twenty African immigrants. As well as interviewing him, we read Sudanese "Lost Boy" Jacob Thon Guot's autobiography, *The Lost Is Found.* Fiction is another important source of understanding the complexities of the immigrant experience. Specifically referenced fiction includes Chimamanda Ngozi Adichie's *Americanah* and *The Thing around Your Neck,* NoViolet Bulawayo's *We Need New Names,* Yaa Gyasi's *Homegoing,* Imbolo Mbue's *Behold the Dreamers,* and Taiye Selasi's *Ghana Must Go.* What may be called African immigrant fiction, although it is really more than that, is especially rich and these books are only a few of those available.[8]

All four authors of this book are themselves immigrants to Kentucky—"from away," as Kentuckians sometimes say of individuals who were not born in the state. Francis Musoni came most recently, in 2011 from Zimbabwe via Atlanta, Georgia, where he studied and lived beginning in 2006. Iddah Otieno arrived in 1996 directly from Kenya for her post-graduate studies at Eastern Kentucky University and the University of Kentucky. Angene and Jack Wilson moved to Kentucky in 1975 for Angene's job as a professor at the University of Kentucky after growing up in northern Ohio and southern Michigan and later living in Liberia, Sierra Leone, Fiji, and just outside Washington, DC. All four authors are quoted in the book, especially Professors Musoni and Otieno, whose interviews are part of the African Immigrants in the Bluegrass Oral History Project, but also occasionally Angene and Jack Wilson, who are "Africans" only in more than fifty-five years of experience, friendship, and passion. We are all referred to in the third person.

Angene and Jack, who were Peace Corps volunteer teachers in Liberia in the early 1960s, continued the friendships they made there and developed many others with Africans over almost six decades. The two initiated this oral history project in fall 2013 and completed the interviewing and indexing of the interviews in fall 2017. However, when they decided to write a book, they knew that they wanted to do that part of the project with African coauthors. As a specialist in migration, Francis Musoni of the University of Kentucky's history department was an obvious collaborator. With over twenty years of teaching and parental experience in central Kentucky, Iddah Otieno, English professor at Bluegrass Community and Technical College, was also an obvious collaborator in writing a book that would also consider African immigrants as families.

In 2015 *A Nation of Nations: A Great American Immigration Story,* written by National Public Radio correspondent Tom Gjelten, was published to coincide with the anniversary of the 1965 amendments to the Immigration and Nationality Act. The "nation of nations" title comes from the Walt Whitman's preface to *Leaves of Grass.* Gjelten's last chapter, "Americanization," begins with a citizenship ceremony and ends by quoting Walter Lippmann's words in 1914: "The great social adventure of America is no longer the conquest of the wilderness but the absorption of fifty different peoples. Immigration . . . may swamp us; it may, if we seize the opportunity, mean the impregnation of our national life with a new brilliancy."[9]

Our book includes echoes of Gjelten's positive story of opportunity and possibilities in Fairfax County, northern Virginia, and agrees with Lippmann about the opportunity for a more brilliant national life. However, we have focused on the second half of the twentieth century and the early twenty-first century, featuring the voices of immigrants from one continent—Africa—who came to and mostly stayed in small cities in a more insular and mostly white southern state, Kentucky. As one interviewed African immigrant said about his prior knowledge of the United States, "You don't hear about Kentucky." Yet they are here. Instead of assimilation or even integration into a multicultural society as the inevitable and preferred goal for immigrants, we consider the possibility of transnationality across borders, with increasing numbers of people living in the borderlands of the world, occasionally having feet firmly planted in multiple nations or at least with strong connectivity to two nations, and yet integrated into the migrated-to society of Kentucky and the United States on an equal basis.

Introduction

A Historical and Theoretical Overview

> Until the lion tells his side of the story, the tale of the hunt will always glorify the hunter.
>
> —Zimbabwean proverb

Following the end of the transatlantic slave trade and the subsequent colonization of the African continent by European powers in the late nineteenth century, the patterns of mobility within and out of Africa changed significantly. As the colonists invested in labor-intensive industries such as mining, agriculture, and construction, Africa witnessed the rise of a migrant labor system, which took workers from areas of low demand to those of higher demand. In most cases this involved the movement of people from rural areas to the mining towns, farms, or industrial cities within the same country. However, it was also common for people to cross colonial boundaries in search of higher-paying jobs in countries such as South Africa, Kenya, Libya, and Côte d'Ivoire, which emerged as major destinations for migrant workers in their respective regions. As such, internal (mostly rural to urban) and regional (intra-Africa) migrations became the dominant forms of mobility during the colonial period.[1] While out-of-Africa migration was very limited, the continent welcomed significant numbers of immigrants from Europe, Asia, and other regions of the world. When colonial rule ended in the 1960s in most African countries, various aspects of the colonially produced patterns of mobility within and out of the continent changed, while some of the migratory trends remained the same.

For the majority of people in Africa—especially those in former settler colonies such as Algeria, Kenya, and Zimbabwe—the attainment of political independence resulted in the removal of bottleneck policies that were meant to reduce competition against the colonists. As opportunities for educational advancement and employment in the cities became available, several countries witnessed rapid increases in urbanization among the formerly colonized populations. This was a result of the expansion of both the rural to urban migration and the intra-Africa (cross-border) migration.[2] While economic factors (such as employment and trade) played a big role in driving the bulk of the population movements in postcolonial Africa (as they had done during the colonial period), some of the cross-border movements involved people with kinship ties in more than one country. Located mostly in Africa's border regions, such people often moved from one country to another in order to stay in touch with their relatives or to attend social events such as weddings, funerals, and others.[3] Therefore their movements, though technically international in nature, had very little to do with the economies of the countries they traveled to and/or from.

As far as migration out of Africa is concerned, the scale was heavily tilted toward the former colonial powers, which maintained varying degrees of influence in their former colonies. In fact, some European powers offered financial scholarships for African students who were trained to be leaders in government departments, the financial sector, and other strategic areas in the former colonies. For example, the British government established the Commonwealth Scholarships and other financial assistance programs that took thousands of African students to London, Cambridge, Oxford, and other centers of British education. Also, African diplomats and employees of multinational corporations found new homes in the former colonial capitals, while thousands of white people of European ancestry abandoned their African countries at the onset of independence. Many of them went to various destinations in Europe, while others relocated to Australia and New Zealand. For example, in 1975 the world witnessed an out-of-Africa exodus of white people from the former Portuguese colonies of Mozambique, Angola, and Cape Verde. Similar developments happened when Zimbabwe regained independence from Britain in 1980. At least one hundred thousand white Rhodesians left the country, fearing retribution from Robert Mugabe, the leader of a former guerrilla movement who was elected prime minister.[4]

The United States had limited migratory connections with colonial Africa. It is estimated that there were about 35,000 Africa-born immigrants in the entire country in 1960. However, this number increased more than 100 percent within a decade, to about 80,000 in 1970. Within another decade, the number of African immigrants in the US more than doubled again, reaching an estimated total of 200,000 in 1980. By 1990, the number had grown to about 364,000 before leaping to around 881,000 in the year 2000. Thereafter, the number increased to 1,607,000 in 2010, and then grew to about 2,293,000 by 2017.[5]

A number of push and pull factors contributed to the increase in African immigrants in the US over the past fifty years, but three probably had the largest effects. The first was the 1970s oil crisis, which caused a global economic recession of a magnitude that had not been witnessed since the Great Depression. The effects of the 1970s recession were probably felt the most in African countries that had recently attained independence from colonial rule and were faced with millions of impoverished citizens. In less than a decade, for most countries, the independence euphoria, fueled by the removal of barriers in education, urban employment, and other spheres of life, was replaced by hopelessness. The same crisis also negatively affected Europe's major economies, leading to the closing up of opportunities that had been available for migrants from the former colonies in Africa. This scenario forced some African people to consider the United States as a possible place to relocate, though the latter's economy was also affected by the recession.[6]

The second factor was the adoption of the US Refugee Act in 1980. The timing of this policy shift was quite convenient for the victims of numerous civil wars and border conflicts as well as military dictatorships that plagued the African continent in the early years of independence. Although it is incorrect to place the blame entirely on external players, the US and Soviet Union's meddling in African affairs (as part of the Cold War) fueled the majority of conflicts that displaced millions of Africans prior to the 1990s. In cases such as Sudan, the civil war began immediately after the country attained independence in 1956 and raged on for decades before the partition of the country into two separate nations in 2011. Along the way, more than 2 million Sudanese who lost their homes and sources of livelihoods fled to different parts of the world. The US, in particular, accommodated thousands of Sudanese refugees, including almost four thousand young men (and women) who came to be known as the "Lost Boys of Sudan."[7]

Thousands of people were also forced to leave Nigeria following the outbreak of the Biafran War of 1967–1970, while many others were forced out of Ethiopia after the overthrow of Emperor Haile Selassie in 1974. With the outbreak of the Somali civil war, the Horn of Africa churned out more refugees over the course of the 1980s and 1990s. The same happened in the former Portuguese colonies of Angola and Mozambique, as well as in countries such as Democratic Republic of the Congo, Rwanda, and Burundi, which plunged into civil wars soon after the end of colonial rule. Although Liberia remained an independent country, it also endured coups and a devastating civil war, as did neighboring Sierra Leone, and thousands of their citizens came to the United States. Overall, the Refugee Processing Center estimates that about 386,586 Africa-born refugees were admitted into the United States between 1980 and 2018.[8]

The third factor was the launch of the US Diversity Visa Lottery (also known as the Green Card Lottery) program, under the auspices of the Immigration Act of 1990. While the primary targets of this program were Irish immigrants, thousands of immigrants from the African continent have also utilized that visa to enter into United States and obtain permanent residency status. As estimates in the *Yearbook of Immigration Statistics* show, a total of 371,722 Africa-born individuals were admitted into the United States under the diversity visa category between 1996 and 2017.[9] Some people who were initially admitted into the country on various kinds of temporary visas (such as student visas) have also been able to obtain permanent residency status through the Diversity Visa Lottery. However, the future of this program has become uncertain owing to President's Trump's public criticism and calls for replacing it with a "merit-based" visa program.

Numbers, Opportunities, and Challenges

Official estimates indicate that the state of Kentucky had just about 1,000 Africa-born immigrants in 1990. By 2017, the number of African immigrants in Kentucky had risen to about 22,300. Compared to larger states such as Texas, which had almost 252,000 Africa-born immigrants in 2017, Kentucky does not appear to be a popular destination for African immigrants. However, the reality is more complicated. The population of Africa-born Kentuckians increased by almost 2,000 percent between 1990 and 2017. During the same period, the number of American-born residents of Kentucky increased by 17.4 percent from 3,651,177 to about 4,285,000, while the total number of foreign-born people in the US increased by about 125 percent.[10] What this means is that between 1990 and 2017, the population of Africa-born immigrants in Kentucky increased at more than sixteen times the growth rate of the entire immigrant population in the country.

As was the case in other parts of America, the number of African immigrants in Kentucky grew in the context of global developments of the 1970s, 1980s, and 1990s, as discussed above. However, other factors specific to Kentucky helped to make this state a major destination for Africa-born foreigners, especially during the past three decades. Of major significance was the role of refugee resettlement agencies. Kentucky is fourteenth in the nation in the number of refugee arrivals compared to other states, and when all eligible populations served by the Office of Refugee Resettlement are included (for instance, Cubans) Kentucky ranks ninth in the nation. Kentucky began receiving its first group of refugees after the end of the Vietnam War in 1975, and since 1994 over 28,500 refugees have been resettled in Kentucky through three agencies with five offices across the state. Refugees are initially resettled in Louisville, Kentucky's largest city, with a population at about 615,000; in Lexington, Kentucky's second largest city, at about 322,000; in Bowling Green, at about 68,000; and in Owensboro, at almost 60,000. Many other refugees have moved to Kentucky after first coming to other states.

The Kentucky Office for Refugees, a department of Catholic Charities in Louisville, is designated by the federal Office of Refugee Resettlement as the nonprofit that administers the state refugee resettlement program and serves as the State Refugee Coordinator's office. It oversees the design, implementation, and coordination of refugee services in the state. Grant funds are awarded to partners across the state for a variety of programs and services such as employment services and career development, English-language training, refugee health assessments and health promotion, and services to older refugees. Although most programs are targeted toward refugees who have been in the US less than one year, refugees retain eligibility for five years from date of arrival.

The Kentucky Refugee Resettlement Agencies include Kentucky Refugee Ministries in Louisville and Lexington, Catholic Charities Migration and Refugee Services in Louisville, and the International Center of Kentucky in Bowling Green and Owensboro. Available statistics indicate that between January 1990 and December 2016, these agencies helped to resettle around 9,889 refugees from

African countries. The majority of these people came from Somalia (about 4,445) and the Democratic Republic of the Congo (about 2,955), two countries that have endured devastating civil wars since the 1960s.[11]

More specifically and recently, in the five years from 2013 through 2017, refugee arrivals in Kentucky from Democratic Republic of Congo led the way with 2,568. Numbers for other African nations include Somalia, 2,128; Sudan, 164; Burundi, 100; Eritrea, 80; Rwanda, 68; and Ethiopia, 67. By city, immigrants from African nations during the years 2013–2017 total Somalia, 1,694; Democratic Republic of Congo, 1,236; Sudan, 164; Eritrea, 80; Burundi, 73; Ethiopia, 64; Rwanda, 33 (Louisville); Democratic Republic of Congo, 870; and Rwanda, 23 (Lexington); Democratic Republic of Congo, 462; Somalia, 434; Burundi, 47; and Rwanda, 12 (Bowling Green); Somalia, 110; and Ethiopia, 5 (Owensboro).[12]

In addition to refugee resettlement agencies, other nongovernmental and state-sponsored programs have helped to make Kentucky a welcoming destination for refugees and other categories of immigrants from Africa. For example, in 2015, the Lexington Fayette County Urban Government established the Lexington Center for Global Engagement (Global Lex), which provides space for various kinds of engagements between the immigrant population and the local people in the city. There is also the Migrant Network Coalition, which brings together local government representatives and leaders of NGOs to engage with issues facing immigrants in Lexington. Schools offer English as a second language (ESL), now often called English-language learning (ELL), and Jefferson County Public Schools (Louisville) has a Newcomer Academy and Bowling Green a special international school. In Lexington the Bluegrass Community Health Center, the Nest Center for Women, Children, and Families, the Share Clinic, Mission Lexington, the Salvation Army Clinic, Crossroads Counseling, the Migrant Head Start, and others provide free or low-cost physical and mental health services to refugees and other immigrant groups. Those who need legal assistance when dealing with issues such as processing applications for permanent residency, naturalization applications, family reunifications, marriage adjustments, and fiancé visas can receive low-cost legal and immigration services from attorneys at the Brandeis Human Rights Advocacy Program (University of Louisville), the Maxwell Street Legal Clinic in Lexington, and the University of Kentucky Legal Clinic.

However, notwithstanding the opportunities that African immigrants enjoy in Kentucky, there are a number of challenges. To begin with, those who left the African continent as free or voluntary migrants had to first obtain a visa of one type or another before they could settle in Kentucky. For those who came on student visas, this meant having to spend some years in school in order to stay in legal standing before they could move on to the work visa, usually an H-1B for the majority of professions or an R-1 for religious workers. For most immigrants, obtaining a work visa is an important milestone because it allows them the opportunity not only to earn income but to apply for permanent residency, which is usually the last step before a foreign-born person can become a naturalized citizen. Although some people move faster than others, the journey to citizenship usually takes several years. For most people who came to the US as PhD students, this means spending about six years on a student visa, about two on a work visa, and then five as a permanent resident, which is a total of thirteen years before they could become eligible to apply for citizenship. Although there are various avenues through which some people can reduce the amount of time between arrival in the US and obtaining citizenship (such as marrying a US citizen), going through such a long process does present obstacles to total integration in American society.

While obtaining permanent residency status under the Diversity Visa Lottery shortens the journey to citizenship, that does not take away the other challenges that come with being an immigrant in this country. Although the lottery targets people with at least a high school diploma and a minimum of two years' work experience, most immigrants need retraining in order to be employed in positions similar to those they held in their countries of origin. Many people have to take whatever job they can find in order to survive while they go through retraining. That can be frustrating, especially for those who leave their country not anticipating having to go through a process of academic and professional assimilation.

For Africans and all other immigrants who enter the United States as refugees, the process is slightly different. While the refugee resettlement process bears the hallmarks of a welcoming environment, it also presents several challenges for integration. The number one challenge that most African refugees face is language. Unlike voluntary migrants, who might learn to read, write, and speak in English before traveling to the United States, many people who come as refugees do not have time and resources to learn English before they arrive or after arrival because they are expected to get a job within ninety days of resettlement. Among the people interviewed for this project, language was a major setback for refugees arriving from Francophone Africa, especially the Democratic Republic of the Congo. Although there are several organizations that offer free ESL/ELL resources to refugees beyond the first ninety days, some people find it difficult to utilize such facilities due to grueling work schedules. While school-aged children might receive extended support with the English language, depending on the county where they are located, their non-English-speaking parents usually struggle to obtain similar educational assistance. People who fled to English-speaking countries such as Uganda, Kenya, Tanzania, South Africa, Zimbabwe, and Namibia before moving to the United States indicated that having a certain degree of English proficiency helped in their transition to life in Kentucky.

As is the case with other categories of immigrants, refugees are often forced to seek retraining after resettlement. While this might sound like an obvious expectation for someone whose education was affected by war or life in a refugee camp, it can be frustrating for people who worked in highly skilled and/or professional occupations before fleeing their countries. The frustration is even greater for people coming from non-English speaking countries. Consider, for example, a former chief magistrate in the Democratic Republic of Congo who had to take up a job in a warehouse because he could not get the same kind of job in Kentucky. Despite the fact that most refugees will become naturalized citizens after only five years in the United States, experiences such as these shape the way they view themselves in relation to the host community.[13]

Another challenge is that since the September 11, 2001, bombing of the World Trade Center in New York by individuals linked to al-Qaeda—a Middle Eastern terrorist organization—there has been a reconfiguration of the migration-security nexus in the United States and other parts of the world.[14] With the emergence of other like-minded organizations such as Boko Haram, Al-Shabaab, and the Islamic State (IS), the fear of terrorism revealed itself in ways that at times fueled the rise in anti-Muslim sentiments. Unfortunately, events such as the 2013 Boston Marathon bombing, the 2015 Paris and San Bernardino attacks, and the 2016 Brussels airport bombing by individuals suspected to be Muslims with ties to terrorist organizations have fueled what is now generally referred to as Islamophobia in the United States and the Western world in general.

Toward the end of 2015, the state of Kentucky became the focus of a nationwide debate over the intersection of migration and security following the resurfacing of a 2009 report indicating that two Iraqi refugees in Bowling Green were convicted of a "terrorist conspiracy."[15] This prompted prominent Kentucky politicians, such as Governor Matt Bevin and Senator Rand Paul, to call for the suspension of the nation's refugee resettlement program until security concerns with respect to Iraqi and Syrian refugees were addressed. In doing so, Bevin joined thirty-one other US governors who argued that the US refugee vetting process was not tight enough to detect potential terrorists posing as refugees.[16] Also, despite being actively involved in the case of one Congolese refugee who recently resettled in Lexington, Congressman Andy Barr—one of Kentucky's representatives in the US Congress—strongly criticized the nation's refugee resettlement program, arguing that helping others should not undermine America's security. Not surprisingly, Congressman Barr voted for the failed HR 4038 (American SAFE Act), which would have paused the program until the US security apparatus could guarantee that refugees from Syria and Iraq are not a security threat.[17]

It was in this context that leaders of Americans First also raised concerns about the resettlement of refugees in Lexington, Kentucky. On November 19, 2015, Dan Rose and Ron Vissing, respectively the president and vice president of Americans First, published a statement in which they called for a moratorium on all immigration to the United States. Citing the Paris attacks, the case of two Iraqis in Bowling Green, and the 2013 Boston Marathon bombing, they argued that the country's security screening was grossly ineffective. They also alleged that the refugee resettlement agencies misdirect taxpayer dollars by paying large salaries to their executives.[18] Americans First repeated the same sentiments in a statement published on August 27, 2016, which dismissed the refugee resettlement program as a "self-perpetuating global enterprise" that does not serve the interest of American citizens. The same statement alleged that many of the refugee claims are fraudulent and that refugees are bringing in communicable diseases (like TB), increased crime rates, and religious, political, and sexual intolerance.[19]

Furthermore, Americans First argued that refugees resettled in Lexington were not *assimilating* into the host communities and that the public school system for Fayette County was losing a lot of money paying for translators and other assistance services to refugee children. Much of the organization's opposition stems from what it perceives to be a lack of transparency in the manner in which Kentucky Refugee Ministries and other refugee agencies use government funds. Americans First was adamant that refugee resettlement does not help American citizens, charging that enrolling refugees in government-funded programs puts pressure on those programs. The organization argued that the use of taxpayer dollars to fund refugee services was unfair to American citizens who may be opposed to the resettlement program. Its members were also concerned that the statistics and identities of resettled refugees were not made public and readily accessible to taxpayers who were unwittingly supporting these programs, further arguing that no refugees should be considered self-sufficient as long as they continued to access government-assisted services.[20] Although these complaints were not directed specifically toward African immigrants, they probably made some of them feel anxious. With the election of Donald Trump as president in 2016, the anxiety among Africans in Kentucky and other immigrant groups in the state and across the country grew deeper.

As immigrants navigate the complexities of everyday life in the US, they carve out survival strategies that reflect an awareness of their status as foreigners. The first general strategy for most of them is to avoid deportation by always striving to remain in legal standing. For some, this may mean being professional or perennial students. They keep studying—moving from one program to another—until they find a job that will help them to change their legal status, or until they obtain their green card through the lottery system. Some immigrants contract "fake" marriages with American citizens and get divorced after obtaining permanent residency permits, which almost guarantees them a clear path to citizenship. In some cases, people simply go off the radar—staying beyond the validity of their visas and then playing hide and seek with immigration law enforcement authorities. Quite often, people in such positions obtain Social Security cards through fraudulent means so they can access certain kinds of services they cannot live without. The list of informal—and sometimes illegal—strategies that immigrants, particularly those undocumented, deploy in order to survive in the US is endless.

For African immigrants in Kentucky, community belonging stood out as the most visible strategy they use to deal with challenges they face as foreigners. In this respect, immigrants from the same African country tend to come together and form community groups with varying degrees of organization. Examples of these groups include Kenyans in Kentucky (KIK), Ndi-Igbo na Kentucky (Igbo People in Kentucky), the Ghanaian Association, and the Congolese Association. Although there are differences from one case to another, these groups usually organize social events and gatherings that bring their members together. When members marry or celebrate birthdays, anniversaries, and other events, these groups become a source of support. They also help to mobilize support for their members in hard times, such as when someone gets arrested or loses a relative through death. Furthermore, groups like these afford their members a platform to share information relating to various kinds of issues that affect immigrant communities. In addition to groups based on immigrants' countries of origin, there are several faith-based African groups, which meet at various churches in Kentucky. For example, St. Luke United Methodist in Lexington offers a Swahili service every Sunday at noon and a multicultural service at 3 p.m. Although these services are open to any interested persons, their leaders and members are predominantly first- and second-generation African immigrants.

Transnationality among Africans in Kentucky

Beginning in the 1970s, scholars have questioned the usability of assimilation as a conceptual tool for understanding immigrants' experiences in host countries by pointing out immigrants' tendencies to keep ties with their countries of origin. As debate on this issue raged on, *transnationalism* became a widely used term in migration studies. As Nina Schiller and others pointed out, scholars viewed "transnational migration" as the more appropriate concept to describe "a pattern of migration in which persons, although they move across international borders, settle and establish ongoing social relations in a new state, maintain ongoing social connections with the polity from which they originated."[21] Put simply, transnationalism refers to a phenomenon whereby people move to a different physical location but remain connected (culturally and otherwise) with their place of origin. In Stephen Castles's words, transnational communities are "groups based in two or more countries that engage in recurrent, enduring and significant cross-border activities, which may be economic, political, social or cultural in character."[22] The idea is that, regardless of how long they may reside in another location or country, migrants never really completely move out of their places of origin.

In this book, we deploy this concept of transnational migration or transnationalism, which Thomas Faist and others also refer to as transnationality, to try to unpack and better understand various aspects of Africa-born Kentuckians' ties with the African continent.[23] Although some of the people we interviewed regularly visited Africa, the term "oscillating migration," which is commonly used by sociologists and anthropologists studying the migrant labor system in Africa, does not accurately describe their connections with their countries of origin.[24] Instead, referring to them as "transnational migrants" helps us to better explore the reasons why Kentucky-based African immigrants keep ties with the African continent. As the accounts in this book show, a multiplicity of factors causes migrants to continually feel like foreigners or strangers in the host country. These can be language barriers or visa conditions that restrict immigrants from engaging in certain activities. Nativist and xenophobic tendencies among the host population can also make immigrants feel as if they belong not where they live but where they came from. In this context, immigrants will strive to maintain ties with their countries of origin in the hope that they will have somewhere to run to if the host environment becomes unwelcoming. For most African immigrants in Kentucky, leading transnational lives is, therefore, a strategy to keep their options open.[25] It is some form of social insurance.

One common trait our interviewees share is that they all have active connections with the African continent. However, as is the case with other immigrant groups in the US and other regions of the world, the forms and levels of connection that African immigrants in Kentucky keep with Africa differ from one individual (or family) to another. Perhaps the most basic way in which African immigrants can remain connected with the continent is through regular visits to their countries of origin. While people who are in the US on various kinds of visas can use this option at any given time, refugees or asylum seekers may return to their countries of origin only after five years of residing in the country. At that stage, most of them will have become American citizens. Given that it can be difficult to visit Africa—due to visa restrictions, financial costs, and other limitations—migrants often find other ways of connecting with the continent.

In most cases, immigrants maintain ties with the African continent through communicating with family members and relatives they left behind. In the 1970s through the 1990s most migrants relied on letters to communicate with loved ones in their home countries. Today they have a wider choice of communication methods. With the advent of the internet and other technological advancements that the world has witnessed over the past two decades, US-based immigrants are now able to communicate with people in Africa using email, Skype, Facebook, Face Time, WhatsApp, Imo, and other methods. Some of these applications come with video facilities, making it possible for immigrants to see their relatives in real time. In addition to maintaining social ties, immigrants also send money, clothes, and other material things to support family members and relatives in Africa. Some also sustain connections by preserving practices and traditions that remind them of Africa, such as their native languages, clothing, and methods of food processing. Some families hold naming ceremonies for newborn babies, while others take their children through rites of passage, such as the circumcision of boys before their twelfth birthday and the so-called coming-of-age ceremonies when they turn eighteen.

Beyond the family level, some immigrants actively participate in national and community development projects in their countries of origin. While some people do this through participating in diaspora voting processes where available, others raise funds for community-based projects and even for political parties of their choices in Africa. Others, especially those who left Africa as refugees, may utilize their being in the US to urge American policy makers to impose sanctions or adopt certain positions in response to developments in Africa. Although some people engage in these kinds of activities as individuals, most immigrants do political work as members of advocacy organizations such as Friends of the Congo. Among other objectives, Friends of the Congo advocates for peace, justice, and democracy in the Democratic Republic of the Congo, where two decades of civil war have claimed millions of lives.[26] By providing details of African immigrants' involvement transnationally, the interviewed immigrants quoted in this book show how technological advances in transport and communication (in the US and Africa) over the past five decades have shaped migrants' experiences of foreignness and advances toward integration in Kentucky. They also reveal how developments in different African countries have shaped the ways in which immigrants relate with their countries of origin as well as their hosts in Kentucky.

In addition to exploring the notion of transnationality, this book makes other significant contributions to a growing literature on African immigrants in the United States.[27] By narrating the stories of their voluntary or forced relocation from different parts of the African continent and (re)settling in Kentucky, our interviewees provide readers with firsthand experiences of the push and pull factors that have increased the numbers of African immigrants in the United States since the 1970s. It is also our hope that the stories in this book will begin to deepen readers' understandings of parenting and family structures among African immigrants in the United States.[28]

Furthermore, these African immigrant stories complicate what "home," "belonging," and "where we're from" mean in a state where these concepts seem particularly important. Former Kentucky governor Happy Chandler is quoted as saying, "I never met a Kentuckian who wasn't either thinking about going home or actually going home."[29] Writers acclaimed beyond Kentucky, such as bell hooks, Bobbie Ann Mason, Frank X Walker, and Wendell Berry, have offered their wisdom about the meaning of "home." In *Belonging: A Culture of Place,* bell hooks first notes what she "did not like about life in my home state (the cruel racist exploitation and oppression that continued from slavery into the present day, the disenfranchisement of poor and/or hillbilly people, the relentless assault on nature)." Then later in the same paragraph she writes, "Yet returning to my home state [after] all the years that I was living away, I found there essential remnants of a culture of belonging, a sense of the meaning and vitality of geographical place."[30]

We wonder how "at home" African immigrants feel in this place and the "culture of belonging." Affrilachian poet Frank X Walker does assert in several early poems the place of black people in Kentucky: "some of the bluegrass is black."[31] In her memoir *Clear Springs,* Bobbie Ann Mason, writing about her family farm in western Kentucky, says: "We've been free to roam, because we've always known where home is."[32] Recent African immigrants have definitely roamed far from their original homes, often for opportunity but sometimes not by choice, driven out of their own countries by war and violence. Finally, according to Wendell Berry, "If you don't know where you're from, you'll have a hard time saying where you're going."[33] This book posits that more than one home, more than one "where you're from" is possible, and that connections to two continents may influence where you're going.

The Structure and Organization of the Book

Chronology is a major part of how this book is organized, and readers can follow individuals from their original home country experiences to the opportunity of coming to the United States, then through their struggles and successes to the contributions they make both in the US and back in their home countries. However, the chapters are also thematic so readers may choose instead to read out of order. Quotations from the interviewees are not cited in the endnotes, but, as mentioned in the preface, readers are alerted at various points to access the oral history interviews online.

In chapter 1, "Origins: Where We Are From," our interviewees tell stories of their childhood, schooling, family backgrounds and careers before they moved to the United States. Through such stories, the chapter not only explores the sociopolitical and economic factors that pushed Africans out of their countries of birth, but also provides information about third countries where some of these people lived before they settled in Kentucky. While many of the "growing-up stories" are happy ones—in countries such as Algeria, Ghana, Kenya, and Malawi—war and forced displacements are major factors in other stories, especially those told by immigrants from Burundi, Côte d'Ivoire, Liberia, and Democratic Republic of the Congo.

Stories in chapter 2, "Opportunity: Why and How We Came," explore various opportunities in the US in general and Kentucky in particular that attracted African migrants. In so doing, the chapter examines a variety of "coming to America stories," such as of a student, a diversity visa holder, a refugee, for economic opportunity, and for love. In some of the stories, young people from Ghana or Kenya or Malawi or Nigeria or Sierra Leone or Zimbabwe arrive in the US in pursuit of higher education—usually at graduate level—and stay for good jobs. In others, the power of love brings migrants to the US to join spouses who were either American citizens or earlier migrants. The chapter also tells stories of diversity visa holders and of refugees brought by the US Refugee Resettlement program through organizations such as Kentucky Refugee Ministries.

Chapter 3, "Struggles and Successes," relates African immigrants' experiences in Kentucky, describing how they utilized the opportunities they found in this state as well as the challenges with which they struggled. Not only does the chapter tell stories of immigrants negotiating new cultural norms, language difficulties, different work ethics and discrimination, it also relates some positive experiences and reasons for appreciating and staying in the United States. Immigrants from Francophone African countries narrate stories of having to learn English after already knowing at least one other European language and often two or three African languages. They describe beginning by working at jobs below their skill levels while adjusting to life in the US. Quite often, this means a change in male and female roles for immigrants, which can be a struggle for some African men. Interviewees also talk about being surprised at the ignorance of Americans about Africa and dealing with racism.

In chapter 4, "Connecting and Contributing to Two Continents," the book examines the connections that African immigrants have with their countries of origin and with Africa more generally, as well as the contributions they make to Kentucky. Immigrants' narratives reveal various methods and tools they used to communicate with people in Africa, including internet-based applications such as Skype, Instagram, WhatsApp, Facebook, and others. Stories in this chapter also show that in addition to sending money to their loved ones, many immigrants contribute to community projects in their home countries, and several are involved at a national level. The contributions to Kentucky include especially starting businesses and educating Americans. In presenting these interview excerpts, the chapter shows how the concept of transnationality plays out among African immigrants in Kentucky, and concludes with a poem by interviewee and coauthor Iddah Otieno.

Chapter 5, "Family and Identity in the United States," engages first with the importance of family for African immigrants and deals with parenting issues, followed by reports on a small number of interviews with young people, the next generation. Then African immigrants' perceptions of identity and belonging in Kentucky and in the United States more generally are examined through answers from interviewed African immigrants to a question about how they identify themselves after they have lived in Kentucky for some time. The chapter reveals the complications of and differences in self-identification. African immigrants respond in different ways when asked, “Where are you from?” For instance, one interviewee—originally from The Gambia—explained that when he speaks to the media, he often says that he is from Louisville, Kentucky. However, another immigrant who has lived in Kentucky for more than a decade always says she is from South Africa. A poem by an interviewed immigrant from Ethiopia who has lived in the US for forty-five years, more than thirty in Frankfort, Kentucky, expresses the ambiguity of being an immigrant. Finally, this chapter updates the story begun in chapter 1 of an immigrant from Malawi and his family.

Chapter 6, “Transnationality in the Present and Future,” concludes the book by describing the current US immigration situation and debates in 2017–2018 and the authors’ case for considering the concept of transnationality.

1

Origins

Where We Are From

> Sankofa. It is not taboo to fetch what is at risk of being left behind. Or return for it.
>
> —Akan Adinkra symbol, Ghana

The question "Where are you from?" is one that immigrants born in African countries are often asked. Their accents and usually dark skins mark them as different, and the geographic and historical ignorance of many Americans about Africa means Liberia may be confused with Libya or Zimbabwe may still be remembered as Rhodesia. A huge continent more than three times the size of the United States and home to fifty-five nation-states, Africa is often compressed into one entity—even one country—by Americans, as by most Westerners. To Americans, proud Congolese or Kenyans or Nigerians often become generic Africans when they arrive in the United States.[1]

However, understanding the stories of African immigrants requires a deeper understanding of where they are from—their home countries and sometimes their ethnicity—in a broader sense than is conveyed by the continent name or even the country name. This chapter shares stories of some lives lived before coming to Kentucky in one or sometimes more of the nations on the continent or in several cases European countries such as Belgium, England, Germany, and Russia. The individual stories have similarities, but they cannot necessarily be labeled as typical because even immigrants from the same country have often had very different experiences.

The chapter begins with a Malawian immigrant's reflections about nation-building, family, education, and jobs in Malawi. Those topics are then illustrated under separate sections with examples from other oral history interviews. Additional sections are "Living in Other Than Home Countries," "We Are Africans, Too" (which includes immigrants from Algeria, Libya, and South Africa, as well as an Indian who grew up in Zambia and an American born in South Africa), and finally "From Countries at War." Readers should note the role of independence from colonial rule for some interviewees, the influence of parents and other family members, the importance accorded education, the often exhibited individual characteristics of ambition and of resilience, and for a number of immigrants the tragedy of involvement in violence and war and sometimes long years in refugee camps. The chapter then comes back to longer individual stories, like the Malawian immigrant story but focusing on four Liberian immigrants' experiences before coming to the United States. As in the opening story, these experiences include nation, family, education, and jobs, but with the added impact of war. The woman in the first of the Liberian stories did not come to the US to stay until she was almost sixty so her story at home in Liberia is a fairly long one. To some extent, Liberian immigrants are unique because of Liberia's long ties to the United States, including specifically Kentucky, going back to the nation's founding. Under the final section, "'Where I'm From,'" is the question "What would African immigrants say if they wrote poems like the 'Where I'm From' poem that George Ella Lyon, one of Kentucky's recent poet laureates, has made famous?"

An Immigrant's Reflections on Nation-Building, Family, Education, and Jobs in Malawi

In the fall of 2016 Robert Chirwa, a US citizen and professor of computer science at Bluegrass Community and Technical College in Lexington, Kentucky, wrote a blog in memory of his father, who died in Malawi at the age of seventy-nine on June 16, 2016.[2] Survived by his wife of fifty-eight years, ten children (ages thirty-seven to fifty-seven) and their spouses, twenty-one grandchildren, and seven siblings, his father is described by Robert as independence fighter, teacher, and parent from whom he learned much that impacted his own life. Where he is from made Robert who he is today, and his father was a central influence. The story of his father also helps explain both Robert's national heritage and his own drive and ambition.

Robert's father, Martin Nkhalambayausi Chirwa, was born in 1936 in a village in central Malawi when the country was under British colonial rule and known as Nyasaland and when the Church of Central Africa Presbyterian, which began in the 1870s with Scottish missionaries, including David Livingstone, was prominent. Martin was ten years old when a teacher was sent by the Church of Central Africa Presbyterian to open a school and a church five miles from his village. First he begged the teacher to let him start school in violation of the age requirement rules—he was too old. Then he secretly earned the 6 pence (about a nickel) needed for school fees and enrolled in school at age twelve. Martin's father was angry because he counted on Martin to herd the cattle, but Martin persuaded him that he could do both school and cattle herding. So every school day Martin rode his bicycle five miles from his village, Fulatira, to school at Chikhutu and, after riding back home, he took care of the cattle. When the inspector of schools came from the church headquarters at Nkhoma, the teacher told the older students to sit hunched over in the back of the classroom to look younger and thus avoid detection. The teacher, Grayson Chikanda, later became Martin's father-in-law and treated him as a son.

After fifth grade, Martin went to a boarding school about thirty miles from his home and in 1957 he passed the eighth-grade government exam. In 1958, at age twenty-two, he started a job as a post office clerk in the southern Malawi city of Blantyre. That same year Dr. Hastings Kamuzu Banda returned from his medical practice, first in England and then in Ghana, to lead the independence movement. Martin quickly became active politically as chair of the local branch of the Nyasaland African Congress, organizing meetings, selling membership cards, and recruiting door to door. The congress strategy of "noncooperation" and protests prompted the British-sponsored colonial government to declare a state of emergency, and in March 1959 the government decided to crush the movement, arresting Banda and other leaders. Martin was arrested on a false charge of embezzling post office money, and although the judge found him innocent, he lost his job.

With his wife Elinart and his first-born son, Martin went back to where he had grown up and continued fighting for independence with what was now called the Malawi Congress Party (MCP). For the next three years, he rode his bicycle around northern Lilongwe selling MCP cards and recruiting members. As Robert wrote in his blog: "People like Martin Chirwa are the reason independence came to Malawi. Their names will not be written in books. They will just be mentioned as 'people' who demanded independence. They will not be studied in history classes. But they are the unsung heroes of the country of Malawi."

By 1962 it was clear independence would be won, and Martin's father-in-law advised him to go to teacher training college in order to pursue a stable career. He graduated from William Murray Teacher Training College in 1964 before setting out on his new career just as Malawi gained its independence. Even as he taught and then became a headmaster, Martin continued to study, by 1968 passing his British

Martin Nkhalambayausi Chirwa, independence activist, teacher, photographer, journalist, and father of Robert Chirwa, in 1982. (Photo courtesy of Robert Chirwa.)

O-level and A-level exams by correspondence through the Cambridge International Program. Martin then became the founder of three new primary schools and several Malawi Correspondence Centers, which expanded opportunities for secondary education.

Born in 1960, Robert now becomes part of the story. After living with his father's in-laws, his Chikanda grandparents, until he was six, Robert joined his family at Matunduluzi, where his father had been sent to start a junior primary school. The first classrooms had grass walls and roofs. Robert's older brother was the only student in the fifth grade, and Robert was one of three students in third grade. Robert remembered hunting grasshoppers, gathering fruit, making toy cars from wires, and taking part in harvesting. He recalled "the natural taste of a ripe *dzaye, psyipsya,* and *matowo* fruit. There was a sense of joy and satisfaction whenever we, the children, caught a big grasshopper after chasing it a long distance. Edification of the character of the children was enhanced by the community of children that ate together, played together, teased each other, and competed in games created by themselves."

In 1970 Robert's father asked to transfer to a more established school and so became headmaster at Nathenje Primary School in a busy trading town. He rented land to grow maize (corn) for the basic Malawian food of *nzima,* but with eight children by now, Martin added taking photographs of people in villages around Nathenje as another source of income. Robert explained that "living at Nathenje opened my eyes to Malawians of diverse backgrounds." He recalled teachers who were Presbyterians, Anglicans, Catholics, Muslims, Traditionalists (followers of indigenous African religions), atheists; male and female; married and single; young, middle aged, and old. "And at least to a child they all seemed to get along." Most shops were owned by Malawians of Asian origin, and Robert also had classmates who were Muslim. The school had very good football (soccer) and netball teams, and good track and field athletes. Robert remembered watching his father, at thirty-plus playing football and that inspired him to play.

In the blog honoring his father, Robert also wrote about what he learned from his mother.

> My mother always told me that I had to do chores ordinarily done by girls because it was my fault that the first four children were boys. I would accompany her to fetch water from the well. She would give me a basket of corn to take to the maize mill to have it ground into flour. She would leave the children with me to baby sit. She tasked me with doing laundry and washing dishes. Perhaps the best moments were in the evening when she was cooking. She would call me to hold the kerosene lamp in the kitchen so she could see the inside of the pot as she was cooking. As she was cooking, she used to tell folklore tales that held my attention so I did not want the cooking to end. She sang some of the best songs as part of the tales. During those moments, she used to give advice about girls, treating others well, being respectful to elders, and being honest.

Robert also did typical boy chores such as building fences and helping with the farming.

In 1974 Robert's father was transferred to yet another primary school. That same year Robert's older brother was selected to go to secondary school, and the next year Robert was likewise chosen, both because of their success on the national exam. In 1978 Martin took early retirement from teaching and became the editor of the monthly magazine *Kuunika* for the Nkhoma Synod in central Malawi of the Church of Central Africa Presbyterian. His father kept on learning, receiving a scholarship to study for a diploma in journalism at Daystar University in Kenya and attending a course in Lusaka, Zambia. At the same time, Robert and his older brother were selected to go to the University of Malawi.

Analyzing the role his father Martin played in raising his children, especially in offering timely advice, Robert wrote: "He was an astute observer of what was going on in each child's life. If he noticed that one of the children was straying off the required progress, he could call that child to his office. I remember him telling me during one of those sessions to avoid politics." By the late 1970s and early 1980s President Banda was becoming more dictatorial and many people were being arrested, and Robert's father also saw the dishonesty and manipulation in politics. Martin told his son about his own struggles and financial situation and advised him to focus on his own goals and not to imitate others. Robert also remembered that his father considered it his responsibility to give each child a first driving lesson. When Robert was twenty-six years old and working in Lilongwe, the political capital of Malawi, his father took him in his used 1970s Nissan out in an open field and began teaching him how to drive.

Robert summarized the lessons from his father as: the journey is multigenerational; balance between country and family is important; and never give up. All Martin's children attained a middle-class lifestyle. Martin contributed to his country by working for independence and establishing new schools in the development of Malawi, and he also made certain his own children were educated. Finally, Martin was a lifetime learner, teacher, and father. Son Robert emulated him.

In his oral history interview Robert talked about his own secondary school and college experience. At that time in Malawi, high school was a privilege for which students paid fees, and only about ten thousand students out of some one hundred thousand who completed primary school were chosen by a government system to get a place in secondary school. In 1979 Robert was selected as one of six students to attend a

Catholic secondary boarding school. Because he was top in his class, he was encouraged to go to the University of Malawi, a privilege that was accorded perhaps one thousand students in any given year in the entire country. In 1983 Robert became the first holder of a university degree on both the Chirwa and Chikanda sides of his family, graduating with a degree in mathematics, which included the new subject of computer science.

After graduation Robert's computer skills enabled him to get a job as a computer programmer at the Commercial Bank in Blantyre. In Malawian and African tradition, he contributed some of his income to his siblings' school fees and took in younger brothers to live with him. In 1986 he went to work for the Central Bank of Malawi as a computer programmer and systems analyst, with the express intention of finding a scholarship abroad for further studies. Other people were going to Britain to study, but "I always wanted something different," Robert explained. When he saw an advertisement for a scholarship sponsored by the Africa-America Institute in the United States, he applied and was one of two chosen out of fifty applicants. With this scholarship he completed a master's in computer science at the University of Kentucky in December 1990 and returned to work for the Central Bank in Malawi until 1993, when he began teaching computer science at the University of Malawi in Zomba.

Like his father, Robert wanted to continue to learn. And like many Americans in the early and mid-twentieth century who had ambitions to leave the farm and small town, Robert was representative of many African young people. He said, "A boy in a village has ambition to leave."

The Influence of National History

More than twenty countries are represented in the oral history interviews on which this book is primarily based, and to some extent their national histories influenced the lives of the immigrants who came to Kentucky. Except for Ethiopia and Liberia, which retained their independence, colonization and independence unfolded differently across the continent, depending on factors such as which European nation was the colonizer (Belgium, Britain, France, Germany, Italy, or Portugal), how attractive a colony was to European settlers (Algeria, Kenya, Rhodesia, South Africa), how long there had been commercial ties previous to official colonization (nations in West Africa), and whether the colonizer was simply bent on conscious conquest (Belgium in Congo).[3] So, for instance, Robert Chirwa's story is different from Francis Musoni's experience in nearby Zimbabwe, where majority-rule independence did not come until 1980, and Marie-Antoinette Sossou's experience across the continent in Ghana, which began the trend toward reclaiming independence for much of Sub-Saharan Africa in 1957.

Like Robert Chirwa's father, Francis Musoni's father was trained as a teacher, in his case by the Dutch Reformed Church of Rhodesia, now the Reformed Church in Zimbabwe. However, after he married more than one wife (he eventually had five wives, including one inherited from a brother), the church would not let him teach, so he became a builder. Musoni's father was head of their village in the Buhera District and had a delicate role during the struggle for independence, which involved two competing nationalist organizations, the Zimbabwe African People's Union (ZAPU) and the Zimbabwe National Union (ZANU), fighting against white settlers who had declared their own illegal independence from Britain in 1965. His father had to deal with both the government army and taking care of liberation fighters who came to the village. One of Francis's brothers served in the Rhodesian army as a way to get a scholarship for secondary school and another brother was a police officer for the government. Francis, who was four years old at independence in 1980, explained how much difference it made when Rhodesia finally became Zimbabwe under the leadership of Robert Mugabe. The government "had massive programs for education and health across the country after independence. They built so many schools, many health centers, and roads across the country and even made it mandatory that every child had to go to primary school for free."

As in Malawi and in Zimbabwe, the creation of mass political parties was crucial to independence in Ghana. This British colony, known as the Gold Coast, was a leader on the African continent with Kwame Nkrumah's in 1949 formation of the Convention People's Party, which agitated for "Independence Now." Ghana achieved independence and fame in 1957 as the first newly independent country in Sub-Saharan Africa, and Nkrumah became prime minister and later president. Free primary education was a national priority. Thus in the early 1960s primary school was a possibility for Marie-Antoinette Sossou even though her mother was a trader of smoked fish and other foodstuff and her father was an immigrant to Ghana from the nearby country of Benin who had no formal education and worked his whole life as a hospital orderly.

Other interviewees also talked about the difference independence made in many African countries. The year 1960 was a banner one, with seventeen African countries gaining political independence, including fifteen former French colonies, except for Guinea, which unilaterally declared independence in 1958. Perhaps most important was the populous, dynamic, and diverse Nigeria. Asimiyu (Sim) Oyetunji remembered the day of October 1, 1960, well. Besides the ceremony with Queen Elizabeth's sister Margaret coming from England to hand over the reins of government in the federal capital of Lagos, there were ceremonies in the capitals of each of the three regions. Sim was the senior prefect in his secondary school, which took forty students to the regional ceremony in Ibadan. He led their group in marching past the premier of the Western Region, Obafemi Awolowo. "We were so excited, clapping, dancing, holding the flag but not listening to the speeches." Sim said, "Free primary education was the key thing Awolowo put in place. He had a vision for the future."[4]

When Sierra Leone, up the coast from Nigeria and Ghana and also a British colony, achieved independence from Britain in 1961, Rosolu John Bankole Thompson was twenty-five years old and a student at Fourah Bay College outside the capital of Freetown. The college was the oldest in West Africa, founded in 1827. He remembered "a national fervor for emancipation from colonial rule. I shared the strong sentiments that Sierra Leone was a self-governing country looking forward to a time of democratic government consolidated by those positive features that would lead to a prosperous country. Hopefully independence would bring benefits that would ensure a country that would prove itself as a sovereign state within the international community."

Former settler colonies like Kenya and Rhodesia suffered much more violence than Malawi, Ghana, Nigeria, or Sierra Leone in the attempt to regain independence. Kenya's struggle was made famous by the Mau Mau, or the Land and People's Party. Explained Armstrong Cheggeh, "I was born in 1956 at the end of the war. The Africans were fighting the British and it was a very bloody and chaotic time. The British were forced to give us independence. They didn't want to say they lost the war, but the Mau Mau, we called them Freedom Fighters—that is what won us independence. Of course, more Africans died than British." Although the British declared "victory" in 1955, it was not until 1960 that the state of emergency was lifted and not until 1961 that nationalist leader Jomo Kenyatta was released from house arrest. Actual independence finally came to Kenya in 1963. Armstrong was seven. "I still remember the independence songs, getting so excited. We sang and danced. It was a fantastic time. We had been born in colonial times, but now we were going to have an African president, Jomo Kenyatta."[5*]

Algeria in North Africa was another settler state. After its conquest of Algeria in 1879, France settled millions of its people on Algeria's coast, so Algeria's war for independence was especially long and brutal. Zineeddine Hamoudi was born twenty years after independence came in 1962. He explained that although the French left behind their educational system, the language of instruction transitioned back to Arabic. He also learned French and English during his schooling, which included a degree from the University of Science and Technology located in the town of Bab Ezzouar, about fifteen kilometers from the country's capital of Algiers. His father had a bakery. As a child he played a lot of soccer and invented games with neighborhood kids.

Libya, also in North Africa, had a different history. It was seized from the Ottoman Empire by Italy in 1911–1912. Then, during World War II, the Allies ousted the Italians and divided the country between the French and British. Libya became independent in 1951 under King Idris al-Sanusi, who in 1969 was deposed in a bloodless military coup by Muammar Gaddafi.[6] Ibrahim Bakoush was born in Benghazi in Libya in 1957, the fifth of six children. As a young man, he studied business administration and accounting for an associate degree. Ibrahim's father was one of the big merchants in the wholesale and retail furniture business, and all his family is still in Libya.

When Nkongolo Kalala, a leader in the Congolese (Democratic Republic of Congo) community in Lexington, spoke about Congo's history at the Congolese independence day celebration in Lexington in 2016, he reminded the audience of Congo's rich natural resources of forests and diamonds, gold, coltan (used in many electronic devices), and uranium (used during the Manhattan Project to develop the first nuclear bombs), and its cash crops of cotton, rubber, coffee, and tea. He also talked about the country's 8 percent growth rate, according to the World Bank, and about the projection that dams on the Congo River could provide power for the whole continent. He pointed out that 1 million people had been displaced as refugees, including some who had resettled in Lexington, and that more than one thousand people were dying each day because of malnutrition. "The problem," he said, "is governance." The problem during colonization was also governance. "Belgium had no experience with colonizing but it had even less experience with decolonization."[7] In fact, until 1908 The Free State of Congo was the personal property of King Leopold, who had claimed it at the infamous 1884–1885 Berlin Conference, which divided up Africa among the European powers—what has been referred to in textbooks as "the Scramble for Africa." This colonial history was followed by post-independence civil war, then the long years of Mobutu rule from 1965 to

1997, followed by another civil war that drew in Congo's neighbors—what some have called "Africa's world war."

Somalia, on the horn of the African continent, has also produced many refugees. In fact, it is one of five countries (the others are Afghanistan, Myanmar, Syria, and South Sudan) that account for less than 2 percent of the world population but 68 percent of the global refugee population.[8] Ismail Ali was raised near the lower Jubba River, where his family farmed fifty acres and sold produce such as mangoes and pineapples in the city of Kismayo. He completed teacher training college before war began in 1991. Much of his family remains in the huge Dadaab camp in Kenya, but he headed instead to South Africa, where he lived for ten years.[9] "I didn't think the war would still be going on twenty-six years later." Another Somali refugee, Khadar Abdullahi, was also born in Kismayo, but in 1991 at the beginning of the war his parents fled with him, then a small child, to Ethiopia.

The national history of Sudan, which gained independence in 1956 as the largest nation on the continent, influenced Jacob Guot's life because he was a member of the Dinka ethnic group in Sudan's black and Christian south. That south engaged in several long civil wars with the Arab and Muslim north until South Sudan became the newest African country in 2011. Jacob was born in 1980 as the oldest son of a farmer who raised cattle, goats, and sheep. From the age of five Jacob helped take care of livestock, driving the animals to public grazing lands in the morning and sometimes sleeping with the cattle. His dog Marol was his constant companion, helping him keep track of the animals and guard against lions, hyenas, or thieves. At seven years of age Jacob became a "Lost Boy" in the spring of 1987 when North Sudan bombed and destroyed villages in South Sudan. Most of the boys were away from the villages taking care of livestock so they were able to run and hide in the bush, and then they escaped by walking a thousand miles east to Ethiopia. Jacob recalled: "You drank your own urine. You ate leaves. For survival."

THE IMPORTANCE OF FAMILY AND EDUCATION

In Zimbabwe Francis Musoni's father valued education, especially for the boys. All of his eighteen sons completed secondary school and his seventeen daughters finished primary school. Although his father was a village head and would have been considered wealthy, the family still struggled financially. Francis remembers walking seven kilometers from their homestead to primary school, often on an empty stomach and without shoes. When an older brother became a temporary teacher, there was a little more money, and that helped. "When I was accepted at a secondary boarding school, my father went to the Social Welfare Department and got money for fees. I wrote a letter to the Zimbabwe Council of Churches and got a scholarship." Still, life at the secondary school was tough. At the boarding school a small supper was served at 4:00 in the afternoon at the school, followed by study hall until 8:00. At night, as students said, "You and hunger are in the same blanket." Francis and a friend decided not to watch the wealthier students eat their extra food at 8:00 but instead return to study hall. As a result, they graduated at the top of their class. After secondary school Francis went to the University of Zimbabwe, where students received a stipend and he even had enough money to buy a dress for his mother every time he went home. He studied history, moving into the Honors Program, and after graduation and teaching second graders for six months, he returned to the university to get a master's in history.

Growing up in Ghana, Marie-Antoinette Sossou had big dreams. "I was a poster child for girl-child education, for what education can do." Marie-Antoinette went on from primary school to get her middle school leaving certificate, but then her father said she should learn a trade. She had other ideas—she wanted to go to secondary school. "While my friends went to high school, I spent one year in a convent cooking for [Irish Catholic] reverend sisters. I saved that money and heard of a late entrance exam for the Zion AME secondary boarding school and told my dad I was going to go. My uncle confronted my dad and asked him why he didn't send me to high school. My dad said he didn't have the money and my uncle said he would pay. But my dad was a proud man and agreed to pay the first fees and I used my saved money for other needs, like books. I did very well and they gave me a lower rate, which allowed my father to be able to pay the fees."

Also in Ghana but in contrast to Marie-Antoinette's experience as the daughter of a fish seller and hospital orderly, Kwaku Addo had opportunities for education because his father worked for the Anglican school system in Ghana. After completing training college his father became a head teacher and later a principal teacher who inspected schools. He called his eleven children "my soccer team," and was intent on providing them a good education. So when he discovered a very successful experimental primary school in his travels as a school inspector, he sent Kwaku and his brother to live with a teacher at that school for fifth and sixth grades. Kwaku then passed the very important common entrance exam and went on to a secondary boarding school, plus two more years to pass his A-level exams. Admitted to all three Ghanaian universities, he decided to go to the Kumasi School of Science and Technology because he was fascinated by biochemistry.

Essa Bokar Sey's father was an Islamic teacher in The Gambia from 1965 to 1996. For both his parents, standards, values, faith, and education were very important. As a youngster growing up in the village, he knew Peace Corps volunteers, and one of them bought him books and encouraged him, saying he could be good in journalism and diplomacy. He remembered the names of two books. "She gave me *Cakes and Ales* by Somerset Maugham. The second book was *The Greening of America.*" Essa got high marks on the common entrance exam at the end of primary school in the village and went to a secondary school that was built in the colonial era to educate the sons of chiefs, leaders for the future to maintain the British system of indirect rule. Essa said that he told American students later when he was teaching in Texas: "If I can make it you have no reason not to make it. English was not my second language. I was born Fulani [Pular is the language], learned Mandingo and Wolof in the streets, studied Arabic at the madrassa to learn the Koran. English is my fourth language." After secondary school he joined the British organization Action Aid for a year and taught primary school and adult literacy.

Princia Itaula-Kifoumba's father was a math professor at the University of Brazzaville in Brazzaville, the capital of all French Central Africa in colonial times and after independence the capital of the Republic of Congo. Her father was also a politician who wanted independence for the small and disputed province of Angola called Cabinda. Both her parents had a love for education. She herself liked reading literature and learning about cultures and remembered reading novels by the famous Francophone African writers Ousmane Sembène and Camara Laye, but her favorite was the classic *So Long a Letter* by the Senegalese writer Mariama Ba.

Nkongolo Kalala was born in Democratic Republic of Congo just before independence and grew up in East Kasai Province after his parents moved from West Kasai Province because of ethnic conflict. His father was a primary school teacher, and both parents always emphasized education. All eight living children graduated from secondary school and two, including him, have PhDs. He went to a Catholic technical secondary boarding school in West Kasai, and then to the University of Kisangani in northeastern Congo, graduating with a degree in agricultural economics.

One's parents didn't have to be teachers to stress education. To Jose

Kazadi's father, who worked for the Commercial Bank of Congo, "Education was a very important matter. He said, 'I pay for your school but it is up to you to learn, to study hard. School is your wife, your children, your future, your everything.'" As a child Jose dreamed about being a pilot and then he became attracted to journalism, probably because his father was always listening to news from around the world, from French radio to Voice of America. However, his father encouraged him to become a doctor so he focused on math and science and after secondary school went to enroll at the University of Kinshasa in the capital Kinshasa. Unfortunately he did not have an "umbrella," or someone to speak for him, and he did not get in. After a year his brother found him a place in the College of Building and Public Works in his hometown of Kananga in West Kasai, and he completed an associate degree in engineering, specifically surveying, in 1994.

Beatrice Mbayo described how she competed with twin boys in another family for top grades in the Catholic schools she attended in the Katanga region of Shaba Province in Democratic Republic of Congo. Both became priests, one in Canada and the other in Congo. "My mom pushed education hard so she gave me every support she could. She used to say 'Your life will be better if you get education.' Thirteen out of seventeen of us finished secondary school. My parents put a lot of effort into education." Her mother, who had gotten a fourth-grade education herself, also made sure Beatrice's father did not marry Beatrice off at age eleven.[10] Beatrice has told her own children how she walked three miles each way to go to secondary school. She had only one pen and divided six copy books into halves for her twelve school subjects. "I tell my children to study hard. Don't let anyone be in front of you."

Gashaw Lake grew up in the time of Emperor Haile Selassie in a family dominated by priests of the Ethiopian Orthodox Church like his grandfather. His stepfather was Lieutenant Colonel Workalemahu of the Selassie government. Born in 1952 near Addis Ababa, Ethiopia's capital, he was educated there and in Eritrea, then still part of Ethiopia, through high school. Gashaw described a classical Christian education with an emphasis on Amharic language and culture, including spiritual music. The education was "Socratic, recitation, memorization. The society, including neighborhood and school, watched to bring out the best in children. The neighbors will look out for you, feel responsible for you to become modest and responsible." He also talked about the influence of his mother. "My mother was a tremendous force for studies. She woke me up at 3:00 in the morning, washed my face, and got me to study."

Both Iddah Otieno's parents valued education. She grew up in the rural village of Okela in Kenya. "My father was an Anglican pastor and my mother a church teacher. Everyone [she was the youngest of ten children] went to secondary school. As the last born I learned from my older siblings." Although four older brothers had gone to university, she was the first girl in the village to sit for the national exam and be accepted at a public university. "Most of my friends married but I wanted to break the mold. I grew up with 'the sky is the limit' attitude. I was proud of being a Luo girl who had this big idea of making it." Iddah's degree at Maseno University gave her certification to teach English at the prestigious Kisumu Boys High School located in Kisumu City, Kenya.

Moulaye Indrissa Barry's father was a doctor at a small hospital in rural southern Senegal and had five wives and thirty-five children, but he died in a car accident when Moulaye, the thirty-second child, was very young and the family broke up. However, Moulaye had a brother who was a teacher and took him to live in the village where he was teaching. But it was his mother who insisted on the importance of education. "She believed that education was the way out for me. She didn't know how to read or write but she knew the importance of education. Because my brother was a teacher he would make sure that I was on the right track, and my mom passed the word that 'he has to succeed. There's no other option.' I did the exam and I came in second. My mom was happy." Moulaye went on to high school in Kolda in southern Senegal. There he began learning English; in fact, in high school three European languages were required. Moulaye was successful in both his national baccalaureate written exam and the oral exam and studied English literature at the University of Dakar. He finished a master's in 2000 with a specialty in African literature.

Getting an education beyond primary and middle school in an African country has rarely been easy, perhaps because of where one lived, often because there were simply not enough opportunities in particular fields for all students, especially for secondary and higher education, sometimes because money for school fees was scarce, and finally because of the crucial importance of exams. Sometimes, as in the case of Robert's father Martin in Malawi, a father did not want a child to become Western educated. In Guinea Hamidou Koivogui's father did not allow him to go to school. He was the oldest and was expected to help his father on the farm. However, Hamidou and his friends became expert dancers, drummers, and acrobats instead, winning contests all over the country. And then Hamidou was chosen to join the prestigious

Guinea Ballet Africaine as a young man and traveled the world, including the United States, in the early 1970s.

Desmond Brown described growing up in a village outside Freetown, the capital of Sierra Leone, with his grandmother, who was both mother and father to him. She raised vegetables and Desmond harvested them and sold them in the market to support the family and obtain money for his school fees. Tambu Chirwa explained that she was "given" to her older sister in the city of Blantyre in Malawi because there was a better chance to get into secondary school there than in her village. She wasn't selected to go to an exclusive boarding school where everything was provided, but she did finish secondary school through a sort of distance learning. Essa Bokar Sey's father did not have the school fee money to allow him to go on to the sixth form of secondary school. Mamadou Savané said that he went to university for one year in Guinea but then there was just not enough money for more education. Efosa Austin Osayamwen talked about the shortcomings of the examination system in Nigeria. "If you don't get into the school you want you have to wait to apply the next year. And then the score on the West Africa exam determines what course you can study." He made four As the first time but didn't pass the math so he studied hard, took the exams again and passed, and then completed a degree in public administration at Edo State University in 2004.

Abigail Unuakhalu, also born in Nigeria and a graduate of Wesley Girls Senior Secondary School in Yaba, noted that it was hard to get to study what you wanted at the university; she really wanted to take accounting but had to study economics. Jose Kazadi hoped to study medicine in the Congo and Kiluba Nkulu wanted to study science in the Congo but those university places were taken, often by students from influential families. Francis Musoni originally wanted to study law at the University of Zimbabwe but that program was full.

Careers in Home Countries

Marie-Antoinette Sossou was an ambitious young woman always striving for more education and more responsible jobs. After secondary school she earned a two-year degree in social work and worked as a welfare officer in Ho in the Volta Region of Ghana for nine years. Then she returned to college to get a diploma in social work and became a probation officer in the juvenile court system in Accra, Ghana's capital. In her work she saw women whose husbands were not supporting their children and juvenile delinquency. So she was part of starting social education programs, including family tribunals that dealt with issues like child

Abigail Unuakhalu in front of her former secondary school during a family trip back to Nigeria in 2018. (Photo courtesy of Abigail Unuakhalu.)

support and custody. In 1990 she had the opportunity to go to Norway for further education. After a year learning Norwegian, she spent four years earning a BA in psychology (with credits transferred from Ghana) and an MA in social work. Returning to Ghana, she worked for a year with the United Nations High Commission for Refugees (UNHCR), repatriating refugees from neighboring Togo. She then became head of the Department of Social Work at the University of Ghana.

Several other African immigrants described distinguished careers in their home countries before immigrating to the United States. Growing up in a "lower-middle-class family" in Sierra Leone with an accountant father, Bankole Thompson felt very fortunate to have two aunts who were teachers. He remembered that when he was eleven he told his father that he would like to be a judge. His persistence and diligence as a student gained him a scholarship to Fourah Bay College. After completing both undergraduate and master's degrees at Fourah Bay in 1961, Bankole taught at the college for four years. Then he received a fellowship to the University of Cambridge where he gained a BA, MA, and PhD in law. He passed the English bar in 1971. Under terms of the fellowship he was appointed a state counselor or prosecutor in Sierra Leone and after five years he was seconded as legal advisor to the Mano River Union of Sierra Leone, Liberia, and later Guinea. In 1981 he was appointed high court judge of the Superior Court of Sierra Leone. Attaining that position fulfilled his stated "academic and professional ambition to contribute immensely to the preservation of civilized values through upholding the rule of law."

After secondary school Essa Bokar Sey served in The Gambia's army for five years, working as a trainer and in motor transport administration. But because he respected his father's urging to continue his education, he entered a pilot program to train teachers of French for The Gambia. After earning an associate degree in French, English, and pedagogy, he was chosen to study in France for two years and then was posted to teach in a secondary school back in The Gambia. He decided instead to apply to the Ministry of Foreign Affairs, and because of his army background, he was selected to be a protocol welfare officer in 1993. In 1995 he began his diplomatic career as first secretary to the embassy in France. He was promoted to consul there in 1997.

Living in Other Than Home Countries

There has always been migration across Africa. In the last 150 years that migration has occurred across national boundaries that were imposed by Europeans and that divided ethnic groups. Sometimes one was born in another country because one's parents had migrated. For example, South Africa's farms and mines drew Malawians and other nationals for work, so Tambu Chirwa was born there. Rwandans left for Uganda because of the 1969 genocide, so Sylvia Uwamaliya Stainback was born there. Sometimes one went to another country to work or to a European country to study and stayed to work; Kennedy Boateng from Ghana is an example of the first and Pierre Ngog and Jose Kazadi are examples of the second. Some Africans, like Essa Bokar Sey and Rahel Bosson's father, represented their countries abroad. As well, violence has pushed people from one country to another country or even several, but war's impact deserves its own section and will be discussed later.

Tambu Chirwa was born in South Africa in 1964, although as a black African baby whose father had gone to work in South Africa during apartheid her birth was not recorded there. Her father was supposed to be a chief in Malawi, but because of missionary influence, he wanted to go to school and did. Being a chief was not possible for a Christian so her father ran away from home. He walked and rode a train through Zimbabwe, where he met Tambu's Malawian mother, whose father was working in the mines, and then went on to South Africa. There he met a white South African who liked him and taught him to be a bricklayer. The family returned to Malawi when Tambu was six years old.

Sylvia Uwamaliya Stainback was born in 1978 and grew up in Uganda as the fourth of eight children in a struggling Rwandan family. Her father had escaped the earlier 1969 genocide in Rwanda and then met her Rwandan mother, who was also in Uganda. Although they were really refugees in Uganda, the children were admonished not to tell anyone they were Rwandan. They grew up speaking the Ugandan language of Lisonga and learned English in school. The family was poor— Sylvia's father worked sometimes in the technical school nearby doing roofing and her mother sold snacks to students and teachers but they did manage to send their children to school. Sylvia remembered, "I would spend a whole year without paying tuition. But my mother was a fighter. She would be in the headmaster's office. 'I know my kids are not paying but I'm working really hard. I've grown some potatoes. We will sell a cow. Just let my children take the exams.'" As a primary school student Sylvia did not wear shoes but did have a pink dress uniform and one exercise book. Then in 1994, after that Rwandan genocide and because things were becoming expensive in Uganda, the parents left their five oldest children, including Sylvia, in Uganda and returned to Rwanda. After tenth grade at age seventeen Sylvia also returned to Rwanda and finished secondary school there. In 1999 she got a scholarship for her university education in Rwanda, beginning with a year learning French, the colonial language of Rwanda, and then majoring in the new field of social work, taking some classes in French and some in English. She did internships with an orphanage and with a micro-credit institution and wrote her thesis on the role of micro-credit institutions in helping women. "It was rewarding. Women are the heart of the family. Women work very hard, like my mother did. They should be given more opportunities. If they are trained, they take good care of their families."

Pierre Ngog, who was born in Cameroon, studied economics for two years at the University of Yaounde, the capital, before receiving a UNESCO scholarship to study printing in the former East Germany just before the Berlin Wall fell. After a year of studying German in the mornings and binding books in the afternoons, he moved to Leipzig in 1990 and by 1996 he had completed both undergraduate and graduate degrees in engineering before going back to Cameroon. Not finding a good-paying job back in Cameroon, he returned to Germany to study information technology. However, the German government said he could not be on a student visa for more than ten years so instead he went to work in the stock market with a French brokerage firm in Germany that needed someone fluent in French and German.

Kennedy Boateng "just wanted a change." After completing his education as a math teacher at the University of Cape Coast in Ghana and his year of national service teaching at a polytechnic school in Accra, Ghana's capital, he went first to Zimbabwe but the economy was not good there in 1987, so he moved on to Botswana, where he got a job teaching math for a year. Because of the economy, the 1980s were a time when many Ghanaian teachers migrated elsewhere in Africa to teach. Kwaku Addo was one of many Ghanaian teachers who went to Nigeria to teach in secondary schools for several years, in his case from 1980 to 1982.

Jose Kazadi had to leave Democratic Republic of Congo in November 1996 because of his political activity as a university student. So he fled to Moscow, planning to be a student. However, the cousin who had promised to help him with funds could not so the university in Russia kicked him out. After he learned some Russian and gained some computer skills, in 2000 Jose and a friend decided to start a magazine to speak for Africans. They established a press identity and started a legitimate business with a Russian friend whose husband was an African as the publisher. They also received some help at the beginning from UNHCR (United Nations High Commission for Refugees) and a French philanthropic organization. The magazine, *My Africa,* included stories about violence against black people by skinheads in Russia as well as trade issues. "We thought about the opening of Russian business to Africa and the opening of African businessmen to Russians because we realized there was some technology Russians have, and Africa could need it. We also had African diplomats paying for pages to announce the birth of children, anniversaries, other life activities. In Moscow during those years I became so powerful." He organized programs for embassies—for example, an art exhibit for the French Culture Center and a Francophone Day of culture and language. He even gave a speech at the Russian Duma (Parliament). "I could be able, from my kitchen, to call one of the high diplomats at the French embassy and recommend somebody for a visa, and they gave it to him."[11*]

Sometimes children lived in another country because of their parents. Born in Ethiopia in 1978, Rahel Bosson moved with her parents to Sweden when she was seven because her father went into politics and became a diplomat. "That was a very rich experience as a child growing up. We traveled all over Scandinavia, Norway, Denmark, Finland. Then my dad was assigned to go to China for a year and we stayed in Sweden on our own, and then my dad was assigned to go to Belgium." After a coup d'état in Ethiopia in 1991 overthrew Mengistu and after 1995 when there was a new government under Meles Zenawi, her father was first called back to Ethiopia and then eventually lost his job. The family chose to remain in Belgium because of her disabled brother. Rahel's mother supported the family as a nurse in a hospital. Rahel and her other brother were able to get scholarships to finish high school at St. John's International School with children of ambassadors and persons working for NATO, and her disabled brother went to a special school that offered physical therapy. "When my dad was a diplomat I was introduced to people like semi–prime ministers all the way to Ethiopian refugees that had PhDs but were working as cleaners. I was able to really experience a spectrum of life and culture there. And it was really interesting to me because over the course of my life I realized that the human condition and the human heart were the same, whether you were the king of Belgium that we met or you were a refugee in your home. We were all the same, you know, like the human soul was the same. And I also realized that fame and glory rise and fall with the change of the season."

We are Africans, Too

"I tell people I am from Africa but they don't believe me," said Samah Sadouki, who was born and grew up in the commercial city of Satif in Algeria. "They think Africa is black people." She explained that she was spoiled by her parents, but she did help her father in his food store. Samah earned a university degree in Arabic literature. A friend of hers told her about her brother Zineeddine Hamoudi. When Zineeddine visited from America, she met him and liked him. Their families agreed to the match, and they were married.

An only child with many cousins, Karin Krain was born in a small town about three hours' driving time south of Johannesburg in what was then Transvaal Province in South Africa, where her father and mother had met while working in a bank. Every few years her father was transferred to a different town in another part of South Africa, but at age thirteen Karin decided to stay in Paul in the Cape Town area to attend boarding school. She recognizes that she had a very privileged childhood, going to one of the best secondary schools in the country and traveling with her family to different places in South Africa for holidays. However, her father's family had struggled, and her father said to Karin: "You will never depend on a man; you will go to college." Although she grew up in the conservative, disciplined Afrikaans culture and was educated in that language, she also had five years of English in high school and at the University of Stellenbosch. Multiple languages have been an important and normal part of her life because her first serious boyfriend and his parents spoke only English and Zulu, and then she married a South African who spoke English (the name Krain came from his Jewish Lithuanian grandfather who had stowed away on a boat). She has raised her children in English with Afrikaans as a second language. Karin got her bachelor's degree in biology and biochemistry because she wanted to work in cosmetics, specifically for Elizabeth Arden, but there were no jobs She began her master's in physiology but switched to pharmacy, and subsequently she and her husband owned their own pharmacy in Cape Town for nine years.

Samah and Karin clearly count as African immigrants because they were born in an African country of parents who were citizens of that country. However, other individuals whose parents are not citizens of an African country may identify as African because of being born and/or growing up as children on the continent. That is the case for Shamik Aikat and Boyd Mpho Hayes.

Because his parents decided to leave West Bengal in India where he was born to take government high school teaching contracts in Africa, Shamik Aikat arrived in Ethiopia when he was eighteen months old. After three years the family moved to newly independent Zambia, formerly Northern Rhodesia. There in Kitwe, Shamik went to both primary and secondary school with a mix of local Zambians and Europeans, as did his sister, who was born in Zambia. After completing a first year of university in Zambia, he decided to go to India to study medicine but, he said, "I feel a large part of me is African, Zambian to be precise. Because I spent nearly two decades of my early life there I feel a strong attachment to Zambia."

Boyd Mpho Hayes was born in Johannesburg, South Africa, in 1993 to American parents who were then living in Botswana. He began

Dr. Shamik Aikat. (Photo courtesy of Jack Wilson.)

school in Maun, Botswana, but then the family moved back to the US for several years before going to Zimbabwe, where his parents worked at Africa University in Mutare. Boyd attended Hillcrest Preparatory School in Mutare for classes 3, 4, and 5. He was an outsider in Zimbabwe as an American but when he returned to the United States and went to West Jessamine County Middle and High Schools in Kentucky, he became an "African" kid with a strange accent who really loved cricket, which he had learned from the family's gardener/cook who took Boyd along with him to visit the black townships. "The transition [to Kentucky] was really tough. I ended up making friends with other outsider kids. One of the only people of color at school is a best friend. People would say, 'You're American, I don't know why you think you're African.'" Boyd was able to reconnect with Africa as a student at the

University of Kentucky, where he joined the African Student Association and took courses about Africa. Through a summer University of Kentucky program he went to Cape Town, South Africa. He went back to Cape Town a second time for six months to work on Web development for a soccer magazine: "the best time of my life." While he was there his middle name—Mpho, meaning "gift"—gained positive reactions from black South Africans, especially those who had the same name. Boyd graduated from the University of Kentucky with a degree in journalism in 2016, and in September 2016 he returned to the continent, becoming a Peace Corps volunteer in Senegal working in agriculture and also with youth, including starting a gender and leadership club in two primary schools.

From Countries at War

War and violence, as well as disease, are only part of Africa's story, although many Americans have conflated and still conflate what they read or hear about events in one country with the entire continent. Angene and Jack Wilson remember being told in 1964, "We're so glad you're back from Africa. Those terrible things happening in the Congo!" They had been Peace Corps volunteers teaching in peaceful Liberia—nine countries and several thousand miles away from the Congo—for two years and traveling around West Africa (Sierra Leone, Guinea, Mali, and Senegal on one trip and Nigeria and Cameroon on another). A twenty-first century example is related to the 2014–2015 Ebola epidemic, which was confined to Liberia, Sierra Leone, and Guinea in West Africa. Parents of children in a Louisville school forced the resignation of a teacher who had returned from a medical mission trip to Kenya—across the continent in East Africa—in October 2014. She resigned rather than submit to a paid twenty-one-day leave and produce a doctor's note saying she was in good health.[12]

However, most 1990s and 2000s stories by interviewed refugees from Burundi and Democratic Republic of the Congo did include escape from war and life in refugee camps before coming to the United States. Some individuals even became refugees as youngsters. For example, Bandushubwange Vanisa, born in a Burundian village in 1986, was only seven years old when war came to her country. She remembers only her house and the nearby Pentecostal church. Her family fled to Tanzania, where she lived in a UNICEF-supported camp in Kigoma Province in Tanzania until she was twenty-one years old and then came to the United States as a refugee with her husband and children. She explained: "The refugee camp was bad. It was in the forest. They didn't allow us to go out."

Tite Niyonizigiye was also born in Burundi. His refugee story is especially complicated, involving three countries besides his own. Ten years old and in second grade when an earlier war came to Burundi on April 29, 1972, he remembered: "We saw houses being burned in the countryside. We started to sleep outside in the bush. We started to run by night and hide during the day because helicopters were overhead shooting." His family crossed Lake Tanganyika to Democratic Republic of Congo, but there was no infrastructure there for refugees. Two younger brothers died because there was no food or medical assistance. He and his parents and sister went on to Rwanda. Because there was no restriction of movement on refugees in Rwanda, he was able to complete primary school in Rwanda, go back to the Congo for secondary school, and return to Rwanda to study social science for three years at the University of Rwanda as one of four Burundi refugee students sponsored by UNHCR. After teaching for a year in Rwanda he returned to Congo for two years to get a degree in sociology at the University of Lubumbashi, graduating in 1989. But that was the year war began in Rwanda, and then war came to Congo in 1994. Tite married in 1995 and fled with his wife and child to Tanzania in 1996. They lived in a refugee camp there until 2007. "In the camp in Tanzania we could not leave unless we had written permission. It was like a prison." However, he was a teacher in the camp and then for three years the principal of a seventeen-hundred-student high school with seventy teachers. So for thirty-three years of his life, Tite was affected by war—in Burundi, in Rwanda, and in Congo—followed by more than ten years in a refugee camp in Tanzania.

Hussein Sombe grew up in a farming family of eight children in a small rural village in the Eastern Region of the Democratic Republic of Congo. After completing secondary school in a larger town, he studied medicine at the University of Lubumbashi for two years until money ran out. Then he taught high school chemistry for several years, but after not being paid for his work he turned to mining gold for three years to earn money to return to the university. When war came to the Congo in 1994 Hussein and his wife and child fled across Lake Tanganyika to a refugee camp in Tanzania, where he helped start a secondary school in which he taught before moving to a second camp where he was education coordinator and a member of the Examination Board. He lived in refugee camps for twelve years.

Kikoko Godfrey is another one among many of the Congolese

refugees who have come from camps outside their home country of Democratic Republic of Congo to live in Lexington. He spent sixteen years in a camp in Namibia with his family; three of his eight children were born there. "Life was not good. You do not have freedom of movement. You have to get permission from the police and a paper to leave the camp. UNHCR is just trying to keep you alive." The camp did have a primary school and a secondary school in English so the "children speak English more fluently than me." After doing food distribution for the Red Cross, Kikoko worked in a health center in the camp. His son Amuri wrote in *Slowly Is the Journey: Stories from Bluegrass Community and Technical College ESL Students,* "Living in a refugee camp for almost someone's whole life is not a small can of Coca Cola or a piece of a wedding cake. There are people who were boys, raised up in a camp, got matured under the same condition, got married and then raised their own family."[13] Amuri was secretary at the Senior Secondary School, from which he graduated. He then taught six- and seven-year-olds at the primary school before coming to the United States.

Born in 1958, Kiluba Nkulu was never a formal refugee but, he said, "Violence has marked my life." He spent his early years on a Brethren mission station called Kiolo in Katanga Province, Democratic Republic of Congo, where his grandfather was in charge after American and European missionaries left at independence in 1960. His primary school education was in Tshiluba, his native language. In 1977 Congo was invaded from Angola, and Kiluba saw people being killed as he walked 150 kilometers home on Easter break from the Methodist high school in Kamina. Some of his friends didn't return to graduate. He also saw people killed on his way to campus his freshman year at the University of Lubumbashi, where he got a degree in 1984 in English literature and language with a final paper on Ernest Hemingway's *The Old Man and the Sea.* After graduation he worked at Barclay's Bank but then decided to teach high school English and then English, French, and philosophy at a Methodist seminary in Mulungwishi, Kolwezi. There he married and his older three children were born. By the 1990s what was happening across the country in the capital of Kinshasa was affecting Katanga Province. His wife's family, originally from Kasai Province, was in danger living in Katanga. In fact, he had to evacuate his wife and the baby and hide them among relatives in Lubumbashi for three months.

Four Liberian Immigrant Stories

A thirteen-year civil war that began in December 1989 is a critical part of the stories of Liberian immigrants in Kentucky. They also have a unique historical connection to the United States and to Kentucky.

Born in 1944, Jemima Natt Roberts immigrated to Kentucky when she was almost sixty years old, and thus her story before Kentucky is a long one. Liberia, her country of birth, was founded under the auspices of the American Colonization Society by American free blacks and freed slaves who first arrived on the West African coast in 1820. There were people of twenty-eight different ethnic groups there already, so in some ways the newcomers, who came to be called Americo-Liberians or Congos, were also colonialists who brought American southern society with them. Kentucky's own Henry Clay, who represented the state in the US House of Representatives and the Senate and ran for president five times, was president of the American Colonization Society for the last seventeen years of his life. Clay did not emancipate any of his own slaves to immigrate to Liberia, but about 770 freed slaves from Kentucky did go to Liberia. Some wrote letters back to their former masters and mistresses, and one, Alfred Russell, was president of Liberia from 1883 to 1884.[14] In the same year Jemima was born, Liberia (which had been independent since 1847—in fact, it is the only African country never ruled by a European power), inaugurated a new president. William V. S. Tubman would remain in office until his death in 1971.

Jemima's parents lived in far western Liberia on the coast in Garraway in Maryland County near a river that emptied into the Atlantic Ocean.[15] (A number of Liberia's place-names are American; there is even a town called Clay-Ashland after Henry Clay and his Ashland estate in Lexington, Kentucky, and a town named Lexington in Sinoe County.) Jemima's maternal grandfather owned a large plantation employing many people that grew cocoa, sugarcane, and rice. Jemima said, "When people looked at us, they would think we were wealthy. We didn't grow up like other children in the village. We didn't really struggle or know hard times." Her father Gregory Natt was a pastor of the Methodist church and the owner of a store. He also had a fishing boat, bought and slaughtered cattle, and traded with the Germans, even ordering clothes from Germany. Jemima told the story of her father buying a kerosene refrigerator. When he lay dying he told his wife not to sell the refrigerator—he wanted his children always to be able to have ice water to drink. She concluded, "My father was respected in the town; he was a straightforward man, a man of principle." Jemima's mother's father had sent her, his oldest child, to the renowned Annie Walsh Memorial School in Freetown, Sierra Leone (it was founded in 1849 and is the oldest girls school in Sub-Saharan Africa), and she was a teacher and seamstress.

Jemima Roberts. (Photo courtesy of Jack Wilson.)

When Jemima was about seven years old her parents decided to send her to live with her mother's sister and husband, who did not have children of their own. "My aunt would become my mother." Since her uncle was with the army, Jemima moved with them to several different places in Liberia's interior. One was an army base where her aunt was teacher and principal at the school. When her uncle was transferred back to Monrovia, Jemima attended a government school, "but my aunt thought I was not applying myself so she decided she wanted me to go to a boarding school."

Thus as a young teenager Jemima started fifth grade at Suehn Industrial Academy, about thirty miles outside Monrovia, which was run by women missionaries from the African American National Convention Baptist Church. A young American couple, Angene and Jack Wilson, in the first group of Peace Corps volunteer teachers in Liberia, taught Jemima and other students English and social studies, including African literature, history, and geography, which they themselves were learning. During one social studies class in 1964 the students celebrated the independence of Malawi.

Jemima remembered: "One thing about boarding school—it taught you to be responsible. Life at Suehn was good because you made a lot of friends, girls from a lot of different places. It was challenging because you had to study to get ahead. Academics was most important, but I didn't like the social aspect. Everything about the opposite sex was bad, so we weren't prepared for adult lives." However, Jemima did fall in love—with Bibi Roberts, the young biology teacher, dean of boys, and manager of the farm at Suehn. They found ways to meet in an empty classroom where he tutored her in math.

Bibi and Jemima married on July 29, 1965, after Jemima graduated from high school, spent their honeymoon upcountry in the Nimba Mountains, and then moved to Cuttington College in Suacoco near Gbarnga, also upcountry. Founded in 1889 by the American Episcopal Church, Cuttington is the oldest private, coeducational, four-year institution in Sub-Saharan Africa. Bibi became farm manager and later taught in the Rural Development Institute, which offered a two-year degree in agriculture. Jemima taught third grade at the government school in the nearby village of Sinyea until 1974, when she was employed at the college in charge of food service. After 1977 she worked in the library cataloguing and ordering books. "That was very good for me because I then decided I wanted to get a college degree." Three staff wives took the entrance exam together and were told they did better than the younger students. Jemima took two or three classes at a time and completed a degree in political science in 1985. From 1986 until civil war began in late 1989 Jemima was assistant dean of women at the college, in charge of assigning rooms to and counseling young women.

Cuttington was a good place to raise a family. Jemima recognized that one of the advantages for their own four children was the excellent American-style school on campus. "The academic environment was very good for our children." Their three daughters (one, whose mother was Bibi's sister, was adopted as a toddler) and one son went for the first eight grades to the campus school and then to St. Martin's Catholic Secondary School in nearby Gbarnga. At Cuttington, "you knew what was going on in the world. You got to meet people like Fulbright professors and interact with them." Health care was also good because of the nearby Phoebe Hospital. Although Jemima regretted that the children had very little interaction with Bibi's family back in the village and that they did not learn a Liberian language, being at Cuttington College "really helped us. The whole family has good memories."

The Roberts were an important and welcoming family on campus. They had many friends, including after 1986 the college president Melvin Mason and his wife Marie, who had been a classmate of Bibi's when she and Bibi attended Suehn Industrial Academy in the 1940s. Over the course of almost three decades at Cuttington College, the Roberts became family for many students. At Bibi's funeral at Christ Church Cathedral in Lexington in early February 2013, some of those students now living in the United States came on a very snowy weekend to honor him and to sing the Cuttington College song at the gathering afterward.

Over the years the Roberts got to know and count as close friends many Americans. For example, the Peace Corps couple Angene and Jack Wilson visited them at Cuttington in 1967 and in 1972 and kept in touch by letter. In 1976 Bibi had an opportunity to do graduate work at Virginia Polytechnic University and the next summer Jemima came to visit him, her first trip to the United States. They toured Florida and Virginia, visiting Orlando and Williamsburg. In August 1988 their son Bibi Jr. came to Kentucky to study biology at Berea College, a coveted destination for international students as the only one of America's top small liberal arts colleges that awards every enrolled student a no-tuition promise.

War started in December 1989 when the Charles Taylor–led rebel movement, the National Patriotic Front of Liberia, invaded the country. Upcountry, where Cuttington College was located, gradually became Greater Liberia ruled by the rebels. Cuttington's students had been sent to Monrovia, the coastal capital, only a few days before the rebels came and took over the college for their training camp. For six weeks Jemima and Bibi and the college president and his wife stayed inside the Roberts' house and slept in one room. They were right to be afraid: when the rebels found a former president of the college, they cut his head off and sliced his body in two with a chainsaw. Miraculously, in May 1992, after being stuck on the campus for a year because of the war, Jemima was able to travel to Monrovia to get a new Liberian passport and an American visa and to pick up an airline ticket to come to Berea, Kentucky, for her son's wedding.

The war ebbed and flowed. Once Bibi and Jemima were in the bush for three months, but they tried to stay on campus and keep things going even when the students were not there. "When things got rough we sent our daughters to Ivory Coast first. Then we came back to Cuttington and finally we went to the town of Danané in Ivory Coast to live as refugees from 1995 to 1998. We had considered going to Ghana because it was English-speaking but rents for housing were too high and we didn't want to live in the camp there. Ivory Coast looked at us as brothers. UNHCR had a center and registered you, but then you could rent a house." A group of about thirty Liberians lived together. Some of the young women bought fish in the market, then seasoned, roasted, and sold it in the evenings. Jemima and others made "light" bread to sell. Friends and relatives in the US sent money when they could. Jack and Angene Wilson sent $100 bills hidden in seed packets to Bibi.

While they were in Côte d'Ivoire, Cuttington developed a Cuttington-in-exile program supported by several US colleges. One was Berea College in Kentucky from which the Roberts' son Bibi Jr. had graduated; their daughter Bindu completed her undergraduate education there. After a peace pact brokered by the international community, there was an election in July 1997 in which Charles Taylor was elected president. The Roberts group was repatriated, the college reopened. Students started registering, with the caveat "Accept the dormitories as they are." So parents fixed the rooms for students. The Roberts had built and moved into their own house off campus in December 1989 weeks before the Taylor invasion. That house was destroyed during the war and so in 1998 they repaired a house on campus to live in. "We graduated one class and then in 2000 we ran to Monrovia and established Cuttington-in-Monrovia. Everybody came down to the capital because rebel groups were beginning a struggle against the Taylor government. Then we went back to Cuttington for several years."

Mulbah Zowah is another Liberian immigrant whose life was affected by the war. He grew up in Lofa County in the northeast of Liberia, the son of a father who was in the military and had two wives and nineteen children. Mulbah started primary school in the village and continued his secondary education at several schools, one a Catholic boarding school, in the city of Voinjama. For secondary school he received the prestigious J. J. Roberts (the first president of Liberia) Scholarship, which gave recipients a stipend and textbooks. However, the war that began with Charles Taylor's invasion of Nimba County in northwestern Liberia in December 1989 reached Voinjama in 1991. "By 1991 Voinjama was under complete military control. There was killing everywhere. People were being raped. It was just total chaos. Everything was shut down completely. And the rebels had a base training child soldiers. It had a big impact on the community because a lot of children had to join the military. It was so bad. But fortunately for me I left Voinjama in the midst of all that trouble and moved toward Monrovia. It was a tough thing to just walk away." Mulbah was separated from his family one night during fighting and didn't see his parents for five years. "Everyone was displaced."

How did Mulbah escape getting recruited by Charles Taylor or another rebel group? "It was just God. Or perhaps it was my desire for something different, for education. My junior brother was recruited by the rebels and he was fighting for the rebels for a while and I was upset about that because I knew it was not a good thing. He stopped and two years later there were a lot of groups fighting so this group came into my village and someone identified him as having fought for Charles Taylor and then he was cut and tarred and they slaughtered him like an animal—it was brutal—in front of my parents, in front of two hundred people they gathered in the center of the village. So I was always moving because I knew I would not have survived if I had attempted to fight." Mulbah was fortunate to finally graduate from high school in Monrovia in 1994. The J. J. Roberts scholarship allowed him to go on to the University of Liberia, but war disrupted its schedule and "sometimes there was only one semester in two years." He started at the university in 1997 but had completed only two years by 2003.

Sam Vorkpor was also born in Lofa County, Liberia, in his case in the village of Giligansiasu as one of seven children, six sons and one daughter, of illiterate farmer parents. After his father died when he was fourteen he went to live with an uncle in Zorzor who was principal of a Lutheran elementary school so he could continue his education. When Sam finished elementary school he went to high school on a scholarship at the Lutheran Training Institute in Salayea, Lofa County. Sam said, "I knew I didn't have a father. I had to be disciplined. Education was number one priority for me. When I was in high school I always studied hard." He graduated as valedictorian, which gave him a government scholarship to either Cuttington College or the University of Liberia.

Sam decided to go to the University of Liberia in Monrovia for a different, urban experience. "Everything my mind was on since sixth grade was to become a doctor." So he entered University of Liberia in 1979 in the pre-medical program and finally finished medical school in 1988 although graduation was delayed until 1989 because of political unrest. The president at that time, Samuel Doe, who as a sergeant had led the 1980 coup, also graduated that year with a master's in administration, just before Charles Taylor invaded Liberia.

In 1990 war came to Monrovia, where Sam was doing an ob-gyn residency at the maternity section of the John F. Kennedy Hospital, which was held by the government.

> A lot of my friends escaped by going to the rebel side, or going to Guinea or the Ivory Coast. But my problem was one of my brothers was then superintendent of Bong County. The rebels were against anyone who was on the government side. And I was getting ready to get married. But we had to cancel the wedding because she was from the tribe that supported Charles Taylor, the other side. Doe on the government side was killing anyone who supported Taylor. So my fiancée came to stay in my apartment and I went to the hospital and changed her last name to my tribal name and made her an identity card with my last name. I told her, "Now you are Kpelle." That's how she survived that war.
>
> Then one day in July 1990 I went to the hospital to see patients and while I was there, Doe sent soldiers. People were taking refuge at the hospital because of the Geneva Convention and most were from the tribe my wife is from. The soldiers brought armed guards in trucks. A lady whispered to me, "We are here to kill all the Gio and Mano." That's the tribe my wife is from. I pretended I didn't understand. There were trucks taking people from other parts of the hospital straight to the airport to kill them. I sat at the ER for a while. After they collected enough people they left and I left. . . . The problem was the war was getting worse. People were just getting killed for anything. Even somebody you had conflict with in the past—they see you, they kill you. Then Prince Johnson [of another rebel faction] took the Freeport and he disciplined his soldiers and said do not harass the civilians. A few people crossed the lines to Freeport, went there, found food, everything was fine. So around 5:00 one morning we went to the other side. It was a time I thought I could die. Charles Taylor was sending rockets into the city.

Sam and his wife found a friend who worked at USIS (United States Information Service) and went with their two children to that building and slept on the floor. "We stayed there for a while until there were some peacekeeping forces who managed to drive Charles Taylor from the city." After the peacekeepers arrived, Médecins sans Frontières (Doctors without Borders) came to Monrovia, and Sam began to work with them as a medical coordinator, from the end of 1991 until 1995.

He was also on loan from them to manage a clinic for Church World Service in 1992.

Abraham Sven-Peters is yet another Liberian who was caught in the war, but his story includes an immediate escape to and work in neighboring Sierra Leone. Abraham's father was a mechanical engineer and his mother a housewife, but in 1978, when he was ten, his parents separated. There were twelve children, six boys and six girls; five of his siblings died during the war. Abraham went to live with an uncle who helped him with his education, and he completed high school in Monrovia in 1989, but "unfortunately we never received our diplomas because the war intensified."

Abraham described walking 150 miles in three days from Monrovia to the Mano River to escape into Sierra Leone. He and his older brother walked with other escaping groups, assuring Charles Taylor's rebels at their checkpoints by speaking Kru that they were not members of an ethnic group the rebels were fighting against. They sold their sweaters to get money to pay the rebels at the border checkpoint at the river. Then they persuaded a guard to let them cross the river to get food by giving him $15 and promising to return. But they kept walking to the town of Zimmi in southwestern Sierra Leone. "Luckily for me," Abraham explained, "at Zimmi, the Red Cross driver had gotten sick and died and they were looking for drivers. They entrusted me to drive the car to Kenema, and they registered us as refugees at a Catholic center there."

Abraham was in Sierra Leone for sixteen years. He did have a family connection in Sierra Leone—his mother had been born there and later married a Sierra Leonean. After Abraham completed a two-month short course in public administration in 1990 in Freetown, the capital, he went to work for a youth organization. Trained in water sanitation, for seven years he built toilets and dug wells in three depressed towns near Freetown. Then he had an opportunity to work in facility maintenance for an American firm servicing West African peacekeeping forces in Sierra Leone for four years, becoming a supervisor the last year.

"Where I'm From"

In 1993 Kentucky poet George Ella Lyon edited her notebook of where-I'm-from lists into a poem entitled "Where I'm From."[16] The idea of using such a list to make a poem took off almost immediately as a writing prompt for workshops and in classrooms in the United States, and since then thousands of people have written such poems. Usually these poems are very personal, often evocative of place as well as people, often of taste and smell.

What tastes would an African immigrant in the Bluegrass write about in such a poem? Would Robert Chirwa write about eating the corn-based staple starch *nsima* with *chombe,* the very tasty tilapia from Lake Malawi? Would Jemima Roberts write about making rice bread and eating potato greens with hot pepper over rice? And/or have they or other immigrants developed any fondness for Kentucky food, perhaps shrimp over grits or burgoo? Living in the United States now—for several years, for many years—how much of their African roots would first-generation immigrants include to answer the question "Where are you from?" Is the answer "both/and" for at least some? However, first the individuals in the oral histories have to arrive, to immigrate. Why and how they came are the topics of the next chapter.

2

Opportunity

Why and How We Came

A bird that is not flying cannot discover where there is harvest.
—Burundian proverb

Both the pull of the United States because of educational and occupational opportunities and the push of economic problems caused by the "structural adjustment" of the 1980s, plus war in African countries like Democratic Republic of Congo and Liberia in the 1990s, resulted in a sizable increase of African immigrants during the second half of the twentieth century and the first decade and second decades of the twenty-first. However, even as early as the 1930s some young people from African countries came to the United States for education, and in the 1960s and 1970s Africans became part of an increasing flow of international students to American universities. Beginning in 1990 the Diversity Visa Lottery provided another pathway to the United States for persons from other countries, including most African countries. Especially in the 2000s refugees who were displaced by war and violence added to the immigrant population, and occasionally Africans were granted asylum. Another visa classification, H-1B, offered opportunities for persons with professional qualifications such as pharmacists. Still other Africans came to the US because they fell in love with an American and/or followed a spouse or another family member in what is known as family reunification.

This chapter includes both long sections about immigrants with similar reasons for coming to the US and short sections that tell more extensive stories of individuals. The first section begins with background history about Africans and higher education in the US, followed by a section entitled "American Higher Education and the African Professoriate in Kentucky." Next are short sections focused on two immigrants: "A Kenyan Immigrant's Story of Education for the Ministry" and "An Ethiopian Immigrant's Story of Becoming a Doctor." The section titled "The Diversity Visa Lottery" describes the experiences of five immigrants coming from Algeria, Cameroon, Côte d'Ivoire, or Democratic Republic of Congo. "For Love and Marriage" focuses on immigrants from Guinea, Nigeria, Rwanda, and Senegal. "Refugee Stories" showcases tales told by individuals from Burundi, Democratic Republic of Congo, Somalia, or Sudan, followed by individual stories: "An Asylum Case" and then "An Ambassador and a Pharmacist." After a section titled "Liberian Stories Continued: Influence of War," the chapter concludes with final thoughts under "The Immigrants Are Here."

Africans and Higher Education in the United States

The history of the United States as an attractive destination for university education by Africans includes several prominent West African leaders who studied in the United States before 1950, although during the colonial period Africans typically studied in the European nation that ruled them. Nnamdi Azikiwe, an important nationalist figure and the first president of independent Nigeria from 1963 to 1966, obtained undergraduate and graduate degrees from Lincoln University in 1927 and 1930 as well as a second master's degree from the University of Pennsylvania in 1933.[1] Like Azikiwe, Kwame Nkrumah, who led Ghana's drive for independence and was first prime minister (1957–1960) and then president (1960–1966), earned a BA from Lincoln University in 1939 followed by master's degrees from both Lincoln University and the University of Pennsylvania.[2] John Karefa-Smart, who worked for the World Health Organization and ran for president of Sierra Leone in 1996 and 2002, gained his BS from Otterbein College in Ohio in 1940, followed by a master's in public health from Harvard University, and then a doctorate in tropical medicine from McGill University in Canada.[3]

Another important precursor to the later more general arrival of Africans coming to study in the United States was the "airlift to America" between 1959 and 1963 of about eight hundred East Africans, mostly Kenyans. It was organized by Tom Mboya, the Kenyan independence leader and trade unionist who after independence served as minister of justice and minister of economic planning and development, and the African American Students Foundation with help from people such as Jackie Robinson, Harry Belafonte, Sidney Poitier, and Martin Luther King Jr. The students included Nobel laureate Wangari Maathai and many other future leaders. Barack Obama's father was not officially part of the airlift but was inspired by it to come to the United States to study and received support from the airlift organizers.[4]

Sim Oyetunji went to a new technical college in Ibadan right after Nigeria's independence in 1960 on a USAID (US Agency for International Development) scholarship; most of his teachers were Peace Corps volunteers. Why did he decide to major in electrical engineering? He explained, "Electricity was the last chapter in the physics book, perhaps because it was the hardest. Being a good student I liked to take whatever was the hardest." Then he had an opportunity to go to the University of Maine through the African Scholarship Program for American Universities (ASPAU), a USAID program established in 1960 to bring Africans to American universities for undergraduate studies.[5] "Fifty-five of us left Lagos in early August 1964 for Boston on an Alitalia flight." Because of an airline strike they were stuck in Rome for five days and got to see its sights. In Sim's physics class in Maine, the course book was the same he had used in Nigeria, and the professor was the author of the book. The professor tested him and gave him credit for the course he had taken in Nigeria, and with other credits transferred from Nigeria he was able to complete a BS in just three years, in 1967. An Iowa State University professor on sabbatical at the University of Maine in Sim's senior year offered him an assistantship and urged him to come to Iowa State for a master's and doctorate in electrical engineering. At the end of his US education the Shell Petroleum Development Company of Nigeria offered him a job. Over the next thirty years he worked for Shell in Port Harcourt and Warri. For two years (1980–1982) he was seconded to Brunei Shell, and for the rest of his career, until 1999, he was a senior electrical engineer in Lagos.

During Sani Abacha's military rule in Nigeria from 1993 to 1998, Nigeria's universities were closed for some months. Because at the time four of his children were university students, in 1995 Sim began to send his seven children for education at various colleges in the United States. They all graduated as professionals in fields such as pharmacy and engineering, and they all remained in the US. In 2008 one of his daughters got him a green card, an example of the US immigration policy of family reunification. In 2011 Sim finally and a bit reluctantly agreed to come to the US to live rather than to just visit regularly. He made Lexington his home because a daughter and son-in-law were working at the time at the University of Kentucky in medical fields. He became an American citizen and joined the Lexington Rotary Club—he had belonged to Rotary in Lagos since 1977. In 2016 his wife Adikat came to join him permanently. At age eighty-one in 2018 Sim had worked part-time or full-time at Walmart for six years, and in mid-August 2018 he came from a 7:30 a.m. to 4:00 p.m. shift at the superstore to share his story

Adikat Oyetunji and Asimiyu (Sim) Oyetunji. (Photo courtesy of Sim Oyetunji.)

with new University of Kentucky international students at the welcome picnic, the fiftieth anniversary of the Lexington Rotary Club's sponsorship of the event.[6]

By the early 1970s Kentucky institutions of higher education too began to host African students like Sim. For example, Nigerians Ezekiel Oke and J. Nesin Omatseye completed their undergraduate degrees at Georgetown College and at Kentucky Wesleyan College respectively and went on to earn PhDs at the University of Kentucky in anthropology and philosophy of education before 1980. Both returned to Nigeria to make their mark at universities there, Ezekiel Oke at the University of Ibadan and Jim Omatseye at the University of Benin in Benin City. In 1980 the two hosted Kentucky and Indiana teachers who went to Nigeria for six weeks on a Fulbright Group Project Abroad led by Angene Wilson, by then a professor at the University of Kentucky. Jim continued his Kentucky connections, returning to the University of Kentucky and Kentucky State University on a Fulbright in 1985–1986 and serving as a professor at Eastern Kentucky University for six years during Abacha's rule in Nigeria in the 1990s. After retiring as dean of the College of Education at the University of Benin, he began leading an effort to start a new university in his home city of Warri. In 2017 Jim was back in Kentucky to visit friends in Owensboro from his years at Kentucky Wesleyan and to arrange for a container of books to be shipped from the International Book Project in Lexington to open the planned university's library.[7]

African students were also coming to other colleges, as is evident in Ron Pelfrey's story. A Peace Corps volunteer in Ethiopia from 1966 to 1968 and a native Kentuckian, Ron wanted to continue contact with Ethiopians when he returned to Kentucky. He found a University of Kentucky directory, looked for Ethiopian names, and found an Ethiopian student who would practice Amharic with him. After a few months, the student invited him to a party in Lexington attended by one hundred or so Ethiopian students from all over the state. At the party a young Ethiopian woman stood out. Ron asked her for a date. They married the day after she graduated from Berea College in December 1975 and settled in Lexington.[8]

Growing up, Ibrahim Bakoush dreamed about coming to the United States. In the late 1970s, "it was what young men in Libya wanted to do, but that dream was always against my father's wishes." After Libya's leader Muammar Gaddafi nationalized his furniture business, his father finally agreed, perhaps because that furniture business would no longer be a possibility for his son's future. Ibrahim already had an I-20 student visa a cousin had sent him from the US, so he went to Tripoli for an interview just before the American embassy was closed and obtained a student visa to come to Hattiesburg, Mississippi, in 1979 to attend the English Language Institute there. He then attended college in New Orleans for a semester before going with friends to Brevard Community College in Florida and completing an associate degree in business there. In 1983 he visited Kentucky for a Ramadan celebration with a cousin's family and decided to stay. Over thirty-three years he has worked at many jobs, from taxi driver to gas station owner to car lot manager. Currently he has his own auto body shop business.

By the 1980s more African students were beginning to stay in the US after graduation. Nkechi Amadife, associate professor and librarian at Kentucky State University, wondered why they were staying and wrote her PhD dissertation at the University of Kentucky based on interviews with nonreturning Nigerian students who originally came to the US in the late 1970s and 1980s. She identified as push factors the disparity in standards of living, a stagnant home economy, lack of resources and incentives for research and stimulating competition, and political instability. The pull factor was expressed by one of her informants: "Western education is the only way one can achieve success or survive in this world."[9]

Although many Nigerians and other students from African countries began to remain in the United States, some continued to return. For example, Noel Nelson Messone took his 1994 PhD in political science from the University of Kentucky back to Gabon and became his nation's ambassador to the United Nations in 2011 and then minister for forestry, environment, and protection of natural resources. Yao Quashigah and Naah Yemeh completed doctorates in the University of Kentucky's College of Education in the early 2000s and returned to leadership positions at the University of Winneba in Ghana. (Naah's oldest daughter, who went to high school in Lexington, began a doctorate at University of Oklahoma in fall 2017 after completing a master's at Western Kentucky University.) Mosoka Fallah returned to Liberia with a PhD in microbiology and immunology from the University of Kentucky and a master's in public health from Harvard to play an important role during the Ebola crisis in 2014–2015. He was one of the "Ebola Fighters" named in *Time's* Person of the Year in 2014 and was subsequently named a "Global Thinker" in the healer category by *Foreign Policy* magazine in its November–December 2015 issue because of his leadership as principal investigator of a research project studying Ebola survivors. Mosoka had started building a clinic in his hometown on the outskirts on Monrovia in 2010 with money from his graduate assistantship stipend and by 2018 was helping several other poor communities build their own clinics as well as transitioning his clinic into a health center with a surgical theater for complicated pregnancies and launching a vision-screening program offering $5 glasses. In 2018 he was appointed as a part-time faculty member at Harvard Medical School.[10]

American Higher Education and the African Professoriate in Kentucky

Except for one person, the immigrant professors interviewed for the African Immigrants in the Bluegrass Oral History Project got graduate (in one case undergraduate as well) degrees at American universities and then went on to become professors in Kentucky universities. They are part of what is a population of well-educated African immigrants in comparison to overall foreign- and native-born populations. An article from the Migration Policy Institute in May 2017 noted, "In 2015 39 percent of sub-Saharan Africans (ages 25 and over) had a bachelor's degree or higher, compared to 29 percent of the total foreign-born populations and 31 percent of the US born populations."[11]

Born in Egypt, Abdelmonem Rizk was probably the first professor at the University of Kentucky born in an African country. Because he died in 2005, his story comes from his daughter Camellia.[12] She recalled that he loved mangoes, pomegranates, dates, and figs and would sometime fix Egyptian food for the family. She knew that as a child her father made soccer balls out of sticks, that as a young man he was a soldier for two years under President Gamal Nasser, and that he then fenced and played soccer all over Europe. He spoke English, Italian, French, and German as well as Arabic. In 1957 he came on a scholarship to Indiana University to get a master's in physical education and met his Kentucky-born wife, who was also a student there. The couple lived in Cairo for a number of years, but after the birth of twin boys, they moved to Lexington in 1964. Abdelmonem got a job in physical education at the University of Kentucky and earned his doctorate there. As a faculty member in the College of Education, he introduced and coached fencing and soccer at the university and supervised physical education student teachers. He believed elementary age children, including girls, should play soccer and so helped found LYSA (Lexington Youth Soccer Association) in 1977. Skip Kifer, also a professor in the College of Education, remembered Abdelmonem as both colleague and mentor. He was "a major source of my soccer education while I was learning the game and coaching young players." His players loved the wonderful Pele films that Abdelmonem showed.[13]

Gashaw Lake came to the United States in 1971, aiming to become a scholar like his priestly ancestors in Ethiopia.[14*] He also admired an uncle who had gone to Oxford and was a well-known poet. He attended university for one year in Addis Abba, but then the university closed because of political unrest. Gashaw arrived in winter two weeks after classes had begun at John Carroll University in Cleveland, Ohio, but the foreign student advisor there arranged for him to begin instead at Saginaw Valley State College in Michigan where classes had not yet started. After he paid his first semester tuition of $648 at Saginaw Valley, Gashaw was out of money and took a job shoveling snow. In Ethiopia, once you were admitted to college finances were taken care of, but in the US he had to wash dishes and clean bathrooms on campus. Because he lacked the money for room and board, he remembered, other students invited him to stay in their rooms in the dorm and he floated from one room to another. An English professor loaned him money for his second semester tuition. Gashaw graduated from Saginaw Valley in

1974 with a major in political science and a minor in philosophy. Then he went on to the University of Oklahoma to earn a master's in public administration and a doctorate in philosophy of education by 1981. In 1982 Gashaw had an opportunity to return to Ethiopia to teach at Addis Ababa University, but he decided to stay in the United States. Before coming to his long career at Kentucky State University in Frankfort in 1986, Gashaw was an elementary teacher, an ESL teacher, and an adjunct professor at Langston University, all in Oklahoma. From 1999 to 2015 he served as dean of the College of Professional Studies at Kentucky State. Originally founded as the state's historically black college, Kentucky State University has had many African immigrant professors over the decades. In 2017 there were five faculty originally from Nigeria, three from Ethiopia, one from Sierra Leone, and one from Egypt.

Three West Africans were among the African immigrant professors who came to the University of Kentucky in the 1990s. Desmond Brown, who became a professor in the retailing and tourism management department in 1995, worked for British Caledonian Airlines after attending a top secondary school in Freetown and passing both his O-level exams and A-level post-secondary exams. He explained: "I liked the tourism area because I did a part-time job for a tour agency. So I decided I wanted to do marketing and business abroad, which were not offerings at the university in Sierra Leone at the time." Why the United States? "The US was a more popular place to go than England among my age group in 1981, with more opportunities. And I had visited England twice, and I felt I would fit in this society more than in England." A Sierra Leonean friend living in Maryland visited "home" and sent Desmond applications to Howard University and Morgan State University in Baltimore from the US. He applied, was accepted, and got the I-20 student visa after sending the first year's tuition, $2,066, to Morgan State, the cheaper choice. "I came with $300 in pocket money and started spending it from JFK to Washington, DC, on Greyhound." After completing a BA at Morgan State, he gained experience in hotel management in Connecticut and Georgia, completed two master's degrees, and tried out college teaching for several years before getting a full fellowship to do a PhD at Virginia Tech. After twenty-one years Desmond retired from the University of Kentucky in 2016 and moved to Bethune-Cookman College in Florida to start a new School of Hospitality Management there.

The journey of Kwaku Addo, originally from Ghana, to professor and later administrator at the University of Kentucky in 1991 was a winding path that included other countries before the United States.

Professor Desmond Brown. (Photo courtesy of Desmond Brown.)

After completing his undergraduate degree in biochemistry at Kumasi Technical College in Ghana in 1981, he received a year-long scholarship to work in research labs in Germany and Switzerland. He then fulfilled his required year of national service by teaching chemistry and biology at a secondary school in Kumasi and after that, because of economic problems in Ghana, he went to Nigeria to teach in a secondary school for several years. While there he received an invitation from the professor he had worked with in the Swiss lab to work in his lab at the University of Alberta in Canada. Before he left Ghana, Kwaku asked his future wife to marry him and went through the initial rites. "I married my wife in absentia and my younger brother stood in for me. My wife joined me in Canada after ten months." But Canada was very cold for both of them and their first child. Kwaku wanted more education, so he next decided to move south to the United States for a master's in biochemistry at the University of Idaho. For his doctorate Kwaku chose something more practical and had the opportunity to work with the renowned food scientist Yshajahu Pomeranz at Washington State University. He expected to enter the corporate world but a friend told a University of Kentucky faculty member about him; her nutrition science department was looking for someone in his field. At around the same time, Kwaku received a job offer from both Frito-Lay in Dallas, Texas, and the University of Kentucky. Why choose academia instead of the corporate world? "Academia had never crossed my mind, but my father was a teacher, so maybe it was in my genes." He spent twenty-two years as a teacher and administrator at the University of Kentucky before taking the post of associate dean for academic programs in the College of Agriculture and Human Sciences at Prairie View A&M University in Texas in 2013.

In contrast to Desmond and Kwaku, Marie-Antoinette Sossou did not originally plan to stay in the United States after getting her PhD. In 1998, while she was head of the Department of Social Work at the University of Legon in Accra, Ghana, she had the opportunity to do a doctorate through the offer of an assistantship for two years at the University of Denver. She went with a promise of sponsorship from the University in Ghana, but a new chancellor later said they had no obligation to her. In order to finish her dissertation Marie-Antoinette had to get work authorization and take out loans. And then she had to pay back the loans. So she took a job at the University of Kentucky's College of Social Work in 2003. She had planned to return—"Let me go back and do so many things." Even after getting tenure at the University of Kentucky, she inquired unsuccessfully about returning.

Francis Musoni was a later addition to the African immigrant faculty at the University of Kentucky. After obtaining his master's in history at the University of Zimbabwe, where he then taught for three years, Francis began looking for overseas opportunities to do his PhD. He first applied to and was accepted at both Oxford and Cambridge Universities in England, but because of Zimbabwe's political situation—it was no longer part of the British Commonwealth—those institutions offered no scholarships. Francis searched for other opportunities via the internet and in 2005 was awarded a four-month fellowship by the Five Colleges (in Massachusetts) African Studies Program. "And that's how I came to the US." At Amherst he learned about the variety of American university doctoral programs beyond the ones like Harvard, which were well known overseas. Francis began his PhD at Emory University in 2006 with full funding, including a stipend, and was hired by the University of Kentucky's history department in 2011.

Another trio of African immigrants became professors at Bluegrass Community and Technical College (BCTC) in Lexington. Nkongolo Kalala, who teaches micro- and macroeconomics, was working in a planning office in the Ministry of Agriculture in Democratic Republic of Congo, beginning research on the connection between food intake and health, when he had the opportunity to come to the United States to do graduate work. In 1985 he came with a group of six from Congo, beginning in Boulder, Colorado, to learn English. After earning a master's degree at the University of Georgia, he came to the University of Kentucky for doctoral work in agricultural economics in 1989 and graduated in 1995. One of his special experiences as a student was participating in conferences in Gabon, Senegal, and Morocco organized by Leon Sullivan to bring Africans and African Americans together.

Robert Chirwa, who had already gotten a master's in computer science at the University of Kentucky in 1990 and had started teaching at the University of Malawi at Zomba, knew he needed to get a doctorate to become an associate professor there. So he returned to the University of Kentucky in the computer science doctoral program in 1996. Life became complicated when his family—wife Tambu and two sons—joined him. (One son had been born when they were in Lexington for his master's degree and the second was born in Malawi.) There were money pressures, such as covering the family for health insurance and paying for his sons to play in soccer leagues. So Robert applied to what was then Lexington Community College and in 1999 the college hired him to teach computer science. "Sometimes you start something one way and it turns into a career and from 1999 until now I have been teaching at LCC, now BCTC." Because the computer science department of the University of Kentucky was not happy with his full-time employment, Robert transferred his coursework to the University of Louisville, where he could complete the program as a part-time student.

Iddah Otieno, who is professor of English and African studies and director of the Kenya Exchange Program at Bluegrass Community and Technical College, came from Kenya to Richmond, Kentucky, in 1996 because her husband had taken a position as a chemistry professor at Eastern Kentucky University. "I had to choose whether to come and join him here. I had been independent." She assumed she would come and teach high school as she had in Kenya, but certification presented roadblocks, so she decided to get a master's in English and African literature at Eastern Kentucky University. She was offered a job at BCTC in 2001 right at the end of that program—"a dream came true." Her second son was born a week later. Iddah began doctoral work in 2004 in the University of Kentucky's Department of Educational Policy Studies and Evaluation. Writing her dissertation on the internationalization of Kenyan institutions of higher education, she completed that degree in 2012 while teaching five classes a semester and having a third child.[15]

Eastern Kentucky University's faculty also now includes, as it has in the past, African immigrant professors. Judge Bankole Thompson, originally from Sierra Leone, was an exception in education, getting all his graduate degrees in England, and his route to teaching in Kentucky was also different. He joined Eastern Kentucky University's Department of Criminal Justice in 1995 after six years at Kent State University in northeastern Ohio. He first came to the United States after the American ambassador heard his speech "The Law, the State, and the Individual" at the Sierra Leone Bar Association's convention in 1986 and invited him to visit for a month. The following year the judge spent fall semester at Kent State University and spring semester at the University of Akron before joining the Kent State faculty. He said, "I had no fanciful ideas about the US. Being an academic lawyer and a judge, my preoccupation has always been exclusively to acquire knowledge about the US as the leading democracy in the world and its commitment to the rule of law, nationally and internationally." He and his wife also wanted their children to take advantage of educational opportunities in the United States. He retired from Eastern Kentucky University in 2014. Since the 1980s Eastern Kentucky University has had about fifteen professors from African countries, including Benin, Ethiopia, Ghana, Kenya, Nigeria, and Sierra Leone. Iddah Otieno's husband Tom Otieno, originally from Kenya, came to Eastern Kentucky University as a chemistry professor in 1995 and became dean of the College of Science in 2016.

One of those who came to the United States for education and eventually joined the professoriate emigrated from his country because of violence and war. In 1994 Kiluba Nkulu was offered a scholarship to study at Asbury Seminary in Wilmore, Kentucky, by the Methodist Church in Democratic Republic of Congo. Although his aim was not to become a pastor, he took advantage of the offer because his wife, from Kasai Province, was of a different ethnic group and as such was a target of people in Katanga Province, where they lived. He had to hide her for three months. The family clearly needed to leave the Congo as soon as possible, and thus instead of going to the University of Witwatersrand

Professor Kiluba Nkulu. (Photo courtesy of Kiluba Nkulu.)

in South Africa to study anthropology, as he had hoped, Kiluba came to the United States with his university degree in English literature and his experience teaching high school and college English, French, and philosophy. After earning his seminary degree at Asbury, he completed a PhD at the University of Kentucky and wrote his dissertation on the educational philosophy of Julius Nyerere, first president of Tanzania. He is now a professor in the University of Kentucky's College of Education.

A Kenyan Immigrant's Story of Education for the Ministry

Armstrong Cheggeh came to the United States for theological education and became a bishop instead of a professor. He went to six theological schools, two in Kenya and four in the United States, and graduated from five. Several factors "created my interest in America": a nearby American mission station in Kenya, a sign announcing that President Theodore Roosevelt had been there in 1909 on his African safari, and being taught by American missionaries and Peace Corps volunteers. So after two years at Scott Theological College in Kenya, Armstrong applied to and was accepted at Oral Roberts University in the US. However, he did not have the money to go. "I struggled for the next four years. I got married and we had our first son. Some friends helped me to apply to Rosedale Bible Institute, a Mennonite institution near Columbus, Ohio, in 1982, right at the time of a short-lived coup in Kenya." Rosedale accepted his two years of credits from Scott College, and after a year he had diplomas in Christian education and pastoral studies.

But Armstrong wanted more education, so he went to Central Bible College (today Evangel College), an Assembly of God college in Missouri, for an additional year. After graduation he went on to Southern California College (now Vanguard College) for a master's in religion. In 1984 he had brought his wife and son to Export, Pennsylvania, where his wife completed a three-year program in Christian education at a small school, and so he moved east to be with his family, now including a second son, and to write his thesis. He was grateful he had taken typing at Scott College—"not a man's thing in Kenya"—but he didn't have a computer so the thesis was not properly finished until 1989, two years after he had returned to Kenya.

Back in Nairobi for fourteen years, he and his wife had three more children and Armstrong continued his education. He completed a master's in Christian ministries in 1993 at the Nairobi International School for Theology (now International Leadership University) while serving with the Campus Crusade for Christ. He did church planting with the Assemblies of God church for ten years and also founded and led a children's center for orphans for seven years. In 1998 he began his own Fountain of Life Church. Then in 2001 Armstrong received a full scholarship from Asbury Seminary in Wilmore, Kentucky, to get his Doctor of Ministry degree in leadership and preaching. This time he stayed in the US so that his children, now in elementary, middle, high school, and college, could finish their education in America. "It was mainly the family—let's take advantage of our time together." But he also discovered that with his connections to churches in America he could do a lot more for his congregations (then fifty, later growing to three hundred) in East and Central Africa by staying in the US as an immigrant.

An Ethiopian Immigrant's Story of Becoming a Doctor

After two years of school in Addis Ababa, Ethiopia, where she was born, three years in Sweden, and then graduating from St. John's International

School in Brussels, Rahel Bosson wanted to come to the United States for her university education. "I was familiar with Africa. I'd been all around Europe. And I thought, 'Why not the culture of the US?' Plus my secondary education was in English." Rahel had always felt called to help the poor and marginalized. "That was really what I felt was my destiny. But there was no way my parents could afford to pay for university tuition in the States." Rahel's mother said, "Well, we'll just pray and let's see what the Lord does."

Opportunity came because Roy McClung, the American pastor who had baptized her at the International Baptist Church in Brussels where her Ethiopian family worshipped, had become president of the one-thousand-student Wayland Baptist University in Plainview, Texas. He arranged a scholarship and other financial assistance to enable Rahel to begin college there in 1996. So Rahel, with visions of New York skyscrapers, flew from Brussels to Lubbock International Airport, with one kiosk, and went on by car to Plainview in West Texas, where she discovered that Americans put ice in their water and don't eat with a knife and fork together. Because Wayland Baptist didn't have a bachelor of nursing degree, after two years she applied to Texas Tech University's accelerated program and got a scholarship there to complete a BA in nursing; she graduated in 2000. Then she did the year of optional practical training allowed by her student visa as a nurse in a hospital in Lubbock while applying for a work permit and a green card. "During that year I felt like God was saying, 'It's time for you to leave Texas.' But I had no idea where I was going." Although she wanted to become a doctor she had become disillusioned. "I didn't see physicians that really loved and cared for patients." She loved psychology and so thought she might do a PhD in behavioral science and behavioral medicine.

While her green card application was pending Rahel decided to travel for three months. As part of that travel she visited Pastor McClung, who had moved to Louisville and asked her, "Well, have you thought about Kentucky?" But she wondered, "Maybe I'm supposed to go back to Africa or back to Europe." She went to see her parents, who were visiting in New York where relatives who had come from Ethiopia as refugees lived. With her parents' encouragement she decided to stay in Louisville after she got her temporary Kentucky nursing license and also discovered she was not required to remain in Texas, where she had petitioned for her green card. She worked as a nurse and applied to the University of Louisville in behavioral science. Rahel switched to the medical school after she became acquainted with physicians "with a heart for medicine similar to mine" in a Bible study group.

She completed medical school in 2011 and her residency there in 2014. Then Rahel became the first director of the Refugee Health Program at the University of Louisville, fulfilling that earlier sense of destiny.

THE DIVERSITY VISA LOTTERY

The Diversity Visa Lottery became an increasingly popular way to try to come to the United States in the early 2000s. It appealed to educated Africans who saw the US as a land of opportunity for more education and better jobs and also as an escape from problems in their home countries.[16] It was also a possibility for an educated adult child over eighteen who could not qualify as a family member under family reunification.

In 2004 Zineeddine Hamoudi applied for the diversity visa during his final year of university in Algeria. He was walking to the train station one morning and saw an internet café that had an American flag and asked, "Why the flag?" The café manager told him about the Diversity Visa Lottery for high school graduates, asked him for the equivalent of $1, and completed the application for Zineeddine online; the only information needed was his name, address, and that he had a high school diploma. Six months later Zineeddine received a letter from the Department of Immigration in Louisville: "Congratulations, you were randomly selected for a diversity visa, which qualifies you to get a green card and be a permanent resident." He went to someone he knew and asked, "Does this sound real?" The friend assured him it was. Zineeddine had thought about going to Europe but never to the United States. "People think of the US as a very far land and as very different." But one brother knew people who had gone to US schools, learned English, and got better professional careers. "Technologically, if you want to succeed, it's better to go the US." He advised Zineeddine, "Go for it." An older brother was skeptical, his father said no, and his mother wasn't sure, saying, "Why don't you go to France, which is two hours away?" He thought about his options for about a month and then Zineeddine filled out the form and sent it back to Louisville.

A year later, in 2005, he received a letter telling him to appear for an interview at the American embassy in Tunis, Tunisia. He remembered the interviewer was very nice, asking him questions in Arabic and French about where he grew up, what he had studied, and then congratulating him and stamping his passport. He paid $750 in onetime fees and gave his uncle's best friend's address in Indianapolis as a contact name. At the interview he met another Algerian, also in electrical engineering and also planning to get an American graduate degree and, after spending Ramadan with their families, they flew together from Algiers to Paris to New York the next month. After Zineeddine completed a master's degree in electrical engineering from IUPUI (Indiana University–Purdue University Indianapolis) in 2010, he became a software developer for a company near Indianapolis and then in 2014 moved to Lexington to work for Lexmark.

Pierre Ngog, born in Cameroon, also applied for and received a diversity visa. Because his wife and two sons were living in France, Pierre was spending every weekend traveling to Paris from his job in Germany in the stock market. So he decided to move to France to be with his family. However, he found it difficult to get a similar job there and while staying at home taking care of his sons he decided he would have to move. In May 2005 "I was surfing the internet and found a website that said, 'Live and work in the United States.' It was for the green card lottery." He had found the Israel-based private company USAFIS, whose website touts that they assist clients from around the globe successfully prepare and submit their applications for a fee. Pierre began filling out the online form but when it asked for money, he thought it was a scam so he didn't finish the application. Thirty minutes later a person from the USAFIS office in Israel called him and said it was real: "Just send 75 euros for three years in the lottery." So he did and two years later, in March 2007, he received an email that said, "Congratulations!" and included a telephone number in Kentucky to call. "My cell phone had free international calls so I called." Someone answered, "Office of the Green Card," and asked his name, age, birthplace, and case number, and then said, "Congratulations, you have won" and asked him if he had received the forms. "But I didn't understand English, and I thought, 'A country where I don't speak English, what will I do there?'" The next day a big envelope arrived in the mail from USAFIS with a form for each member of the family. "But who can explain how to fill them out?" he wondered.

USAFIS gave him the name of an attorney in New York who charged $3,000 for assistance. Pierre would fax forms to the attorney, who would fax them back, and that went on until everything was correct. Then he was assigned an interview time the following March. He chose Cameroon for the interview because his two older sons were there, and then the embassy in Yaounde could send papers to Paris for his wife and two younger sons. Pierre arrived by himself in 2008; his wife and children followed some months later. After his arrival he completed an associate degree in accounting and finance and did some substitute teaching.

Venus Niza and Aka Kpla, both from Côte d'Ivoire, also won the lottery. The impetus for their leaving was Côte d'Ivoire's brief civil war and its effects on the country. Venus had graduated from secondary school in 2007 and then studied physics and chemistry to obtain an associate degree at a university in Côte d'Ivoire's capital Abidjan, but the university was closed for two years during disputed presidential elections and civil war and there were no jobs. "I was in depression." Her fiancé, who had been a friend through high school and college, suggested applying for the diversity visa and when she got the visa they got married. "I thought it was a joke. I thought the only way I could come was on a student or tourist visa." They came to Lexington, arriving on June 12, 2012, because a friend in their church in Côte d'Ivoire knew a Congolese pastor in the International Christian Church in Lexington. She has worked for Amazon and takes classes at Bluegrass Community and Technical College. Venus has found it frustrating that Kentuckians often seem to think that "everyone has come as a refugee." They don't seem to know about the diversity visa, but she knows more than ten people from various countries who came to the US that way.

Aka Kpla already had a master's degree, a job, a wife, and a child when civil war began in 2011 in Côte d'Ivoire. He remembered life was good growing up. "We lived in harmony." When the war started, his family had a difficult three months because they lived very close to an army base. "We didn't have money, food, or drink. My daughter cried all the time. We didn't know whether we would live or die." After the fighting, he went back to work but because of the war and its effect on the economy, he decided to look for another country to live in. His wife knew about the process of moving to Canada because her best childhood friend had emigrated there, so they investigated that option, but it was very expensive. "My small sister told me about the diversity visa, which required only paying for the visa and the airfare. She applied many times but never got chosen." Aka, however, was chosen; he applied in 2012, was accepted in 2013, and came to the United States in 2014. He works at Amazon and has taken courses at Bluegrass Community and Technical College.

Fiston Boyita Bo Malinga graduated from high school in Kinshasa, Democratic Republic of Congo, in 2000, but he didn't have the money to go on to college. When his American father, Gary Liebert, who had been a Peace Corps volunteer in Congo in the early 1980s, reconnected with him, Fiston was older than eighteen and didn't qualify as a family

Fiston Boyita Bo Malinga and his father Gary Liebert.
(Photo courtesy of Gary Liebert.)

member under family reunification. His father paid for him to study law for two years at the University of Burkina Faso in Burkina Faso's capital Ouagadougou and then applied for a diversity visa for him. Fiston filled out forms at the embassy that asked for a criminal background check, health records, school records, and a medical examination. Finally he was interviewed by the American ambassador who, he remembered, asked him about his studies. Fiston came to Louisville and lived with his father for several years. He took some classes at Jefferson Community College but then stopped because of his work schedule and finances and began working as an electrician.

For Love and Marriage

African immigrants have also come to the United States because of love and marriage. African men fall in love with American women. African women fall in love with American men. African women follow their husbands.

In 1992 Mamadou Savané (Sav), like other unemployed young men in Conakry, the capital of Guinea, was looking for an opportunity to go to the United States, Canada, or Europe. He already had brothers in Europe and in the US. One weekend he went to a party in the town of Kindia with a friend who was dating a Peace Corps volunteer and met Rachel Gibson, also a Peace Corps volunteer. After learning the next day that Rachel liked him, he took her on their first date that evening: an Indian movie and a meal prepared by his friend's sister with a nice piece of meat the young men had gotten at the funeral feast for Sav's grandmother that afternoon. Sav went back to Conakry and Rachel to her village, but they had another date the following weekend, "and that was it." In love and nearing the end of her Peace Corps service, Rachel decided to take a six-month job with USAID and moved with Sav into Sav's mother's home in Conakry. Although it was culturally inappropriate, his mother was willing to do that for her son. Getting married in Guinea turned out to be complicated, and Sav told Rachel, "Besides meeting you, I was trying to come to America." She helped him get a visitor's or tourist visa. His brother, who was driving a taxi in New York City, sent him money for an airline ticket, and he arrived in New York on March 21, 1993. Sav stayed with his brother until Rachel finished her USAID job, visited her sister in England, and flew to New York. She didn't know whether she or America was most important to Sav. But he was there to meet her at the airport and they took a train to Cincinnati and then came to Lexington, where Rachel had lived and worked before her stint in the Peace Corps. Sav got a job at the Campbell House Hotel and then worked at both the Hyatt Regency Hotel and UPS for seven and a half years, continuing at UPS for another seven and a half years, including for a year and a half after he opened his restaurant, Sav's Grill and West African Cuisine, in September 2008.

Moulaye Indrissa Barry also met and married an American woman. After completing his master's degree he went back to his village in Senegal to bury his mother, who had died from cancer, and to support his grandparents by teaching English, but "the money was not good." In 2001 he had an opportunity to use his English in Senegal's capital Dakar, where he worked for $200 a month at a company that cleared and transported shipping containers. He had always wanted to live in an English-speaking country, even applying to a university in England, but his visa was denied. He also applied to several universities in the United States, but then "9/11 came and everything stopped." So he concentrated on his job. He worked there until 2006, when he met his wife. She got his paperwork started for a visa, and he then chose to come to the US because a change of government in Senegal caused the South African company he was working for to leave the country. Like Sav, he had dreamed about America as the place to be. "They come because of the dream," he said, speaking of immigrants like himself.[17] With encouragement from his wife, he got an assistantship and a scholarship for two years to complete a master's degree in the University of Kentucky's French department. Then he got a graduate teaching certificate and worked as a translator for Kentucky Refugee Ministries and then as an adjunct professor at Georgetown College and Transylvania University.

Sylvia Uwamaliya Stainback met her future American husband when he visited Rwanda. When she was a senior in college, her uncle, who worked as a driver for the National Conservation Services, asked if she wanted to go out with him and a visiting American doctoral researcher from Florida State University for lunch and to visit Virunga National Park. "I was the host, I had to talk, so I guess I made an impression. I was in awe of how much he had accomplished, but I thought that was it." But he said he would call her from the States—and he did. They talked about their dreams, including her desire to get a master's degree. He asked her if she would like to come and visit the United States, offering to pay her plane fare. When Sylvia was advised by the embassy that it would be easier to get a student visa than a tourist visa, her future husband arranged for her to apply to the Center for English at Florida State, and with a bank statement from his parents, her acceptance was assured. In Rwanda Sylvia was working for the nongovernmental organization Women with Women International in micro-credit. She completed her undergraduate thesis in August 2005 and the next day flew to the US. After her marriage in 2006, Sylvia got a graduate degree in administration and leadership in 2008 at State University of New York–Plattsburgh, where her husband was teaching, and later did an online certificate at Northeastern University in teaching English as a second language. After their move to Kentucky she taught ESL at Eastern Kentucky University and the University of Kentucky. In 2017 the Stainbacks moved to Miami, where Sylvia reported that she was teaching ESL and also learning Spanish.

African women sometimes followed their husbands, like Iddah Otieno from Kenya, whose husband preceded her by a year as a professor at Eastern Kentucky University, and Tambu Chirwa, who came with her husband Robert from Malawi when he attended the University of Kentucky for graduate degrees. Abigail Unuakhalu met her husband when a mutual friend introduced them while he was visiting Lagos, Nigeria, where she lived. They married in 1995 and in 1997 he brought her to Frankfort, where he was already a professor at Kentucky State University. Abigail had never thought about coming to America. She came from a very modest family, and she had heard some horror stories about America, where marriages fall apart, where people have to work so hard, where people live in one or two rooms.[18] "I didn't want to experience that. But he came so genuinely." Still, her family was cautious and one of her brothers talked to some people in the United States and did a kind of background check. Abigail arrived with her undergraduate degree in economics and transferred enough credits to complete a degree in accounting at Kentucky State University, enabling her to get increasingly responsible jobs as an accountant in state government in Frankfort.

A different experience of following a husband comes from Alice Kamadjou, who told her story on a Bluegrass Refugee Voices radio program in March 2017. Originally from Cameroon, she had migrated in her late teens via ship to South Africa, where she worked selling bread and braiding hair. There she met her future Congolese husband, who was then living in Malawi as a refugee. She agreed to marry him after he proposed a third time but they did not live together after their wedding in South Africa because he had to return to Malawi. Then he had the opportunity to come to the United States as a refugee. He filed an application for her to join him under family reunification. Two years later, in February 2017, in the midst of the confusion over President Trump's travel ban, her flight was canceled and then rescheduled, but on February 21 she arrived at Bluegrass Field to be welcomed by Kentucky Refugee Ministries and her husband, whom she called her gift. "He was dressed in a suit and had brought flowers."[19]

Refugee Stories

Refugees and their stories became prominent in the 2000s in Kentucky, especially as Kentucky Refugee Ministries grew in Lexington and Louisville. Numbers of Congolese and Burundians became noticeable in Lexington and Somalis in Louisville. In contrast to other immigrants, they often came from refugee camps in countries other than their countries of origin.[20]

The "Lost Boys" of Sudan were one of the earliest large groups to come to the US from refugee camps. Sixteen thousand Lost Boys who had left Sudan in 1987 survived their one-thousand-mile walk and reached Panyundo Refugee Camp in Ethiopia, where both UNHCR and the Red Cross helped them. Jacob Guot was one of them. However, when Eritrean rebels attacked the camp in 1990 they had to run again, back to Sudan. A lot of people died crossing the Gilo River. Three boys Jacob was running with were shot by Arab militia. After six months the Lost Boys fled to Kenya. "We thought we came here for life," but the Turkana people who lived near Kakuma Refugee Camp wanted food that the United Nations was giving refugees, and they killed Jacob's cousin and many others. Besides Sudanese, the huge camp eventually included Burundians, Rwandans, Ugandans, and Somalis. Jacob was in that camp for nine years. He wrote in his autobiography: "I learned much about people from different cultures and how they think. As a good student, I learned the basics of math, science, English, geography and the Bible, as well as arts and crafts. Since I was good at socializing and storytelling, I often sat under a lean-to or a shade tree and attracted a crowd of people with whom to talk."[21]

In 1999 the United States agreed to bring some of the sixteen thousand "Lost Boys and Lost Girls" in the camp to America so they could further their education. Before the events of September 11 closed the program, four thousand young Sudanese came to the US. They had to go through a screening process in Kenya, including a medical examination. Their airplane tickets cost $850 and each had to sign a promissory note to pay the money back within six months.[22]

As a twenty-one-year-old with a seventh-grade education, Jacob arrived in a very cold New York on March 6, 2001. He remembered being scared because he saw breath coming out of people's mouths. "I thought people were burning over here." The next day he flew to Houston to begin an American life. Jacob completed his undergraduate education at Lancaster Bible College in Pennsylvania and came to Asbury Theological Seminary in Wilmore, Kentucky, in 2012. He graduated with two master's degrees in 2016 and then organized African Sunrise Communities, which works for peace and reconciliation in East Africa. Jacob also went through a difficult process to bring his wife to the US. He returned to South Sudan to marry her in 2006 and then, after he became a US citizen in 2007, he took her to Kenya to begin the process to get a visa. His wife almost gave up. He remembered the two years it took as "a terrible process," afterward giving "me a pain in my heart." As of 2017, he and his wife and three children lived in Wilmore, Kentucky, where she was a star ESL student.

Originally from Democratic Republic of Congo, Kikoko Godfrey described the process of coming to the United States as a refugee from the camp in Namibia. He had been there for eight years. He said, "I didn't have any hope. So in 2005 I went to the authorities and said, 'I'm getting older and my children have no opportunities.'" Eventually he and his wife and the children older than fifteen were all interviewed. They passed. "I was lucky." Where he would go was not his choice, but he was very happy when he learned the United States was the family's destination. "I knew the US was peaceful, that education was good, that there were opportunities for education and jobs for my children." Eight years after he had first inquired, on November 27, 2013, Kikoko and his family came to Lexington. Kikoko does housekeeping at the Family Care Center and his wife works in housekeeping at the University of Kentucky. Like a number of other refugees, he has gone through certified nurse assistant training.

Beatrice Mbayo escaped when the rebels came to Kongolo in Democratic Republic of Congo in September 1999, running at night with her eight-year-old-son. But tragically, she was separated from her husband, whom she never saw again. She and her son walked from Kongolo to Lubumbashi on the government side. Beatrice was pregnant and the baby was born with club feet at the camp of displaced persons near Lubumbashi. After sixteen months, the Red Cross there urged her to go where she could get help for her baby, so they rode on trucks and buses from the Congo through Zambia to Harare, Zimbabwe, where they registered and then were taken to the remote Tongogara refugee camp, where they lived for about five years. "We had a school under a tree," she explained in her interview. But "more than 2000 refugees had to fight every day at the well to get one bucket of water. The heat was unexplainable and all year long."[23] She described a dream in which she had two passports, Canadian and American, and the Canadian one was fake. After a Zimbabwean doctor told her that she should go back to her own country with her handicapped child because Zimbabwe already had its own children needing surgery, the social worker at the camp felt sorry for her. From that struggle Beatrice seems to have gotten fast-tracked to come to the United States in 2006. She was a case manager at Kentucky Refugee Ministries in Lexington for a time, then worked as a certified nursing assistant doing home visits in the mental health area.

She has completed her certification to be a medical technician, and is currently working at a senior citizen facility.

Khadar Abdullahi's Somali family also had the opportunity to come to the United States because of a child with a medical problem. His infant sister had a critical heart problem and the United States finally agreed to take the whole family in 2005 when other countries would not. The infant sister had four open-heart surgeries at Korsair/Norton Hospital in Louisville and at thirteen years old in 2017 said she wants to become a surgeon when she grows up to help American children. Khadar was fourteen when he arrived in the US. He graduated from Waggener High School in Louisville and then he studied to be a pharmacy tech through National College. He would like to go back to school to be able to work in public assistance, but as the oldest of twelve children, Khadar has had to work to help support his family so his siblings can go on to college.

Between 2005 and 2008 the United States agreed to take about nine thousand individuals from three refugee camps in Tanzania, mostly Hutu refugees who had left Burundi in 1972 and were not welcome to return because their land had been redistributed and they would be viewed as outsiders. Having been in a camp in Tanzania for ten years and out of Burundi for thirty-three years, Tite Niyonizigiye was one who qualified for relocation to the US. He went through three interviews with UNHCR and then an interview with US immigration. One day in 2007 names were posted, and "I was among those, but I didn't know where I would go." In November 2007 he and his family went to a Transit Center and on December 17, 2007, they flew to the US and arrived in Lexington two days later. His sister-in-law had preceded him four months before and two sisters came earlier to North Carolina. A scholarship paid for Tite to do his master's at Asbury University in Wilmore, Kentucky, and at the time of his interview he was working toward his certification as a social worker and looking for a job in social work. In spring 2019 he was working at Amazon at night (he had been there for ten years and valued the benefits package) and doing interpreter work in the daytime, as well as being the pastor of a new Pentecostal church.

An Asylum Case

In 2002 Jose Kazadi encountered a Congolese arms buyer for the first President Kabila who discovered Kazadi's role as a journalist, which led to people following him and threatening his life in Russia. Jose told the story.

> So a Congolese official came to Russia on a secret mission. The Congo was engaged in a war with the rebels and he came to buy a plane, an aircraft that will be capable of carrying helicopters so he can pursue rebels in the jungles, so they can push back the rebels. He was in Moscow for two weeks with all these official paper documents. He couldn't get anywhere. And the language barrier made it complicated for him. So someone who knew about it said, "Why don't you help him because you have those connections?" So I said, "Okay, no problem. But I need to get a guarantee from the official at the Congo Embassy in Moscow that this is something I can do. And if I do it, they have to pay me a commission." So once I got a guarantee I sent my colleague from the Cameroon to meet him instead of me and he could see the aircraft, his dream come true. But I told my Cameroon colleague never to talk about our magazine. Don't mix journalism with business.

However, eventually the Cameroon colleague did mention the magazine to the Congolese official and even gave him a copy of the issue in which an article Jose had written described Russia missing an opportunity to do weapons business with Congo because of Congo's bureaucracy.

So the deal fell apart. "The guy was gone. Business was missed. I was attacked and threatened. That's why I'm in the United States. I wanted to be involved in things of the country, so I have to choose either living or not living. I'm in trouble for the magazine. I was so afraid that everyone I love is getting into jeopardy now. So the [American] embassy took the case. They studied it, and they granted me a resettlement in the US." Jose came to Lexington in 2004 with his Russian wife and two sons. He completed a degree at the University of Kentucky in foreign language/international economics in 2012 and has worked for Xerox since 2012 as well as doing business importing food products from Africa and the Caribbean.

An Ambassador and a Pharmacist

Essa Bokar Sey first came to the United States in 1998 to support The Gambia in its role on the United Nations Security Council in New York City. His subsequent appointments included ambassador to France with accreditation to Russia, Spain, Portugal, Greece, Hungary, and UNESCO, and ambassador to Taiwan with accreditation to the

Essa Bokar Sey. On his left is a picture of him as ambassador from The Gambia with President George W. Bush on the wall behind him. (Photo courtesy of Jack Wilson.)

Philippines and Indonesia. And then in 2002 he became ambassador to the United States with accreditation to Mexico, Cuba, Brazil, and Venezuela.[24*] He met President George W. Bush on four or five occasions, "a man I can call a friend. It was just a natural connect. When I became a citizen he wrote to me." Essa particularly recalled the Iftar dinner at the end of Ramadan at the White House. "People don't know things like that are happening in this country, the respect for Islam. After you pray you can join the president and sit at the table." He also described how he was able to "get his country back in the good books" by not being defensive, by being natural and objective, and so satisfying the human rights criteria so the United States would allow The Gambia to be part of the Africa Growth and Opportunity Act.

Then in 2003, when "things soured" between him and the president of The Gambia and he lost his job, Essa was offered a house by a good friend in Houston. He lived there with his family until he got the appropriate papers to begin to work and later move toward citizenship. In 2006 he moved to Louisville with his wife and two sons, nineteen and twenty-two. The older son has cerebral palsy and is in a wheelchair. Essa has worked as a Walmart business representative, a substitute teacher in the Jefferson County Schools, in the credit department of a bank, and finally as a contractor for Mid Atlantic Professionals, working with the US Department of Defense.

Karin Krain and her husband owned an independent pharmacy in South Africa for nine years. In 2003 a change in the law regarding dispensing fees meant there was no profit margin in the business, especially with chain pharmacies coming in to compete with the independents. Rite-Aid Pharmacies was recruiting in South Africa and "the choice was clear." Karin came to the United States on an H-1B visa, which allows employers to hire highly skilled foreign workers in particular occupations. It was a time when some other white South Africans were leaving for New Zealand.

Rite-Aid sponsored the Krains for work visas and green cards in the United States, and Karin saw the move as an opportunity for herself, her husband, and their children. The first offer was in Napa, California. She flew to San Francisco and took the required exam but discovered how prohibitively expensive houses were in the area. Then Rite-Aid offered Kentucky, promising to get her and her husband visas and green cards in just eighteen months. All they knew about Kentucky were the horses and Kentucky Fried Chicken, but they could see the advantages: "Kentucky was beautiful," the University of Kentucky was a public institution, and the cost of living was reasonable. So Karin and her family arrived in 2005, and she began her work in Kentucky with Rite Aid. She is now pharmacy director associate of the ambulatory pharmacy services department at the University of Kentucky.

Liberian Stories Continued: Influence of War

The stories of the four Liberians related in chapter 1 and continued here illustrate the variety of reasons and the variety of ways immigrants from just one country have come to the United States: to get an education, to escape danger in the home country and get asylum in the US, as a refugee, and on a visitor's visa. In their stories the long Liberian civil war of 1989–2003 was the important backdrop.

For Mulbah Zowah the aim was education. In 1995 he escaped war in Liberia's capital Monrovia by joining sixteen thousand others on the infamous cargo ship that languished for nine days on the ocean before being allowed to land at Takoradi, Ghana. He remained in a refugee camp there until 1998 when, after Charles Taylor won the presidential election, war waned and he was accepted at the University of Liberia. However, he returned to Ghana after each semester because it was safe, there was internet, and he could work. "I was always hoping to travel to the US to get an education." So Mulbah googled tuition-free colleges and found Berea College, which has a long history of accepting African students.[25]

After submitting his paperwork to Berea College in 2003, Mulbah got an email saying he was accepted and then the packet with his I-20 immigration form arrived. However, the war had started up again in Liberia and the American embassy was closed in Monrovia so he couldn't do a visa interview there. Mulbah sold what clothes he had, but was still $7 short of what he needed for a plane ticket (his first plane ride) to Conakry, Guinea. He waited until the airline took pity on him and allowed him to board. He arrived in Guinea with no money but found a fellow Liberian who took him to the American embassy, where he obtained a visa. Berea College, whose international student advisor was tracking his movements through the region via telephone calls from Mulbah, sent him an airline ticket and he arrived the day before classes began in August 2003, with the clothes on his back, his documents, and malaria. He graduated in 2008 as a nurse and has since worked in various medical settings, including as a dialysis specialist, in Kentucky and elsewhere. In 2019 he was preparing to take his board certification examination as a family nurse practitioner and working on a doctor of nursing degree online.

Sam Vorkpor's experiences with the war in Liberia led him to decide in 1995 to come to Pecos, Texas, where he had a cousin who was also a family doctor. "Charles Taylor was now in Monrovia. I had to find a way to get out of here. I couldn't tell anybody except my wife because of the risk involved. I stayed with my cousin, took all my exams. Then war broke out again in Monrovia." His wife didn't want to follow him initially but he was able to gain asylum and pressured her to leave. She and their children came to Pecos in 1997, and she decided to go to school and become a nurse. Sam said, "I tried to get into a residency, but I had to compete with all these American grads. My grades were not way up there." Sam was advised that his documents from his medical education and his experience as a doctor in Liberia didn't mean much in the United States so he should get more education in the US.

"So I took a loan in 2001 and did a public health master's degree at Meharry Medical College in Nashville, Tennessee. My wife told me what I make will take care of the family. I took the test for pharmacy tech and got a job at CVS to pay the rent. The director for the preventive medicine department wanted someone to collect data for a research project. I worked hard and impressed him. I wanted to get into a residency and he saw how serious I was." Sam was accepted for a residency in preventive medicine but began September 1 rather than July 1 because the college wouldn't accept the letter saying he would get his green card in four to six months. It wanted the actual physical card. "Life is determination," Sam said. He remembered the college put him "on call" the first day and he didn't know how to put information in the computer because there were no computers in the hospital where he had worked in Liberia. He had to learn the system. After getting his master's in public health and finishing a year's residency in preventive health, he was still not satisfied. He wanted more training. So he applied for a residency in family medicine at the University of Connecticut in Hartford and completed that program in 2008.

At that point Sam got a job offer from Wellmont Health Care System in southwest Virginia and worked there from 2008 to 2012. Then he worked with an ER group for a year but he wanted to be an outpatient and inpatient doctor and move somewhere for a good education for his children, who were in middle and late elementary school. "My older son wanted to play football and he liked University of Kentucky. He said when I get there the football program will be better." They moved to Lexington in 2013, and Sam now practices clinical medicine at Manchester Memorial Hospital, an Advantage Hospital in Clay County. The older son began his sophomore year at the University of Kentucky in fall 2018 as a pre-med student. The younger son, a junior in high school in 2018–2019, wants to be a lawyer.

When Abraham Sven-Peters lost his job in Sierra Leone with the closing of the American firm he worked for because the peacekeeping mission was completed, he decided to apply through UNHCR as a refugee. "Luckily for me, the US gave opportunities for Liberian refugees. It was a two-year process. I had to write a paper about the political reasons I couldn't return to Liberia." He was chosen by Kentucky Refugee Ministries and came to Lexington in July 2005. Wesley United

Methodist Church sponsored him, his Sierra Leonean wife, whom he had met when they both worked on the Mercy ship (a hospital ship that provides life-saving surgeries for people where medical care is nearly nonexistent) in 1998, and his son. He has worked as a caregiver for people with mental disabilities with several different organizations, but is doing online coursework in criminal justice and would like to work in security.

In May 2003 Cuttington College, where Jemima and Bibi Roberts worked, started a program in Monrovia because of rebel activity upcountry. "But by the end of June everything was getting so tense." The rebels were closing in on Taylor. "The war was almost on Broad Street. Bibi was getting kind of fragile. My nephew said you just need to pack and go. We called the St. Stephens people [the Episcopal church in Richmond, Virginia, which had supported them for many years] and they sent money for plane tickets to the US through Ghana." So on July 5, 2003 Jemima Roberts, then fifty-eight, and her husband Bibi Sr., then sixty-eight, arrived in the US on visitor's visas, as they had a number of times before. They came to Lexington to stay with their son Bibi Jr. and his family, uncertain about their future. "People are so weary with the war," Jemima said when columnist Merlene Davis interviewed them a month later for the *Lexington Herald Leader*. "You get up in the morning, you hear guns shooting. Go to bed at night, and your head cannot rest on your pillow. People are shooting. You wake up in the middle of the night guns shooting." No wonder Jemima thought the fireworks she heard the night they arrived in Lexington were guns. Would they stay? Jemima didn't like being dependent on her son, and "it would really be difficult at our age to start our lives all over again. America is not an easy country. You have to work so hard." Her husband said, "I would rather be home than here, but if there is no way out, then you try to make life where you are."[26] And they did decide to make a life in the United States.

The Immigrants Are Here

In the novel *Exit West,* Mohsin Hamid uses doors to indicate the migration of his refugee couple from country to country.[27] Sometimes the place is named—London in England, Marin County in California—and sometimes it is not. Perhaps the couple's birth country is Pakistan or Syria, or perhaps it is whatever country the reader wishes it to be. Chinese immigrant to the United States Jess X. Snow describes migration as magical and natural and defines immigration as "imagination given a destination."[28]

Most of the immigrants interviewed for this oral history project found at least some open doors after they arrived in the United States. But while migration has been a natural process for thousands of years, is migration magical? Is the destination of America as immigrants had imagined? What was different from the culture and country into which they were born? What adjustments were hard? What do they miss? What do they value here? Who and what has helped as they have learned to live in their destination—Kentucky? The occupations of the interviewed immigrants have usually been included in this chapter, but what do the immigrants themselves think counts as success? In sum, how have migration and immigration turned out for the individuals who told their stories for this oral history project and this book? The next chapter deals with all these questions.

3

Struggles and Successes

> One does not cross a river without getting wet.
>
> —Zulu proverb

Getting to the United States is just the beginning of the immigrant experience, and very soon expectations meet reality. "An Italian friend in Malawi had told me the US is supposed to be like waking up in heaven," said Tambu Chirwa, who was joining her graduate student husband, but of course it was not. Coming to do a graduate degree from Zimbabwe, Francis Musoni found "ordinariness" rather than heaven. The immigrant was a "completely newborn starting life," said Bandushubwenge Vanisa, a refugee from Burundi. "I had to reconstruct myself. Everything was different," said Sylvia Uwamaliya Stainback, who came to marry an American she had met in Rwanda. Former ambassador Essa Bokar Sey from The Gambia said: "The United States has two ambassadors, *CNN* and Hollywood." But he could show a visitor who expected New York and Miami, with much concrete and many lights, places that were as "bush," with as many trees, as parts of West Africa. Mamadou Savané from Guinea agreed. "People know about America from movies. To see the reality, it is totally different."

Whether they first come as students, refugees, diversity visa holders, or on a tourist or another kind of visa, immigrants go through the first days and then the months and years dealing with cultural and language differences, getting an education or reeducation, finding a job and perhaps a second job to have enough money to live, often confronting ignorance and discrimination, even racism, usually discovering some helpful American people and institutions, and usually becoming successful, however they define success. This chapter begins with "First Days," followed by "What Is Difficult?" "Ignorance and Racism," and "Who and What Has Been Helpful?" The last two sections are titled "What is Success?" and "One Success Story."

First Days

Memories of first days and weeks in the US are vivid for most immigrants. Many, as evidenced in the previous chapter, can cite the date they arrived. Their experiences vary but even for those who have been to the United States before or who have helpful friends or relatives or groups such as Kentucky Refugee Ministries or the Rite Aid recruiter, culture shock is real.

Karin Krain arrived in Lexington from Cape Town, South Africa, on September 14, 2005, with her husband, three children aged twelve, ten, and eight, and eighteen pieces of luggage. It was almost midnight and there was no one to meet them at the airport. Customs in Detroit had gone through all their luggage and they had missed their earlier flight. Karin called the Rite Aid recruiter in California who arranged transportation to their hotel in Richmond, Kentucky. The next morning they took their children to Model Lab School. "We are still jet-lagged and tired and everything is strange and people driving on the other side of the road. For the kids it was such a shock, here in school already. The middle and the younger ones had a very hard time understanding the dialect. So many words were different, *post* instead of *mail*. Sometimes we drove on the wrong side of the road. But we got through it."

Zineeddine Hamoudi arrived in New York City on November 16, 2005, with the new Algerian friend he had met getting his diversity visa who had a friend in the city. That friend gave the newcomers a subway map and showed them where to get food, advising, "Start your life." But Zineeddine quickly saw that New York would be an expensive place to live and, after spending a week seeing the sights, he took a Greyhound bus twenty hours west to Indianapolis, where his uncle's friend met him and invited him to stay in his apartment for several months. He remembered the cold—thirty-two degrees was cold in Algeria.

Beatrice Mbayo arrived in Lexington on July 21, 2006. "We don't know where we are going as a refugee. I had documents that said Bluegrass Airport. When we were landing, my [second] husband and I were looking at the green fields and there were no houses. I told him, 'We will be farming for white people.' But people met us at the airport, and the people and Kentucky Refugee Ministries were so welcoming and ready to help, and I made friends in the first three months. Learning and listening to English was a challenge. Learning how to drive was a challenge." Working forty hours a week with children and no family to help was very hard. Beatrice lost her first job at University of Kentucky food service because she spent so much time with her younger son, who was at Shriner's Hospital for 150 days for surgery on his club feet to enable him to walk.

Tite Niyonizigiye and his family arrived as refugees in Lexington on December 18, 2007. The Great Recession had begun. "The picture we had in our country was not what we saw when we came. Outside we were thinking that the United States is a great country, a powerful country, a small paradise on this earth where life is easy. What I was thinking was completely different. When I was thinking life was easy it was not true." He saw homeless people. He learned there was not medical insurance for everyone. "When we came it was around Christmas and some offices were closed. Kentucky Refugee Ministries was more basic then. During those holidays we did not have enough food. Ah, this is the United States! Wow, how is that possible?" Then he learned that in three months they must begin to pay rent for their apartment. He got a job working at Lexington's Amazon warehouse on March 31, and on April 1 he started paying rent.

Six months after he got his diversity visa, Pierre Ngog arrived in Maryland on May 17, 2008. He was waiting for his pregnant wife and four children to come. He called a woman he knew at the University of Kentucky, and she said, "With a whole family, Maryland is too expensive. Housing is cheaper here." So he came to Lexington by Greyhound and she took him to a staffing place to get a job. "I did not understand English. My first week job I gave up on Friday—to clean up the car parts. I remember, I thought, 'That's how I will live in America?'" Then he had a job on an assembly line for eight or nine days. That was hard because he did not have a car to get to the place. After trying yet another job, he started to work for Armco Packaging. "That was a hard job, too." Pierre had been working in banks in Germany.

What Is Difficult?

Elisha Mutayongwa came to Lexington in 2005 as a seventeen-year-old refugee from Democratic Republic of Congo via a camp in Uganda. He wrote about his arrival later for the previously mentioned book *Slowly Is the Journey,* a collection of writing by ESL students at Bluegrass Community and Technical College in Lexington.

> The new life had begun in the United States and I was so scared even when I knew that the struggle was over. There would be no more days going without meals or shelter but, "How will I be in America?" I thought. "Will I ever catch up with their culture?" I

> watched people walking so fast, going up and down and none of them looked like they were enjoying the American life. It was as if everyone was on the run for something. It didn't look as enjoyable as I had expected.
>
> I tried to talk to some people but their English was way different from mine. I had a hard time communicating with them because they had to think hard about what I said before responding to me. It felt so hard and challenging and I didn't feel welcome at all. Everyone I met asked me, "Where are you from?" I started to ask myself, "What will it take for me to feel at home one day?" Yet this is my final destination and I have to make it my home somehow.[1]

Indeed, language can be an important barrier, especially at the beginning. Fiston Boyita Bo Malinga, who spoke French and Lingala, arrived in the United States from Democratic Republic of Congo in October 2008. He flew into Houston and went through immigration, giving workers there his sealed envelope from the American embassy. They didn't ask him any questions, but he missed his flight to Louisville, where he was to meet his American father, and he needed help to book another flight. "I met a helpful guy from Finland at the airport who went to school in France so he speaks French and now lives in the US. That was a relief because everything in the airport was in English."

Sometimes the language issue is idiom. Nkongolo Kalala, also from Democratic Republic of Congo, remembered going to a McDonald's restaurant after arriving in Washington, DC, as an international student in 1985. He ordered from the menu on the wall but then was asked, "For here or to go?" The McDonald's employee said it so fast he didn't understand and then the employee ignored him and said, "Next?" So he went to the end of the line, observed what others did, and was able to answer "Here" when he got to the front of the line again.

The differences between British and American English also cause difficulties for Africans from former British colonies who learned English in school. British spelling and vocabulary are often different from American spelling and vocabulary, and spoken American English has many accents and regional expressions unfamiliar to Africans. Aka Kpla from Côte d'Ivoire found American accents difficult to understand. "Georgetown [Kentucky] accent is different from Lexington accent. Sometimes I get only one word." Venus Niza, also from Côte d'Ivoire, wished people would make more of an effort to understand a person whose accent is different. As novelist NoViolet Bulawayo's Zimbabwean immigrant protagonist in *We Need New Names* explains: "The problem with English is this: You usually can't open your mouth and it comes out just like that—first you have to think what you want to say. Then you have to find the words. Then you have to carefully arrange those words in your head. Then you have to say the words quietly to yourself, to make sure you got them okay. . . . And then the problem with those who speak only English is this: they don't know how to listen."[2]

Individuals from all walks of life in African countries—professors and teachers, doctors, pastors, and taxi drivers—concur. Professor Marie-Antoinette Sossou came to the University of Kentucky from more cosmopolitan Denver, where it was easier to fit in and took on the challenge of being a minority and a Ghanaian teaching white students. "I had no idea what I was walking in to. My life is always about taking on challenges. Retreating is not an option. I just threw myself into everything." But on her first evaluations her students all said, "We don't understand her." Trained as a teacher in Ghana, Kennedy Boateng has his Kentucky teaching certificate and has done substitute teaching and tutoring but had problems because of complaints about his accent. Medical doctor Sam Vorkpor from Liberia found that some people "rate your ability by your accent. Having a different accent doesn't mean I don't know what I am saying." Bishop Armstrong Cheggeh from Kenya said some people think that "if you sound different you are stupid." He has been "talked down to" in churches by white people with less biblical education than he has. He said, "Brains do not have an accent." Ibrahim Bakoush from Libya laughed as he recalled an incident that occurred when he was a taxi driver. A car stopped him on Nicholasville Road in Lexington to ask for directions and when the occupants heard his accent, one said, "Oh, he's not from here. He wouldn't know." He let them continue on—in the wrong direction.

Language is a particularly hard barrier for older immigrants who have more trouble learning a new language and fewer opportunities for ESL classes. The lack of English develops into a more serious problem if the older immigrant is trying to pass the citizenship exam. But learning English is crucial for immigrants of all ages. Ironically, African immigrants almost always come to the United States with multiple languages. Jose Kazadi's list may be the longest; he spoke Tshiluba, Lingala, Swahili, and French in the Congo before learning Russian in Russia, and now speaks English and Spanish, having learned the latter as part of his degree at the University of Kentucky. He is not unusual. Being multilingual is useful for individuals like Kiluba Nkulu, originally from the Congo, and others who are among the dozens of interpreters who work for Lexington's Fayette County schools, translating for parent-teacher conferences and dealing with issues of behavior and trauma. Jemima Roberts was able to use her Grebo, one of Liberia's over eighteen languages, in a court case involving an immigrant who could not communicate well in English. However, since the United States emphasizes one language—English—being bilingual or multilingual is not particularly valued. Pierre Ngog's ability to read, write, and speak French and German and to speak his Cameroonian language Basse as well as English could at least be an inspiration but is not. Pierre was delighted when he found that a member of his church speaks German. The United States is also a very different experience for Karin, whose first language is Afrikaans and who came from South Africa, where there are eleven official languages. Her husband is an English-speaking South African and they made the decision to bring up their children in English, but Karin is sad that her children won't be able to read her Afrikaans cookbook. "The language is lost."

Vietnamese American writer Viet Thanh Nguyen states: "The immigrant, the refugee, the exile, and the stranger who comes to these new shores may already have a voice, but usually it speaks in a different language than the American lingua franca, English. While those who live in what the scholar Werner Solors calls a 'multilingual America' speak and write many languages, America as a whole, the America that rules, prides itself on trenchant monolingualism."[3] So learning English becomes a first job for immigrants if they do not come with it, and clearly those who can already speak, read, and write English, such as those coming from former British colonies, have at least a beginning advantage. English as a second language or English language learning courses, whether informal or for credit, are critical for long-term adjustment and success. As Moulaye Indrissa Barry said: "You can't make it without English. The language is capital for someone who wants to live in America."

Loneliness is another problem encountered early on, perhaps especially for women who come on spousal visas with several restrictions. Abigail Unuakhalu said, "It was very difficult at first" because she was lonely and cold after she came from Nigeria to join her husband in Frankfort, Kentucky's state capital. She had come from the huge bustling city of Lagos to tiny Frankfort. Because she came in 1997 she could only write letters home, not use the internet, and calling on the phone was very expensive. She watched a lot of television for the first three months, becoming a fan of Oprah, but eventually she found friends in other Nigerian and African families who took her places before she started an accounting degree, had a baby, and learned to drive. Tambu Chirwa remembered loneliness as most difficult, too. She felt she had lost her freedom. In Malawi, "you might have a tiny house but the whole outside was yours. I was happy to see snow but I realized quickly I was almost locked in the house." As the spouse of an international student she could not work, and it was hard to do shopping or laundry without a car.

Associated with loneliness is the difference between an emphasis on community in African culture and on the individual in American culture. Kiluba Nkulu talked about missing the communal life in the Congo. He has fond memories of growing up on the lively, people-filled Kiolo mission station with his grandparents. He explained that community is "a shelter, a place where you find yourself belonging. People know you, they understand you. They can understand your struggles. They can lend a hand without any prejudice." In the United States that sense of community was lacking for his family. Moulaye Indrissa Barry said, "Loneliness is permanent here because you go to work and come back home and go to bed, wake up in the morning [and begin again]. You always feel that loneliness. In my country, Senegal, once you step in there the community is around you. You have people all the time around. Here is more individual, everybody is in his own house, own car. We have the comfort, houses, big car, but what you miss is the family warmth, the community warmth."

Related to the African concept of community is Efosa Austin Osayamwen's experience the day after he arrived in Dallas from Nigeria to go to Baylor University for a master's in business administration. Efosa was staying with a friend who had gone to work and so he decided to go for a walk. "I thought I was still in Africa. I saw these little kids playing in the water fountain and they beckoned to me. I was there with them, cracking jokes. They asked me my name and I asked theirs. They were excited, I was excited. In Africa your kids are safe. I never knew that children were not supposed to talk to strangers. Ten minutes later the police came and said, 'What are you doing with these kids?' I told them, 'I am a stranger and a student, staying with my family friend. I just flew in last night.' They followed me to the house to see my papers. They said, 'Where we are from you can be someone who can abuse, abduct them.'"

Differences between African cultures and American culture are many. In fact, in an analysis of what Craig Storti calls building blocks of culture and communication styles American culture and African cultures are almost always at or near opposite ends of the continuum.[4] For example, as Kiluba Nkulu points out, Africans prize community. Desmond Tutu, South African Nobel Prize laureate, explains community further in his definition of *ubuntu,* which "recognizes that my humanity is bound up in yours, for we can only be human together."[5] Americans, on the other hand, stress the importance of the individual and being self-sufficient, independent. Personal freedom is highly valued. Still, Africans on the continent also recognize individual effort, and certainly African immigrants have to in order to be successful in the United States. Both the importance of community and the importance of individual effort are illustrated in the following Akan (Ghana) proverbs: "A person is not a palm tree that he should be self-sufficient" and "Life is as you yourself make it."[6] In terms of communication styles, Americans are usually direct, while Africans are more indirect, and it may be appropriate to have an intermediary, someone with the influence of what Nigerians call "long legs" and Congolese call "an umbrella" to get something accomplished. Americans also tend to ask personal questions immediately on meeting someone, which Africans would never do, such as "Are you married?" or "How many children do you have?" "And we may have just met. It's too much!" exclaimed Moulaye Indrissa Barry.

Interviewed African immigrants talked about differences with Americans in the way they viewed property, personal space, friendship, eye contact, time, and gender. Rahel Bosson, who came from an Ethiopian family and an international high school experience in Brussels to live in a dorm at Wayland Baptist University in Plainview, Texas, found ways in which her Ethiopian culture was different from American culture in the first three concepts.[7*] In terms of private property, she thought, "Whatever was mine was theirs and whatever was theirs was mine" in her shared dorm room. "It created a huge issue. They said, 'This is mine' and 'This is yours,' and it was very hurtful. I said, 'We need to talk and have an understanding because for me that's not how I think.'" The concept of personal space was another example. "I can get really close to people. I kept walking and they would back away and say, 'Stop, this is my personal space. That is your space.'" Another difference was the idea of friendship. "We become lifetime friends, not just friends for a season. In the dorms everybody loved me and they gave me a Texas name. But then the semester changed, they're in different classes, and they just totally disappeared."

Iddah Otieno learned very quickly that "Americans love their space. I missed knocking on a neighbor's door and drinking tea." She laughed and said, "I learned that if you drop by they may meet you at the door with a dog because you didn't call." Abraham Sven-Peters knew something about communicating with Americans because he had worked for an American company in Sierra Leone, but it was different being in America. He learned not to walk into another's personal space, that he should make eye contact, and that "time is so crucial." Bandushubwenge Vanisa thought the most distinctive difference involved concepts of time. "If I come to visit you in my country, I can stay all day. In this country you have to make an appointment. Also in America you have to look someone in the eyes. In my country you don't look people who are older than you in the eye."

However, Bandushubwenge was impressed with the commitment to equal rights for women and men. "In Africa men are first and then women and children. Many men from Burundi call America 'women's country.' Here you can't beat your wife." Beatrice Mbayo also noted, "In Congo you can beat your wife. In America you can't do that." She found that some African men didn't want to adapt to both men and women working. "Men need to understand this culture is different. They want us to work but they don't want to share responsibilities. When I came here I had to go through a divorce after my first year here, and I had to survive and take care of the children. Now I am a strong, independent woman. I think men need to understand this culture is different and take things that are good here, mix good things from America like freedom and independence for women and the good things from Congo like the food and dress."

Sylvia Uwamaliya Stainback talked about a broader experience with diversity in the United States.[8] "I was in a diverse place where I came from [Uganda, where she grew up, and Rwanda, her home country], but the diversity here was white, black, Asian, individuals from countries I didn't know existed, like Mongolia. Back home, the issue of gay marriage is taboo. I studied about it as a dysfunction." Moulaye Indrissa Barry, who came from a conservative Fulani Muslim family in Senegal, said: "Everything is modern and done completely differently than in my country. I've learned to be less judgmental about unmarried couples, tattoos, homosexuality. I will respect everyone's practice as long as they respect mine."

Just understanding the American systems in terms of jobs, child care, health care, and education is hard. Aka Kpla came on a diversity visa in 2014 from Côte d'Ivoire, where he had worked in supervisory positions for nine years after obtaining undergraduate and master's degrees. His wife had education and work experience, too—an associate's degree in accounting and a job at an oil company for seven years—but they agreed he would get a job and go to school and she would stay home to take care of their two children. In his 2016 interview, he pointed out, "It's easy to get child care in Africa—a grandmother, an aunt. Here it is expensive." After staying three months with a cousin in Maryland and finding no jobs, Aka came to Lexington and found a job paying $10 an hour at Amazon the first day. He left after three weeks for a job paying $14 an hour for a contractor at Toyota. He stayed there for a year and a half but "one day I was sick and they called 911 and the ambulance took me to Georgetown Hospital. I was only there for two hours and the bill was $5,000," he explained incredulously. He didn't have $5,000 so the hospital arranged a payment plan of $50 a month. However, he then discovered that his credit score had gone way down. "I tried to find money from friends but it was a lot of money. I finally called my cousin in Kenya and explained this is my problem—to clean my credit score. He sent me the money in one week. This is why I quit Toyota." Aka went back to Amazon and then had health insurance for himself, for which he paid $38 every two weeks, but he couldn't afford the several hundred more dollars for his wife. He does appreciate taking courses in English as a second language at Bluegrass Community and Technical College and was taking classes in industrial mechanics. "The system is better here than Côte d'Ivoire because you can work and go to school at the same time." He has talked to someone about translating and evaluating his Côte d'Ivoire degrees because he understands he needs American credentials to do well in the United States.

A challenge for African immigrants, especially for those who come with previous education and job experience and for whom English is a second, third, or even fourth language, is finding a good job. They may have to retrain, get new credentials, or move into a new field. Although there are many opportunities for education in the United States, finding a job with appropriate status and decent pay can be difficult. Jose Kazadi is an example. In Russia he was a journalist who partied with diplomats. He came to Kentucky as a refugee in 2004. "It's life starting from scratch." He went to an interview at the Amazon warehouse. "The interviews run like, 'You are so smart. You can even be in HR.' I say 'I know, but I need money.' I started work as picker. I picked for Amazon customers for almost six months until they found out that I had these computer skills. They asked me if I can become a problem solver, which is the guy who corrects any shipment that has a problem and defect." He worked for Amazon for eight years. But Jose also decided to get an American education and graduated with honors from the University of Kentucky with a degree in foreign language and international economics, including study abroad in Costa Rica. As noted earlier, he added

Spanish fluency to his English, French, Russian, Tshiluba, Lingala, and Swahili.

More evidence of the issues of language, credentials, and jobs can be found in a qualitative study of refugee parents from Democratic Republic of Congo and Burundi published in 2012 by social work professor Marie-Antoinette Sossou, one of our interviewees. Although participants in her focus groups were grateful for resettlement opportunities and other services in the United States, they identified the intertwined issues of unemployment, lack of recognition of professional credentials from countries of origin, and limited English as problems. Resettlement emphasis on refugee employment within three months gives short shrift to learning English and disregards the skills immigrants already have. So they take menial jobs, such as housekeeping.[9]

A 2017 case study of refugee resettlement in Kentucky by Allyson Ferry, community empowerment specialist for the Kentucky Office for Refugees, raises similar concerns, especially related to women. In response to UNHCR's decision in 2013 to prioritize women who appear to be at risk, increasing numbers of vulnerable single women with children from the Democratic Republic of Congo and some other African countries are arriving as refugees. Although these single women are helpfully registered for KTAP (the Kentucky Transitional Assistance Program), that program requires that they volunteer thirty-five hours a week and that requirement, as well finding someone to watch small children while they work, limits their time in ESL classes and cultural orientation. From her survey of Kentucky refugees arriving from all sending countries, Allyson Ferry identified employment (48 percent of individuals who had been in the US for five years had full-time jobs), transportation to jobs, language access, especially in taking the driver's test, and mental health issues as refugee concerns. She referenced an assessment of the Somali community in Bowling Green, Kentucky, which highlighted unmet health needs and lack of language access and overall cultural competency even when mainstream mental health services were available, and she also noted that single women from Democratic Republic of Congo have often been victims of sexual assault during war and thus need appropriate mental health services.[10]

A discussion in January 2017 with three women at Westminster Village, a section 8 apartment complex in Lexington where more than forty refugee families, mostly from Democratic Republic of Congo, live revealed a variety of struggles that illustrate some of the points in Ferry's study. One single mother with a twelve-year-old son was focused on passing the written exam to get a learner's permit to drive. She had failed it twice. Her first two languages are Swahili and French but the test is in English. She had training in Democratic Republic of Congo as an accountant but was working at Aramark washing uniforms. She hoped to bring her eighteen-year-old son and her parents to the United States. In September 2018 she reported that she had passed the driver's test, gotten a better job at Quad Graphics, and was beginning an ESL course at the community college. Another single mother, with six children, the oldest twenty-three and the youngest in middle school, was in a refugee camp in Tanzania for nineteen years. She leaves on a bus at 7:30 a.m. for an hour of travel to her job making soap. She explained that the older children helped the younger ones with schoolwork. A mother with five children, the youngest a year and a half and the oldest in middle school, knows enough English to function at her job but said, "I am young and can do more." She plans to take classes at the community college when her youngest child goes to school. She has an advantage unavailable to the single women; she and her husband try to schedule their jobs so one or the other is at home with the children. Also the family has a car so she can take her middle school child to the library for school assignments.[11]

Clearly the two-parent family had an easier time. Clearly there is a tension between getting a job quickly and learning enough English to get a good job and/or go to school and thus more easily become integrated into the community.

Ignorance and Racism

African immigrants are often amazed by the questions Americans ask, from "Have you seen lions?" to "Did you come by bus?" While he was driving a taxi in Lexington, Kennedy Boateng said he was asked questions "which make you want to shake your head. 'Do you have streets? Do you have houses in Ghana? Do you wear clothes?' And some of these people have gone to college!" He tells people you can just google and find pictures of the real Ghana on the internet. Efosa Austin Osayamwen discovered that people who have not traveled outside the US may relate to him in a "cold way" and think Africa is a country. They ask questions like "Do you wear clothes in Africa? Do you live in trees?" Realizing that television has portrayed Africa as home to AIDS and poverty rather than shopping malls, he suggests that questioners go on YouTube to see his home city of Benin in Nigeria. Karin Krain said a neighbor asked, "Do you have furniture like us?" She encourages people to visit Cape Town, South Africa. Sim Oyetunji's wife Adikat recognized that less educated

Americans know little about Africa, just as less educated Nigerians in a village might not know much about the United States. Kiluba Nkulu was a mission interpreter talking to church audiences about Democratic Republic of Congo when he first came to Kentucky. His conclusion: "You have to be patient and generous. There is no room to get offended." Still, because of America's reputation as the leader of the world, Africans are surprised by the ignorance of many Americans.[12*]

Venus Niza found few people have heard of her country, Côte d'Ivoire. She also has to explain that she is not a refugee but has a diversity visa. She came with several years of university education in science and is continuing that education, loving the science equipment in her courses. Labeling can be a problem, especially for someone who may come with credentials and accomplishments but may be assumed to have been poor or even illiterate. Skilled and unskilled immigrants and refugees alike may work in similar jobs at Amazon or UPS because the new immigrant or refugee may be just beginning to learn English or may need to get a new credential or more education to qualify for a better job. And Americans usually ask, "Where are you from?" rather than "What do you know? What are your skills?" So your national origin sometimes seems to determine what you deserve. An immigrant from the Democratic Republic of Congo (who wished to remain anonymous) talked at a meeting of African immigrants about the burden of "otherness" and the "making of strangeness." He knew that African immigrants had a reputation for resilience but was not convinced that hopelessness made people more resilient.

Most African immigrants come from countries where, except for under colonial rule, people who look like them have always been in charge and thus they may not be as sensitized to discrimination as African Americans. Gashaw Lake explained that he came from the dominant culture in Ethiopia. However, during his undergraduate years in Michigan in the 1970s, he was considered black working class and experienced racism. He felt he had chosen to come and could not complain. "It comes with the package." He also said, "Education was salvation," and "I know who I am" and "I have my [Ethiopian] legacy." Francis Musoni, who arrived in the United States in the mid-2000s, explained that he grew up in an environment in Zimbabwe where there were no white people; in fact, most of the people even had the same last name as his. So as a graduate student he didn't always see the discrimination—a library checker looking at his bag on the way out but not those of white students ahead of him, for instance. He said, "I never thought of myself as 'black' before coming to the United States."

African immigrants definitely encounter discrimination and racism based on skin color and on the negative image of the African continent long held by Americans. Venus Niza talked about her husband being denied promotions at his place of employment that others with less experience got. Hamidou Koivogui, the dancer-drummer from Guinea who lives in Louisville, remembered being called an "African nigger" when he lived in Cincinnati. Mamadou Savané, also from Guinea, remembered being called the "n-word" once when he walked in a bar in Lexington. Robert and Tambu Chirwa remembered some people shouted racial slurs, yelled, "Go home!" and spit on them as they walked back to their apartment off the University of Kentucky campus when Robert was a graduate student in the 1980s. Even Karin, who is a white South African, described a neighbor in Richmond, Kentucky, who told her family "to crawl back in the black hole of Africa where we came from," and she also mentioned insults from a patient in Lexington. Marie-Antoinette Sossou from Ghana said she had not experienced "in-your-face racism," but she noted, "I am not sure people distinguish one black person from another. You talk with someone for sometime one day and the next day they don't even seem to see you."

Khadar Abdullahi from Somalia noted a lack of understanding by some Americans about Muslim worship differences and food restrictions as well as the dress of Muslim women. He described his mother being pushed aside at a grocery store and being told, "Go back where you came from." However, Khadar has successfully educated a local pizza owner in Louisville that because Muslims do not eat pork, his pizza shouldn't be cut with the same knife as a sausage or pepperoni pizza. Jacob Guot, originally from Sudan, had bad experiences in Midland, Texas, with police always asking for his ID, not being able to rent an apartment until a white person intervened, and finding unfriendly churches. Someone asked, "Why do you keep coming here when no one will sit beside you? Do you know nobody likes you?" He answered, "Do you know Jesus was not an American citizen?"

In *Tears We Cannot Stop: A Sermon to White America,* Michael Eric Dyson points out that African immigrant and African American experiences are different because the African immigrant does not have "the common history of oppression that binds black Americans together." He sees Africans as having "arrived from societies where they enjoyed equality without regard to color. Thus they arrive with great assets, skills, and experiences, allowing them to compete in the American marketplace. These black immigrants faced no color barriers to human capital like those we face in America." He concludes: "Neither can we discount the exotic appeal of foreign blackness."[13] That "exotic appeal" may apply to white Americans who became host families for international students as part of university hospitality programs begun in the 1960s to welcome students from all over the world. Some white American families became close to African students for a lifetime, as Gashaw Lake describes in the next section.

Another, usually unspoken, barrier between the African immigrant and African American is that the latter occasionally reminds the former that some black Africans sold other black Africans into slavery.[14] That is the complex story tackled by Yaa Gyasi in her novel *Homegoing,* which traces three hundred years of Ghanaian and American history. In the last chapter she deals specifically with differences between recent African immigrants and African Americans. The Ghanaian immigrant father of teenage Marjorie, who is based on Gyasi's own experience growing up in Alabama, explains why calling someone *obroni,* or white person, in Ghana was "an innocent act, an interpretation of race as skin color" because Ghanaians "were the majority, theirs was the only skin color for miles around." But to her dismay Marjorie's African American high school English teacher calls Marjorie African American and insists that in the United States "black is black." Marjorie, however, knows that "at home, they had a different word for African Americans. *Akata.* . . . *Akata* people were different from Ghanaians, too long gone from the mother continent to continue calling it the mother continent," and she wonders if perhaps she has been gone so long that she is becoming *akata.* At the request of her teacher Marjorie writes a poem for the high school's black cultural event: it describes the split yet "sister skin" of Africans at Cape Coast Castle, some of whom were whipped and shipped across the ocean, where they became slaves.[15]

It is important to point out that African Americans did journey back to Africa over the centuries, from men like Paul Cuffe and Martin Delany, who were involved in the nineteenth-century African emigration movement to Liberia to individuals like W. E. B. DuBois and Maya Angelou, who went to live in Ghana after its independence.[16] African Americans have also celebrated their African heritage, whether in observing Kwanzaa or giving their children African names. In *Between the World and Me,* written as a letter to his son, Ta-Neshi Coates explains the origin of the name he and his wife Kenyatta gave him: Samori, after Samori Toure, who struggled against French colonizers. He also describes his education at Howard University in African history, learning about Mansa Musa of the Mali Empire and Yaa Asantewaa of the Ashanti, among others.[17] The film *Black Panther,* which drew huge enthusiastic audiences in both the United States and in African nations in early 2018, may portend a renewed connectedness to and pride in the African continent by African Americans. However, *Black Panther* has had to deal with issues of cultural appropriation and creative theft, including on its original soundtrack.[18]

One other historical point in the relationship between African Americans and Africans: it is telling that during the debate about the 1965 immigration reform, "Senator Holland of Florida asked 'Why, for the first time, are the emerging nations of Africa to be placed on the same basis as our mother countries—Britain, Germany, the Scandinavian nations, France, and the other nations from which most Americans have come?' In fact, the 1960 census showed that Americans of African descent outnumbered Scandinavian Americans by a margin of two and a half to one, and there were more African Americans in the United States than there were Americans whose origins lay in Italy, France, Netherlands, Belgium, Austria, and Switzerland combined. For the senator from Florida, however, the nations of Africa were not among 'our mother countries.'"[19]

In any case, as the earlier examples illustrate and as Jane Madembo described in her essay "The History of Racism I Didn't Want to Share," African immigrants do encounter both racism and confusion about the importance of race in the United States. Madembo had identified as an African, not an African American, yet she writes, "Now that I have accumulated my own catalog of racial incidents, racism is more real to me than words on paper. . . . Now that I am an American citizen, American history is part of my history. I have to bear the burden of its past, present and future."[20] Ilhan Omar, the first Somali American Muslim woman to become a state legislator, as a Minnesota state representative in 2016, and who then won a seat in the US House of Representatives in 2018, explained how she sees the difference between living in an African country and living in the US. "Somalia is a majority black Muslim country and so is the camp in Kenya. When you're growing up in an environment where your faith and race are not topics of conversation, it's really hard to come to an environment where all of that means something. Being black in the US means something. There's a history. Being an immigrant, a refugee, Muslim—all of those things represent an otherness that is not typical or easily confined into the social fabric of this country."[21]

As Chimamanda Ngozi Adichie shows in her widely acclaimed novel *Americanah,* identity is a context-specific phenomenon. Not every person who is presumed to be black or African thinks of herself or himself that way every time. Just as Ifemelu—the main character in Adichie's novel—"discovers" that she is black when she migrates from Nigeria to the United States, many people think of themselves differently depending on where they are.[22] In an earlier interview with the *Washington Post,* Adichie stated that she (not a fictional character in her novel) actually realized that she was African when she moved to the United States, adding; "Whenever Africa came up in my college classes, everyone turned to me. It didn't matter whether the subject was Namibia or Egypt; I was expected to know, to explain."[23]

African immigrants in this oral history project also talked about the relationships of African immigrants and African Americans. Rahel Bosson confirmed difference between African immigrants and African Americans. "I don't have the deep roots of history. So the sense of offense hasn't been as great, but I've experienced discrimination, even from African Americans initially because of the way that I speak; the way that I act is different." Once in New Orleans as she got off a bus a group of black girls and boys walked up to her and said, "'What are you? You ain't black, you ugly, you ain't black.' They were pulling my hair. Sometimes Caucasians don't really view me as black but I am black." And she understands racism. She knows her uncles and other family members from Ethiopia now living in the United States have faced more discrimination than she has, perhaps, she speculates, because they don't speak English as well. Then there is the marriage question. Rahel remembered conversations in Texas when a friend said that Africans and Caucasians can be friends but not marry. "I realized that was the litmus for true racism—if you're okay for your family member to marry someone of another race, then you're truly not racist." She understands it was difficult for her husband to tell his family that he wanted to marry an African, but once he told them she was "fully embraced. They had the Ethiopian flag hanging in their house when I went to visit them."

Kennedy Boateng, who has adopted two African American boys to add to his two biological children, was straightforward about what he sees as a difference between the groups. He tells African Americans that he came to America from Ghana without money or a house and now he has both. "Don't be blaming people all the time. Work hard to make yourself better. Don't spend too much energy on what happened." He says: "If you keep looking back you cannot go forward. I tell my fellow black Americans: stop watching soap operas and get a job."

Robert Chirwa remembered a very good experience when his family joined a Kwanzaa celebration at the University of Kentucky that created a unity with the African American community. But he suggested there is a "kind of love/hate" relationship between Africans and African Americans.

> White American missionaries came to Malawi and ministered and you come here and there are white churches and black churches and people are separated by where they live. If you come here like I did to a university, the university will have host families to welcome you and most of these are white, and these host families can take you to their church so your first experience with integration into American culture is not with the African Americans. By the time you realize you are in the different community and there is a totally other community that you could have identified with, sometimes your roots have perhaps gone too deep in the first direction. So there is a sense among African Americans that Africans tend to distance themselves from blackness and prefer to be white. That creates a bit of a conflict. And if I meet an African American on the road they assume I have come here to great opportunity from nothing.

People do not realize Robert had a degree from a university in Malawi in mathematics and computer science before he came and that he had worked in a bank in Malawi, and had a house and money there. "If an institution has classified jobs so most African Americans are janitors they feel something is wrong. Why are African Americans not professors?" Instead, many colleges and universities have hired African immigrants to meet their diversity requirements. Like many other colleges and universities, when Bluegrass Community and Technical College wanted to increase its numbers of African American faculty members in the 1990s, especially in certain fields, they hired Africans such as Robert Chirwa in computer science and Nkongolo Kalala in economics. Robert is still the only black member of his department.

As for dealing with ignorance and racism, immigrants who have been in the US for a number of years have advice for newcomers. Desmond Brown from Sierra Leone said: "When people get to know you as a human being, discrimination seems to go away." But he recognizes that African Americans born here have different experiences. Iddah Otieno from Kenya said: "Some people might dismiss you for the color of your skin," but a proven track record makes the difference. "I've learned that as long as I'm competent I don't have to change the way I talk. I embrace the challenges." Jose Kazadi from Congo said: "I see the world as a big pot of flowers, of different colors and size and beauty. And the

Creator is glad about it. People from east to west, I never felt them bringing me down. When you work hard you can make it no matter the obstacles of racism, discrimination that come against you."

And racism and discrimination do keep coming. Shaista Vally, an ophthalmologist at the University of Kentucky who immigrated to the United States from South Africa when she was seven years old, spoke at the Lexington Fayette Urban County Government Council meeting in August 2017 as one of fifty-five citizens, almost all in favor of moving the Confederate statues in front of the old courthouse. "From the moment I stepped foot in the US, I've been told with mouths and fists that I'm not 'American-looking enough,' that I should 'go back to where I come from,' that there is no place for people like me in the states. My skin color oppressed me in a third world country and continues to oppress me in a country that is supposed to be the land of the free. I can't believe I'm standing here in 2017 fighting for the same principles I fought for in 1994 in South Africa in the land that is supposed to advocate equality, life, liberty, and the pursuit of happiness. Prove it to me. Take down the Confederate statues and show the world what Americans really fight for: freedom."[24]

Nigerian chef Tunde Wey's story on National Public Radio about his 2017 experience at Big Switch Farm in Egypt, Kentucky, offers the possibility of crossing racial and cultural boundaries. Although Wey, who "travels around the country staging pop-up dinners where Nigerian comfort food and discomfiting conversations about race in America are on the menu," arrived with an unflattering image of eastern Kentucky, he enjoyed the visit and the potluck. He found that "the food commingled congenially. My Nigerian jollof rice, cooked with bauble of fresh tomatoes and local sweet red bell pepper varietals of the reddest swatch, picked just a few hours earlier from the farm's high tunnel, shared comfortable space with Lora's chicken and dumpling dish. . . . There was something intimately familiar about Appalachian food. The flavors were honest, reminding me of my relationship with food from my people." His host Lora Smith said, "We talked about our experiences of having to serve as arbiters and translators of our culture and place to Americans with no direct experience of where we come from, but who more often than not hold opinions and assumptions based on stereotypes."[25]

Who and What Has Been Helpful?

Zineeddine Hamoudi remembered that people of varied backgrounds were helpful after he arrived in Indianapolis from Algeria in 2005. "I am shy and don't usually ask for help but people here from African countries tend to help new immigrants without any reward. If you are new they feel the need to help." He got a bus pass and rode the bus to learn about the city and make connections. One day a Pakistani bus driver asked him where he was from and whether he was looking for a job. He told him about a person who owned shops in the downtown hotels and showed him the Embassy Suites Hotel. Being a cashier at the gift shop there was Zineeddine's first job. He took ESL classes for the first year, prepared for the Graduate Record Examinations, and made contact with the Asian graduate school admissions advisor at Purdue University who helped international students. His favorite job while working at the hospital during his graduate school years was patient transportation because he felt he was doing helpful work and met people from different backgrounds.

As Zineeddine found, immigrants themselves are often the helpers. Sylvia Uwamaliya Stainback, who came from Rwanda to marry her American husband, said: "I can't imagine coming here and not knowing anybody. Someone took my hand and showed me the way. It's a complex system. I see that in the [ESL] students I teach, the immigrants I see. I try to show them the way. Give a ride to the Social Security office, make a phone call for you. Lots of anxiety builds up, especially when you have a heavy accent and you are trying to explain yourself all the time. Sometimes you shut down. It takes time to process, calm down, know how things work. It took me a whole year to fully understand the complexity of the country and the systems. It's a continuous process. Every day you learn something."

Helpful people are crucial, especially at the beginning when immigrants may need someone to be what Vanessa Grossl calls an "in-between advocate" in order to navigate the system. Vanessa is the multicultural affairs program specialist at the Lexington Global Engagement Center (Global Lex for short), an office of Lexington Fayette Urban County Government. She offered as examples how to find medicine for elderly parents and how to help a man who arrived with bullets in his legs. The personal touch is important. She and her husband helped a refugee from Burundi who completed a Job Corps program in Simpsonville, Kentucky, and was trying to pass his certified nursing assistant exam with transportation and finding furniture at garage sales for his apartment. In March 2019 Vanessa organized six tables at Global Lex for the one-day On the Table community-wide discussions concentrated on equity, social inclusion, and race relations. She focused on inviting immigrants, another example of being an "in-between advocate."

Craig Borie is an example of someone with that personal touch and a long-term commitment to refugee families who also is clear about how much he has gained from the relationships. The manager of Shoulder to Shoulder Global at the University of Kentucky, which sends faculty and student brigades to Santo Domingo, Ecuador, to improve health and well-being, and a Peace Corps volunteer in Nicaragua in the 2000s, Craig first volunteered with Ethiopian and Sudanese refugees in Denver. When he moved to central Kentucky and was working for Toyota, he found Kentucky Refugee Ministries and began giving English lessons to a Congolese family. After that family moved to Ohio he became acquainted with Burundian families, taking them grocery shopping, helping them buy cars, teaching them how to drive, and answering questions about how university loans work. "Once you're in the community, you get involved," Craig said. "I feel at home, I connect with Africans, the way they greet me, invite me to eat, the way they expect to help each other and say, 'We call that living.' I'm usually the only *mzungu* [white person] at events, but I have made a family here. I'm part of their lives. I think they would say that I am nice, helpful, know a lot, but also that I complain a lot—for instance, about the need to eat healthfully—and I don't like to spend money." Craig often stops in to see the Alfani family on his way home from work, sometimes eating with them, and he has become a special mentor/friend to their young son, even taking him to New York City while other members of the family went to Burundi. He has watched the father go from working at Krispy Kreme after he arrived in 2007 to getting his commercial driver's license (Craig studied for the exam along with him) and driving for Werner Trucking to owning his own truck.[26]

Among the interviewees, both Karin Krain from South Africa and the Chirwas from Malawi told stories of discrimination and of racism, but they also talked about the importance of American friends. Karin said, "We met Americans that really extended their hands to us." She could call an American friend for help when the school phoned her at work saying her child was sick; that friend picked up the child. The Chirwas appreciated friends they made through their sons' soccer teams and at church. Iddah Otieno said, "Americans are very friendly. I've met people along the way who have been really ready to lend a hand, teachers I still keep in touch with, my Lamaze coach, who is my kids' godparent. I have meaningful relationships." Besides the fact that he had had Peace Corps teachers and attended American-related schools and churches in Kenya, Armstrong Cheggeh thought that beginning his American education at Bible colleges smoothed the way for him to adapt to the United States. They were conservative, holding values similar to his own. “The Mennonite women [at Rosedale Bible Institute near Columbus, Ohio] are like Kikuyu women.”

Sometimes particular people were crucial, as Pastor Roy McClung was for Rahel Bosson. For Essa Bokar Sey, the particular people were the couple Mark and Rachel Neff, who became friends when he was the ambassador from The Gambia in Washington, DC. The Neffs had experience in and a passion for Africa, and the three worked on projects together. “When things soured between me and the president of The Gambia, Mark moved out of his house in Texas, took an apartment, and told me, ‘Stay here with your wife and children and have a day care in the house’ until you get your papers. I can’t just forget that.” Essa also listened to his advice about moving to Louisville to be with his whole extended family rather than chasing after international jobs. For Gashaw Lake, the Bourdow family was special. When they discovered he didn’t have a place to stay, they invited him to live in their basement. “A Catholic family, they had seven children and I was number eight. God was absolutely taking care of me when I had no other place to go.” The father owned a trucking company in Saginaw, Michigan, and Gashaw worked there repairing truck tires. They gave a party for him when he got married. In his Frankfort home he has framed photos of the Bourdows and himself as a young man, and he calls them Mother and Father Bourdow.

Kwaku Addo, who became the first faculty member at the University of Kentucky from Sub-Saharan Africa in 1992, gave credit to Preston Mercer, the person who hired him. “He was very supportive. He believed in me. I felt so welcomed, and I never had any problems.” Kwaku connected to other Africans when, not long after his arrival, he became advisor to the African Student Association. Of course, Kwaku had the advantage of numerous cross-cultural experiences before coming to Kentucky, having lived and worked not only in his home country of Ghana but also in Nigeria, Germany, and Canada and getting his graduate degrees in Idaho and Washington State.

An American spouse or family member already in the US could also be an important help. Moulaye Indrissa Barry was grateful to his American wife. “She had her own house, her own job. So I came to a cocoon, you know. I wasn’t very worried about the next day.” She told him, “‘You are educated. You should go to school.’ I’m very grateful because she opened my eyes. She said, ‘I’ve seen a whole lot of immigrants coming here and working in different places and they don’t get an education.’ She was telling me that education is the way out in this country. If you have education, you have choice, you have freedom. And I listened. When you come to America at a certain age, where you are established in your own country, you have to start everything afresh. And it takes courage to do that, you know."

For Jemima Roberts and her husband Bibi Sr., the essential person was their son Bibi Jr., who had come to Berea College for his education and after graduation lived in Lexington with his African American wife and two young daughters. Jemima and Bibi Sr. lived with their family for several years before moving to senior housing downtown. As a social worker, Bibi Jr. was able to link his parents with health resources and part-time jobs available for senior citizens. Jemima worked at Lexington's Senior Center as a receptionist and Bibi Sr. worked at the Lexington Housing Authority and later as a foster grandparent. Because their son had become a citizen, through family reunification they could then apply for citizenship and become citizens themselves in 2011.

African immigrants who are already settled in the US also help newcomers. For Venus Niza and her husband, who came on diversity visas from Côte d'Ivoire, a Congolese pastor in the International Christian Church of Lexington was the key person. He paid for their plane tickets, hosted them in his home for three months, and helped them get settled.

For refugees, as explained in the introduction, specific organizations such as Catholic Charities and Kentucky Refugee Ministries with federal funding from the Kentucky Office for Refugees provide the important initial help. Churches have also been helpful. For example, small rural Pisgah Presbyterian Church in Fayette County sponsored Kikoko Godfrey and his wife and ten children, giving them a car and so many clothes they didn't have to buy any. Kikoko said, "Let me say this freely, not just because I am talking to you. Americans are good." The Godfreys became members of that church. When Pierre Ngog first arrived he walked from his apartment off Richmond Road to downtown Lexington and found Second Presbyterian Church, "where God opened the doors for me. I am somewhere now. I am in America." He had belonged to a Presbyterian church in Cameroon. Second Presbyterian unofficially sponsored the Ngogs since they were not refugees but on diversity visas. The church paid their rent for six months, gave the family beds and many gift cards to buy food and other things, and held a baby shower for the Ngogs' daughter, born in 2008 after they arrived in the United States. The church also raised money for and worked on a Habitat house for the Ngogs. Pierre remembered the time he was working at Walmart, doing his 160 sweat equity hours for Habitat, and going to school as a very stressful time. "Without Second, I would have had my stroke [suffered in 2014] earlier." Kennedy Boateng and his family also qualified to work on and receive a Habitat house.

Schools are clearly critical in especially helping the children of refugee immigrants. To help students learn English and get extra academic help when they first arrive in the United States, Newcomer Academies have been organized in various school systems around the country, including Louisville, Kentucky. In 2017–2018, Fayette County Schools were prepared to open a Newcomer Academy if they had enough new refugee students, but they did not. Meanwhile, the school system, which in 2018 counted ninety-four languages among its 5,835 ELL students and has 104 ELL teachers who are also certified in a subject area, is providing professional development for staff about an emotional/trauma service delivery model, has inaugurated a new curriculum for English language learning from *National Geographic*, and has increased monitoring of English learners long term to prevent dropping out and bolster success.[27] Warren County Schools in Bowling Green, Kentucky, has opened the GEO International High School, which "serves a multilingual community of new learners of English to prepare them for graduation, college and beyond. Students develop English in a rigorous, academic, collaborative environment through partnerships with the Warren County community."[28]

The multiyear–funded Project Place: Partnerships for Learning, Achievement, and Classroom Engagement, led by two University of Kentucky College of Education professors, Kristen Perry and Susan Cantrell, and working with teachers in Fayette, Clark, and Scott Counties in central Kentucky, views families as equitable partners in learning. At the 2018 World Refugee Day Summit presentation in Lexington, the two professors and an elementary school teacher explained how teachers were intentionally learning about families' linguistic and cultural knowledge and providing opportunities for reading at home.[29]

Yet it is usually individual teachers and others who make the difference. In Fayette County, some schools in particular have accepted the challenge of welcoming African immigrant students. For example, the Family Resource Center coordinator at Picadome Elementary School and the Youth Services coordinator at Jessie Clark Middle School were proactive in 2016–2017 in getting to know incoming students from the Westminster Village section 8 housing complex who were being transferred to their schools. In spring 2017, the elementary school Family Resource Center coordinator Ebonee Brown noticed that parents could not easily come to the school to pick up food donated by Glean

Kentucky so she arranged for delivery directly to the Village. During the summer of 2017, the Youth Services coordinator Gabriel Brown at Jessie Clark Middle School went to the Village one night a week to play soccer with the incoming students and get to know them. He also arranged for On the Move Art Studio to hold a program at the Village during the summer. Gabriel got a grant to bring seventeen new students to the school for a week during the summer so they could attend regular classes with math, science, reading, computer, and art teachers. The school staff at the middle school received training in how to talk with children who had suffered trauma and how to use the foreign-language line, a translation service available on the telephone, but the highlight of the training was two Congolese soccer players from Henry Clay High School talking about their experiences. Both coordinators planned events for families at the Village targeting clothing and school supply needs. During fall 2017, Gabriel signed the students up for Backpack Buddies, which provides food for weekends, and organized a weekly tutoring/basketball/dinner program for the new students. Gabriel also made home visits at Westminster Village accompanied by a Congolese American college graduate, whom he encouraged the school to hire as a para-educator and who provided critical language and cultural help. Most important seemed to be individual relationship building with students and their parents.[30]

Again, African immigrants themselves are often the most important helpers. Country groups serve a role in keeping a community together and in offering advice for adapting to and in the United States. A Nigerian association in Frankfort meets regularly and has a big party for October 1 Nigerian Independence Day, and there is a bigger association in Louisville. When Armstrong Cheggeh spoke at the Kenya Community in Kentucky's annual holiday event in December 2016, he urged the gathered Kenyans to develop strong relationships with Americans and to recognize cultural differences, including the American view of children's rights and treatment of women. He talked specifically to the men about not clinging to African male roles. "You don't become a woman if you take the job that is available," he said. He described his experience learning to change diapers and cook. Jemima Roberts serves as the "Old Ma" for the Liberian community, with other elders offering advice to couples with marital problems or difficulties with children. She has also made presentations on Liberia's July 26 Independence Day about Liberian history to refugees who may have spent most of their lives in camps outside Liberia. She and other Liberians support each other by attending graduations and weddings (she has even acted as mother of the bride) and sympathizing with Liberians who have lost a loved one. Although there are not enough immigrants from some countries to support an association, just the opportunity for a small group of Malawians to get together once in a while and talk in Chichewa and eat *nsima,* chicken, and samosas is special. Country group events always include food.

African churches are another opportunity for fellowship, and sometimes immigrants go to both an American church and an African church on a Sunday. For Francis Musoni, becoming part of a Zimbabwean church in Atlanta during his years there as a doctoral student offered a sense of community he had missed. During the service he could sing in Shona and hear the drums. Kennedy Boateng from Ghana appreciated the Grace Fellowship Church in Lexington because other churches were "too quiet" for him. He was ordained as a minister there in 2012 and started Christ Ambassadors International. They have two services, one in Nepali, one in English, and in the evening he helps at the Liberian service, playing the drums and sometimes giving the message. Kiluba Nkulu points out, however, that the multiple Congolese churches for the many Congolese in Lexington delay immersion. "People get caught up by the comfort of being around people who speak your language and that doesn't advance you. There is more appreciation of life when you are mixed with other people. You need to be prepared for the reality of life."

For Muslims, the mosque is important in their lives. Ibrahim Bakoush from Libya is active in the mosque on South Limestone in Lexington. "In the mid-1980s one shelter at Jacobson Park would be enough to break Ramadan for the Muslim community," he said. "Now it takes Heritage Hall at the Convention Center." Ibrahim explained that Lexington was the place for Libyans to come in the 1990s because the community was very close knit. They have the same background, all involved in opposition to Gaddafi. "On holidays like Ramadan Libyans from elsewhere come to Lexington and sometimes Libyans from elsewhere move to Lexington because of the close community." Sim Oyetunji from Nigeria prays at various mosques in Lexington. The closest place to his home is at the Universal Academy, the Muslim school in south Lexington.

What Is Success?

Ideas about success comes from the interviewed African immigrants themselves. Although when he was a translator at Kentucky Refugee

Ministries, Moulaye Indrissa Barry saw people, mostly older people, who "were expecting something they did not see," he concluded, "In America, whoever comes in here, no matter who you are, black, yellow, wherever you came from, you can succeed. And that's the dream. They know they will have a place as long as they play by the rules, do the right thing, they will succeed. Nobody has ever said to me, 'I'm not going to give you a job because you are coming from X.' They ask, 'Are you competent? Can you do it?' Whatever work, you get paid." Rahel Bosson's advice is not to "isolate yourself and stay within your community only, creating a mini refuge, and hanging out with the same people. You can do okay but not become very successful." Iddah Otieno said, "I've learned to pick and choose. I don't expect my friends to call before coming and there is always extra food to share. But I've learned to keep time. I've learned new things—there is a lot to learn in this culture. I am a work under construction."

And success needn't be measured in huge accomplishments. Kikoko Godfrey, a refugee from Democratic Republic of Congo, said: "I can sleep without thinking about war. My wife can work." Abraham Sven-Peters, coming from Liberia via Sierra Leone, also as a refugee, said, "It is a blessing to be in America and be able to get a job, I can put food on the table. I don't have to bribe someone to get a job." Aka Kpla, who took advantage of the diversity visa option, talked about his good experience buying a car. "I worked six years in Ivory Coast and I couldn't buy a car, but in this country I could buy a car easily because the bank gave me a loan. And one year after I buy a second car for my wife. I live in this country two years and I get two cars."

Sometimes success is knowing how the American system works. Tite Niyonizigiye from Burundi told about going to get recertification for food stamps. The caseworker had lowered his amount for food stamps, perhaps because he was working part-time, but he had taken English classes and could read and write and saw there was an opportunity for an appeal, so he emailed her and she verified her decision. Then he sent his email and hers to Frankfort and got a letter back stating that her decision had been overturned and she was no longer his caseworker. "I got justice.'

Many immigrants have embraced the opportunity for education and the choices available for them and their children to pursue that education. Bandushubwenge Vanisa, from Burundi, worked as a certified nursing assistant. At the time of her interview Bandushubwenge, the divorced mother of two boys and two girls ranging in age from two to ten, was a student at Jefferson Community and Technical College pursuing a nursing degree. Tite Niyonizigiye, also from Burundi, completed a master's in social work and was proud of the educational success of his wife and seven children. Kennedy Boateng, who got his university education in Ghana, was also proud of his wife, who began with her GED and is now a nurse (RN), and his children, the oldest an engineering student at the University of Kentucky and a daughter in Fayette County's STEAM Academy who wants to be a lawyer. Abigail Unuakhalu from Nigeria wrote in a September 2017 email: "My first daughter is a sophomore now in UK, majoring in biology/pre-med and minoring in Spanish. She is doing well and enjoying her life as a Wildcat. We are so proud of her."

What do anthropologists, psychologists, and cross-cultural professionals say immigrants and other people living in a culture different from their own need to be successful? In his essay on recent African immigrants, Nigerian American anthropologist Emmanuel Babatunde looks at the African worldview and concludes that "residual elements of African culture such as kinship bonding, network of reciprocal trusting relations with a positive deviance in favor of not failing gleaned from proverbs, worldview, short stories and songs constitute the foundation of resilience in the African immigrant." They "imbue the recent African immigrant with an almost fanatic refusal to fail as a function of the positive deviance in favor of succeeding." Babatunde also makes the point that across various African cultures "a reasonable person is hardworking, enduring in the face of adversity" and that "a major measure of a responsible adult's life is the extent to which the twin principles of a sense of honor and abhorrence of shame are applicable in his or her life."[31]

Adikat Oyetunji, who with her husband Sim Oyetunji brought up seven children in Nigeria, all of whom are now living in the United States, explained that responsibility has been traditionally taught to children, with growing responsibilities expected of them at succeeding ages. Girls of six to eight, for instance, would be expected to watch younger children and at ten not to cook the stew, perhaps, but to warm it up and serve it. She taught both her daughters and sons to cook, and she remembered a son writing her a thank-you letter from the United States for teaching him that skill.[32] As Babatunde points out, proverbs are instructive, for instance: "A person is not rewarded for having a brain but using it" (Cameroon); "The sound of the drum depends on the drummer" (Mozambique); and "If you want something done, do it yourself" (Tanzania). And yet another with a different but relevant message: "When the drumbeat changes, the dancers must adapt" (Burkina Faso).[33]

In her book *The Middle of Everywhere: The World's Refugees Come to Our Town,* Mary Pipher, who worked with refugees as a cultural broker and a therapist in Lincoln, Nebraska, describes twelve attributes of resilience that apply to immigrants in general, maybe even Americans in general: orientation toward the future, energy and good health, the ability to pay attention, ambition and initiative, verbal expressiveness, positive mental health, the ability to calm down, flexibility, intentionality, or being thoughtful about choices, lovability, the ability to love new people, and good moral character. She writes: "Few refugees had all the attributes, but the ones who were successful in adapting to America had many of them."[34] Certainly orientation toward the future shows in the commitment of many African immigrants to further their education. And as one listens to the oral history interviews, one can hear the verbal expressiveness of many immigrants. Sylvia Uwamaliya Stainback shows the flexibility. "Here I am in a country where all is interesting and fascinating to me. I had an open mind, just ran with it. You adjust things you were thinking." Rahel Bosson is an example of being thoughtful about choices as she moved from a small Texas college to a university, tried nursing in a hospital, considered and reconsidered and considered again becoming a doctor, and then achieved a goal of helping people as the director of the Refugee Health Program at the University of Louisville. In 2018 Rahel and her family, including a son and two daughters, moved to Boston, where she was completing a second residency in psychiatry at Harvard's MCH/McLean program, open to whatever the future holds.

Of course, Americans living overseas also experience cross-cultural adjustment. Although several of the skills on L. Robert Kohls's classic list for Americans who adjust successfully to living abroad are not appropriate for adaptation in the United States—low goal/task orientation, for instance—other items are similar to those on Pipher's list, such as communicativeness, flexibility, and warmth in human relationships. And two of Kohls's favorite skills might be added to Pipher's list: sense of humor and the ability to fail.[35] One can hear the sense of humor in listening to some of the interviews. Both sense of humor and ability to fail are evident in how immigrants talk about dealing with American supermarkets, brimming with confusing choices of bread and detergents, when they first arrived. They also sometimes use humor in answering questions Americans ask about Africa. "Yes, every morning I play with lions in my backyard" and "Yes, I sit in one tree and watch my television, perched in another tree." Sim Oyetunji recalled a student in Maine asking him, "I've heard Africans live in trees. What about the children?" His answer: "They live on the leaves."

Dr. Rahel Bosson and husband Chris, daughter Aster, son Hanoch, and baby daughter Adonai. (Photo courtesy of Rahel Bosson.)

Another relevant concept for immigrant success is grit, defined by psychologist Angela Duckworth as "passion and perseverance for very long-term goals. Grit is having stamina. Grit is sticking with your future, day in, day out, not just for the week, not just for the month, but for years, and working really hard to make that future a reality. Grit is living life like it's a marathon, not a sprint."[36] In fall 2013 ESL students at Bluegrass Community and Technical College were introduced to the concept in a first-level writing class by watching Duckworth's Ted Talk about grit. Out of their essays came the book referred to earlier, *Slowly Is the Journey*, referencing a Swahili proverb: "It doesn't matter how slowly you are getting along because with time you get to where you want to go."[37] That proverb also fits with Babatunde's point about a "refusal to fail."

Twenty of *Slowly Is the Journey's* authors are from the African continent—ten from Democratic Republic of Congo and also individuals from Burundi, Central African Republic, Ghana, Liberia, Republic of Congo, and Togo. Beatrice Mbayo is featured in nine selections of poetry and prose. Her essay "We Are Grit" begins: "Grit means. Be determined to achieve. You need a clear vision of what you need to do and how you need to do it. An accomplishment is a result of perseverance," and continues to describe her walking to leave the Democratic Republic of Congo with a sixteen-month-old son, who could not walk, on her back and a nine-year-old son. In her long poem "My Heart Is Bleeding," Princia Itaula-Kifoumba remembers June 5, 1997, when she was fourteen years old and the private militia of the president attacked the general population in Brazzaville, the capital of the Republic of Congo. Princia, who was a refugee in Gabon before becoming a refugee in the United States, also uses the word *grit*, writing, "I want everyone to be gritty, Grit that together we can, changes can be made, Grit to vote for happiness, Grit to help these children on the street, with tears on their face and broken hearts."[38]

One Success Story

His American Peace Corps volunteer wife Rachel was Mamadou Savané's role model. "I learned a lot from her," he said, especially how she developed her silversmith business over the years by going to craft and art fairs before opening Savané Silver in downtown Lexington. Sav remembered their first years in Lexington.[39*] "That was a very scary time. I would have gone back to Guinea during those first two years. We didn't have anything. Our meals were macaroni and cheese and peanut chicken and rice. I had to change from a tourist visa and pay $200 to get a temporary work permit." His brother loaned him the money. He took ESL classes in Bradley Hall at the University of Kentucky but then had to focus on finding a second part-time job at UPS beyond working full-time at the Hyatt Hotel when he learned Rachel was pregnant. Their son was born in 1994 six weeks early, when they were visiting Rachel's family in Iowa. Because the baby was so early, Rachel was flown by helicopter from the small Iowa town to a hospital in Omaha, Nebraska. Sav had to drive back to Lexington by himself.

However, after years of working at hotels and UPS and grilling

The Savané family in 2011: Bangaly Orion Savané, Mamadou Savané, Hadja Diaka Souaré (Mamadou's mother), Rachel Savané, Diaka Grace Savané, and Kanny Yvonne Savané. (Photo courtesy of Rachel Savané.)

Cornish hens and baby back ribs for family and neighbors, Sav attained his dream in September 2008 and opened the doors of Sav's Grill and West African Cuisine on South Limestone, very near the University of Kentucky campus. With walls covered with art and artifacts and an African map in French that shows his home country of Guinea, the restaurant offers those on campus and many Lexington residents the opportunity to try peanut goat and attiéké salad. This is where the four coauthors of this book met regularly to eat and to talk about the book's progress. In fact, at a lunch in May 2017 Sav witnessed each of the four contracts for this book with the University Press of Kentucky. Said Sav in his oral history interview: "Only in this country can you start from nothing and be someone. It's been wonderful. I see myself as a lucky guy. With the courage I have, I never gave up. There are so many opportunities out there." But his grit came from Africa.

So how do Sav and others keep connections with their birth countries? What do Sav and other African immigrants contribute to the Lexington or Louisville community, the Commonwealth of Kentucky, the United States? Answers to those questions are the topics of the next chapter.

4

Connecting and Contributing to Two Continents

> It is not where you are but what you do there that matters.
> —Rwandan proverb

The hard-won success of African immigrants accrues to more than the individual. Success of Africa-born immigrants often redounds to the communities and countries from which they came through remittances and more formal connections and projects. A 2018 United Nations Conference on Trade and Development (UNCTAD) Economic Development in Africa Report focusing on intra-Africa migration for structural transformation describes the diaspora's intra-continent contribution to development as including community projects, philanthropy, investment, heritage trade, tourism, and technology and knowledge transfer.[1] The diaspora abroad, specifically in the United States, makes similar contributions: for example, Abigail Unuakhalu helps her extended family back in Nigeria, Beatrice Mbayo supports her Dreams of My Homeland project in Democratic Republic of Congo, and the Vorkpors have invested in apartments in Monrovia. While African nations have lamented a brain drain, the United States has benefited from a brain gain in professors, beginning in the 1970s, including those in the oral history project on which this book is based: Gashaw Lake from Ethiopia, Desmond Brown from Sierra Leone, Kwaku Addo and Marie-Antoinette Sossou from Ghana, Robert Chirwa from Malawi, Nkongolo Kalala and Kiluba Nkulu from Democratic Republic of Congo, Iddah Otieno from Kenya, and Francis Musoni from Zimbabwe. The United States has also become a more colorful, richer mosaic, thanks to the cultural enrichment in food, art, music, and literature, and Kentucky itself "becomes a little more like the rest of the country and the world" in terms of diversity, as one of the interviewees pointed out. These connections and contributions illustrate how African immigrants are acting in a transnational social space.

The first section of this chapter, "Connecting and Contributing to Africa," uses answers to questions asked in the oral history interviews about continuing connections to countries of birth to discuss contributions to those countries, to Africa. The second section, "Finding Family," tells the story of a family spread over four countries: Liberia, Sierra Leone, the United States, and England. For the third section, "Connecting and Contributing to Kentucky," the chapter draws on answers to the interview question "What do you think are the contributions of African immigrants to Kentucky?" The fourth section, "A Bishop and a Judge," focuses on Judge Bankole Thompson and Bishop Armstrong Cheggeh and their transnational careers and lives. Iddah Otieno's poem "Borderland," which expresses the idea of living in between, concludes the chapter.

Connecting and Contributing to Africa

"You succeed but you have to bring others up with you," explains Iddah Otieno. "We have to help. I have a house in Kenya. Just take me home when I am older because I don't want to be in a nursing home. I pray for good health so I can go back and forth." Iddah supports a lot of people, both "nieces and nephews and orphans for school fees and general maintenance." She enabled her mother to have electricity and other amenities at her home in Okela Village. Iddah is not unusual. Almost all immigrants send money, known formally as remittances, back to their families. As Abigail Unuakhalu, who was the first of her family in Nigeria to come to the US, said, "I am so blessed to be in America because it has opened so many opportunities for me and I have been able to help my extended family back home." A sister had just visited her in Frankfort before her oral history interview. Some immigrants go beyond their families to build schools or develop small nongovernmental organizations or partner with already existing organizations such as churches that can raise funds and other help for African projects from both immigrant and nonimmigrant Americans.

It is important to point out the immense contribution of remittances by immigrants to African as well as other countries in the world. They can be a critical part of a country's GDP, as for Liberia in recent years. In 2017 it was the top African remittance-receiving country as a percentage of GDP, at 25.9 percent. Nigeria topped African country recipients in terms of total dollars, with $22.3 billion in 2017.[2] Sometimes help travels the other way, such as in the case of Aka Kpla's cousin, who sent him $5,000 to pay his hospital bill. And often immigrants are helping parents and relatives who earlier helped them get to America.

Some examples of immigrants who have supported relatives but also started and/or worked through and with various organizations to make a difference in the countries from which they emigrated are Moulaye Indrissa Barry from Senegal, Kiluba Nkulu and Beatrice Mbayo from Democratic Republic of Congo, Kwaku Addo from Ghana, Robert and Tambu Chirwa from Malawi, Iddah Otieno from Kenya, and Jacob Guot from South Sudan.

Moulaye Indrissa Barry said that "once you get here you start slowly but soon you will begin to help people back home." He helped with school fees for a younger brother and sister. Then when he went back to his village in Senegal for a visit he saw kids on the street and so "today I have a school in Africa with three hundred kids and twelve paid teachers. And I started that from my own money." When he was interviewed in March 2014 he was also planning to start a computer school and had already shipped twenty desktop computers to Senegal. "So these are things when you are here, you are able to give back to your country."

Kiluba Nkulu had already sponsored education for children who were not members of his ethnic group when he was teaching in Congo, and they "became part of my family." With that background, in the United States he decided to be a Good Samaritan and establish a program that would sponsor training of needy people back home. The program is called Micheketi, which means young palm tree in Swahili and is a symbol of independence. The idea is that people are trained so they can get a paying job and become self-reliant, then realize they need to also become a Good Samaritan, helping others in their turn. So far Kiluba has supported two medical doctors who did their training in Lesotho and South Africa.

Beatrice Mbayo struggled with depression and flashbacks after she came to the United States and her therapist suggested that she return to Congo for a visit, which she did after she became a citizen in 2011.[3*] "I met a lot of women and saw how blessed I was in America. I was healed when I returned." Beatrice realized she needed to do something to help women who, like her, had been victims of rape, so she started Rêves de Ma Patrie, or Dreams of My Homeland. She has built a school in Lubumbashi to provide education for children and a place for women to meet. She goes almost every year for conferences with the women and speaks with them regularly by phone. Beatrice talks passionately about the need for people to know what is happening in Congo. "Women are being raped every day. I know how that feels. Stand and do something. We can do something as a global community."

Kwaku Addo, who was professor in dietetics and human nutrition as

Professor Kwaku Addo and wife Esther. (Photo courtesy of Kwaku Addo.)

well as associate dean of the graduate school for eight years and then interim chair of merchandising and textiles at the University of Kentucky, and his wife Esther developed connections between Kentucky and Ghana through the building of a school called Kentucky Academy in Esther's home village. Beginning in 2005 Kwaku took students and sometimes faculty on a two-week study tour to Ghana each summer. The study tour includes service learning at the Kentucky Academy, reading stories to children, and helping in the feeding program. One summer they painted a building on the campus, named Kentucky, blue. Other University of Kentucky faculty got involved, including a colleague of Kwaku's who asked that her wedding guests, in lieu of gifts, contribute to the academy so it could start the feeding program. The Kentucky Extension Homemakers Association adopted the Kentucky Academy as a multiyear international fund-raising project that brought electricity, new furniture, and a dining pavilion to the academy, and the Student Dietetic and Nutrition Association and the Panhellenic community added their help.[4]

As members of Second Presbyterian Church in Lexington, Robert and Tambu Chirwa inspired other members to travel to Malawi on mission trips in 2007 and 2010 and to then convince church members to support various projects. As Robert has described the process: "We go and learn and listen. Then we come back and fund things that have life-changing impact." Among the results of the 2007 trip were the funding of a dormitory at Livingstonia Theological Seminary as a part of a tithe from Second Presbyterian's capital campaign and a scholarship for a theological student from the mission budget. In 2007, through the Alternative Christmas gifts, individual Second members gave more than $4,000 to fund two shallow wells, eight secondary school scholarships, seven bicycles for seminary students, five days of drugs for the hospital, twenty-one hospital deliveries for babies, and school supplies for an orphan care center. Alternative gifts in subsequent years bought desks for the primary school in the village where Tambu grew up, and then the mission committee began funding secondary school and nursing scholarships on an annual basis. The 2010 trip resulted in the renovation of the roof of the primary school that Robert attended as a child and support for a young theological student who spent a month in Lexington offering his gift of music. Then in 2016 the construction of a classroom block at Robert's primary school was funded by part of a tithe from another Second Presbyterian capital campaign.

Through Okela School Charities from 2005 to 2015, Iddah Otieno, along with her colleagues from Bluegrass Community and Technical College, equipped the secondary school science lab, installed a water collection system, bought a generator, donated a laptop, built a classroom for the early child development program, established a feeding program, and sponsored two local students through university education. The ten-year project was funded through fund-raising initiatives and personal donations. Additionally, BCTC has donated over two thousand books in the arts and sciences to Maseno University through the Kenya Exchange Program, which Iddah directs.

When he returned to Zimbabwe for fieldwork for his dissertation in 2009–2010, Francis Musoni helped organize the Muzokomba Old Students Association for the secondary school near his village in Buhera, Zimbabwe. Since its formation, the association has donated sports equipment and books and computers to the school as well as sponsoring the renovation of classrooms and the drilling of a borehole that provides water for the teachers, students, and community around the school. The association has a Facebook page with more than a thousand subscribers. In 2010 Francis also helped pay national exam fees for ten high school students who had the best results in school-based tests in history. When he lived in Atlanta, Francis helped organize Zimbabwe

Professor Francis Musoni giving books from Lexington's International Book Project to students at the primary school he attended in Zimbabwe. (Photo courtesy of Francis Musoni.)

Atlanta Initiative, whose purpose was to assist community development projects in Zimbabwe, for example, donating clothes and educational supplies to an orphanage in Zimbabwe's capital, Harare.

Jacob Guot worked with a number of local ministries when he lived in Houston. He co-founded the Sudanese Community Fellowship Church, and he headed Sudan Aim Foundation, which collected donations from different churches for Sudanese communities.[5] More recently he founded Africa Sunrise Communities as a faith-based, nonprofit organization in Wilmore, Kentucky, with the mission of restoring communities, empowering refugees, and reconciling relationships in East Africa. On a 2017 trip to Uganda's Kiryandongo Refugee Camp, where about fifty-three thousand South Sudanese refugees live, Jacob decided an important need there was support for orphans. He planned to set up a local nongovernmental organization there to establish a group home for ten to twelve children aged four to ten, while trying to raise money in the US.[6]

As Jacob's experience suggests, there is a huge difference in how connected African immigrants can be with their birth countries because communication with and travel to the African continent are both so much easier in the second decade of the twenty-first century than even twenty years ago, and certainly easier than when African students came in earlier decades. Thus Kwaku Addo went back to Ghana in 1992, ten years after he first came to North America, and then several more times in the 1990s, but beginning in 2004 he was able to return each summer. In 2010 he took the whole family, including his three daughters, to experience the same tour in Ghana he organized for American students and they also spent a week in his village and in his wife's village. When he was interviewed Kwaku said he read *Ghana News* every day online and called several times a week to talk with his siblings and his mother. "We have a house in Ghana that is rented and have bought some land near the beach on which to build a retirement home."

Supporting family in various ways is a part of African culture. Sam Vorkpor adopted the daughter of a sister-in-law who died in childbirth and brought a boy from Liberia to live in Lexington; he is now on his own in Texas. Sam is in touch with sisters and cousins who are in Liberia. He has a home in Monrovia and has taken his American-born sons back to Liberia so they "can relate to Liberians and to appreciate what they have here." His wife goes to Liberia several times a year to manage apartments they own in Monrovia. Francis Musoni pays boarding school and college fees for the daughter and son of his brother, who paid most of his secondary school fees. He also sends presents to family members at Christmas. Because of his concerns about being on a "black list in Congo," Jose Kazadi did not go back to Congo until he was a US citizen, but he returned in 2010 and in 2012 for the funeral of a brother and is in contact by phone, Viber, Skype, email, and Facebook with his mother and sisters and brothers. Efosa Austin Osayamwen talks to his family in Nigeria for an hour once a week. He recognized that if he went home "they will expect gifts of money, shoes, cologne to say I love you, I have you in mind." Sylvia Uwamaliya Stainback goes to Rwanda every year and has taken her son several times. "There is no distance now with family." Her father has visited her in the United States.

Refugees and other immigrants who have come recently phone family as often as they can. Venus Niza is in contact with Côte d'Ivoire through Facebook, phone, and WhatsApp. She reads news about the country on the internet and sends money back. Khadar Abdullahi talks frequently to members of his Somali extended family still in the refugee camp in Ethiopia. Ismail Ali, who also came as refugee from Kenya, has children still in Dadaab Refugee Camp in Kenya whom he hopes to bring to the US. He keeps in touch with them by cell phone. Hamidou

Koivogui talks by cell phone with brothers and sisters back in Guinea. He has gone back with his current American wife and brought one daughter with special needs to the US and is trying to bring a grandson. Francis Musoni communicates regularly with his mother and siblings through phone calls, text messaging, and WhatsApp. They have a family WhatsApp group where they discuss various issues and developments in the family and the country. The group is also a platform to share jokes.

Sometimes the connecting and contributing becomes a two-way street. As well as keeping up with relatives and friends in the United States through regular phone calls, Jemima Roberts talks on the phone with her daughter and her sister in Liberia about once a week. In the 2010s her sister Ellen Natt has several times a year visited the United States and often Lexington because of her membership on a United Methodist Church Commission for Planning Conventions. Ellen worked for the Liberian Ministry of Agriculture for many years before the civil war, was the superintendent of Grand Bassa County from 2000 to 2003 and, like Jemima, has children in both the US and Liberia. During her fall 2018 visit she was able to connect with an aquaculture specialist in Kentucky's Department of Agriculture who was preparing to travel to Grand Bassa County for the first time to work on an aquaculture project there.

Immigrants also think both about how they can invest in their home countries and what they may be able to contribute to their countries in the future. Kennedy Boateng is building a house in Accra, Ghana, and trying to invest in a business. Francis Musoni has bought land in Zimbabwe's capital and two other cities to build houses, and during his several-month visit in summer 2017 built a house on one of those properties to rent out. Although he is a US citizen, Mulbah Zowah has thought about "perhaps one day doing consulting and going back to Liberia to help rebuild the medical system there." He has now built a house in Liberia and wants to start a clinic. Zineeddine Hamoudi would like to move back to Algeria eventually. "If I go back, one of the things I am planning is to try to convince using English as a second language instead of French because of its importance in technology and research, and communication with the United States for mutual help." His wife Samah Sadouki talks to her family every day on Skype and also hopes to return to Algeria someday to live. "I love my country," she said. In 2017 they were in Algeria for nine months caring for an ill family member. They also wanted to be there for the birth of their second daughter.

There are other ways to keep a connection to and make a contribution to one's birth country and to other countries in Africa. Gashaw

Lake has been back to Ethiopia only a few times because of the political situation, but he taught his three adult daughters about their Ethiopian heritage and to speak the Amharic language every Sunday when they were growing up. He looked forward to the future publication of his book of poetry in Amharic. In addition, he was honored with the 1988–1989 Ethiopian Human Rights Award as well as being declared a Grand Officer of the Imperial Order of the Ethiopian Lion for his outstanding work to improve human rights and national unity in Ethiopia. While Nkongolo Kalala has not been back to Congo, he has done professional consulting for the International Fund for Agricultural Development in Cape Verde, Gabon, Morocco, Senegal, and South Africa.

Related to the 2017 hopeful change in government in The Gambia, former ambassador Essa Bokar Sey maintains an active online journal and Facebook page and conducts programs via YouTube and Radio Hello Gambia. In June 2018 Essa went back to The Gambia, appointed by the government as head of public relations in the Office of Islamic Cooperation (OIC) Secretariat. A first job was to organize The Gambia's hosting of a conference of the OIC, which is the second-largest international organization in the world, after the United Nations, with fifty-seven member states. It was formed in 1969.

Desmond Brown, originally from Sierra Leone, has particularly enjoyed his work in Ghana. He volunteered twice with the nongovernmental organization Winrock International to help develop hospitality and tourism curricula at two two-year colleges and in 2002–2003 taught and did research at University of Cape Coast as a Fulbright scholar.

Finding Family

Abraham Sven-Peters, who grew up in Liberia, is now in contact by phone with his father, whom he had not seen for thirty-five years and whom he thought had died during the war. He was able to find him because he met in Lexington Jemima Roberts's husband Bibi, who knew Abraham's father was alive—he was the mechanic in Gbarnga, Liberia, who had repaired vehicles for Bibi at Cuttington College.

However, Abraham's really amazing story is about trying to link his mother and her sister, who have never met. His grandfather, his mother's father, was a "Kru man," one of the Kru sailors from Liberia who worked up and down the West African coast. "He believed in taking your property with you wherever you go," so he took his three-month-old daughter, Abraham's mother, with him back to Liberia when his job on a British ship taking *piassava*, straw used to make brooms, to

England was finished. For many years "my grandmother struggled to find my grandfather. Finally in December 1975 a Sierra Leonean professor who was going to Liberia to teach at the University of Liberia went to my grandmother's house for a blessing for his new job. She told him, 'I will write a letter and I believe the spirit will bless you and you will find her'" (the daughter and Abraham's mother). When the professor arrived at the University of Liberia, the president took him around to introduce him to the staff, including those at the cafeteria. Abraham's mother was working there and so she introduced herself to the professor as having been born in Sierra Leone. He realized her name was the same as the one on the letter he carried and so gave the letter to her. "My mother cannot read but she kept the letter," and ten years later in 1985, when Abraham was in high school, his mother showed him the letter. Abraham wondered, "Who is my grandmother? How can I find her?" So he wrote a letter to his grandmother at the address on the envelope, thinking she was still alive. When his mother's sister came from England where she lived to the family house in Sierra Leone to visit, she was given Abraham's letter but she never wrote Abraham, perhaps because she was angry that Abraham's mother had never sent a reply to the original letter from her mother in Sierra Leone.

Still, Abraham kept his grandmother's letter, carrying it with him when he escaped to Sierra Leone at the beginning of the war in Liberia in 1990. Abraham did find the family house and met his great uncle Thomas Walker, who took him to his grandmother's grave. Abraham said, "I believed I had a responsibility to bring my mother and her sister together." After he came to the United States as a refugee in 2005 and then became a citizen, he brought his mother to the US on a green card in 2014. "It took ten years to persuade my aunt to accept her sister. I said, 'I really want you to meet. I haven't seen my grandmother, my other relatives. The only thing I can see is you.'" Finally his mother's sister began to send some money from England to his mother. With that money Abraham bought his mother a sewing machine and suggested she make a shirt for her sister so her sister could see that although she was illiterate she had talent. In 2018 Abraham was still hoping that the sister, his aunt, might come to the United States someday to meet his mother. He is grateful to have "the ability to put the family together."

Connecting and Contributing to Kentucky

African immigrants also contribute to Kentucky, which benefits from their work in many professions and jobs, from professors and doctors and engineers but also from those who serve as caregivers of the elderly and sick and mentally handicapped and those doing minimum wage jobs in housekeeping at the hospitals or as factory or warehouse workers. For a number of years Zineeddine Hamoudi worked as a contractor with Lexmark, helping to program the motherboard of their printer. As Robert Chirwa points out, coaches love the young Africans who grew up playing soccer. And many Americans have learned from Hamidou Koivogui, the now older man who never went to school but who danced for the world-touring Guinea Ballet Africaine and then spent decades in the United States, most recently in Louisville, teaching African dance and drumming.

From the perspective of African immigrants, one of their most important contributions has been to educate Americans—not only about Africa but about themselves. Fiston Boyita Bo Malinga from Congo said, "Africans help Americans understand the outside world," and he added that perhaps when Americans "see people from other countries appreciating this life they would not take their life here for granted. They see people who really want to live here, who are proud to be part of the US and are ready for anything to improve the economy, the country." Several immigrants talked about what they think Americans take for granted. Karin Krain from South Africa appreciated the willingness of Americans to help others and wasn't sure that Americans understood how perhaps rare and special that was. "When there is a national disaster it is amazing how much Americans extend help. They contribute what they can." She was district manager for Rite Aid in eastern Kentucky when a tornado hit West Liberty, including the pharmacy. "It was heartwarming to see people helping. America is such a beautiful society and community." She wondered if foreigners are more appreciative, even patriotic because they understand the good qualities of U.S. society compared to other countries.

When Beatrice Mbayo was interviewed on Lexington Community Radio the day before the November 2016 election, she talked about how important voting was. She had grown up in Democratic Republic of Congo thinking President Mobutu would be president until he died. "Here my voice will be heard. Voting is a right. You need to stand and vote."[7] African and other immigrants noted the importance of the rule of law and the right to protest in the United States. Both Americans born in the US and immigrants participated in rallies supporting immigrants, such as one in Frankfort, the capital of Kentucky, in March 2017. One of the organizers for the Lexington rally that spring was Ibrahim Bakoush's daughter, then a high school senior.

Some immigrants come from countries where institutions and rights are not necessarily as strong as in the US and appreciated the fact they could protest. Ibrahim Bakoush, who came from Libya more than thirty years ago, told a story about being stopped by a policeman for speeding. He disputed it in court and the issue was worked out. "That would not happen in many other countries." He also talked about equality of opportunity in the United States. "That is a value a lot of people born here don't think about. My son and the son of whoever is here have the same opportunity. Where in the rest of the world, for example, would a person of color come, meet a Caucasian lady, have a child, and that child become president." Besides voting, African immigrants who have become citizens participate in other ways. In scheduling an interview with retired electrical engineer and American citizen Sim Oyetunji, not only his full-time work schedule at Walmart but also his jury duty had to be considered.

Shamik Aikat from India via Zambia pointed out that immigrants are willing to do jobs others will not. He and Sam Vorkpor from Liberia are two medical doctors who are committed to working with patients in rural and eastern Kentucky. Sam says that these people "need me." In family medicine he has an obligation to local people who come to Manchester Memorial Hospital in Clay County, the poorest county in the state. He came from a rural area in Liberia so he is comfortable there. Shamik told stories about patients who have "paid" him by singing a country song or bringing him a gift of milk from their cow. He described a particular "warrior, striving spirit mentality" that African immigrants bring. Abraham Sven-Peters from Liberia via Sierra Leone thought "Kentuckians could learn about the importance of self-control, determination, and hard work."

Karin Krain was one of a number of interviewed African immigrants who talked about "just the diversity we bring" as a contribution to Kentucky. As Jose Kazadi from Congo said, "Diversity is good for the country and the economy." Rahel Bosson from Ethiopia said, "People have learned from me that there is not one way." Armstrong Cheggeh from Kenya noted that African immigrants were "making Kentucky more of what America is. Having more people from other places opens minds here about others. People learn, okay, they are just like us."

Abigail Unuakhalu talked about the numbers of Nigerian faculty at Kentucky State University—"the students love them"—nine Nigerians working in state government, and also Nigerian medical doctors. Individuals have said to her, "Oh, you are from Nigeria. Do you know Dr. So and So? He took time with my child."

Kennedy Boateng, originally from Ghana, pointed out that African immigrants "are teachers, doctors, and working in other fields. All are contributing to build the state in one way or another. They contribute by paying taxes; they spend money.[8] They want to own their own houses. Their kids are going to grow up and become productive citizens. Refugees too want to help themselves." Ismail Ali, a refugee from Somalia, said, "Refugees are contributing by working, paying taxes, buying in shops, opening businesses, and doing good things." He and his wife would like to go into farming to grow for a market or bring goods from other places to sell in Louisville.

Like immigrants in the United States from all over the world, African immigrants start their own businesses.[9] Many engage in what may be called heritage trade. Selby's Tropical Food Market in Lexington caters to African immigrants, selling a wide range of mostly food items. One can find Maggi bouillon cubes, Vita Malt, and Malta Goya in bottles and big cans of Ovaltine and Milo, digestive biscuits and shortbread highlanders, goat meat and dried fish, fresh yams and plantains, ginger and tomatoes, as well as bags of *banku* mix and ground *fufu* in the freezer, boxes of cocoyam *fufu* mix and plantain *fufu* mix, and bottles of mango nectar, guava nectar, and passion fruit juice on the shelves. Afrikan herbal soap is next to Irish Spring soap below Dettol first-aid antiseptic. Fanti cloth bags hang on one wall. One can also send money through MoneyGram back to Africa. The store owner Angela Selby banters good-naturedly with customers. She came from Ghana, completed a business degree in Atlanta, and met her husband, also from Ghana, there. He is an anesthesiologist. Other Lexington stores owned by African immigrants include Mama's African Market, Africa and Caribbean Imports/Cuisine Take Out & Delivery, and Karibu International Market, which is Nkongolo Kalala's business near the University of Kentucky campus.

An article about Elizabeth Kizito in the *Tops Louisville* magazine begins: "Elizabeth Kizito, Louisville's Cookie Lady, walks around with a basket on top of her head. That's marketing! What really counts is what's inside her head." The oldest of the thirty-six children of a businessman father who owned a bakery, Elizabeth came to the US from Uganda in 1972 to complete high school and then earned a degree in environmental health from Eastern New Mexico State University. She came to Louisville, the hometown of a man she met at college and married, and started selling cookies at Fourth and Broadway in 1983, and later at Slugger Field and the Kentucky Derby. On the Saturday morning of Labor Day weekend in 2017, wonderful smells wafted out of her small bakery on Bardstown Road, a business now worth almost $500,000.

Professor Nkongolo Kalala in front of his African store in Lexington. (Photo courtesy of Angene and Jack Wilson.)

Boxes of cookies that only moments before had come hot out of the oven were being packed to sell at WorldFest on the riverfront and also at a soccer game and a flea market. As well as cookies (chocolate chip, of course, but also Mt. Kilimanjaro ginger and nine other kinds), she makes brownies, biscotti, muffins, and granola and sells African crafts. On her website Elizabeth writes about what was appealing about America. "Everybody seemed to believe that they could make a better life by working hard." On her blog, among other topics, she has educated Americans about Uganda, encouraged fund-raising with frozen dough, and explained that man cannot survive on cookies alone and thus should buy some Kizito granola.[10]

Another African vendor at the Labor Day weekend 2017 WorldFest in Louisville was Eden & Kissi, a food and beverage company and caterer owned by a couple from Côte d'Ivoire. They use locally sourced ingredients to make food that is an Afro-Caribbean fusion with a French touch. Their hibiscus drink is sold in bottles with a bright descriptive label reading: "Amazing Hibiscus is a specially prepared drink, from our secret family recipe. . . . For many centuries, the hibiscus flower has been consumed for its natural ingredients, wonderful flavor, and numerous health benefits." The drink is known as *bissap* in Côte d'Ivoire.

Sav's Grill and West African Cuisine near the University of Kentucky has had a wide reach, now educating people in central Kentucky for more than a decade about one kind of African food and about Guinea. As he says, "This restaurant represents my country. Just because of my business, people are learning. Teachers have also brought their classes, freshmen wanting to learn how to start a business." Sav has also opened Sav's Chill across the street, where he makes gourmet ice cream in flavors that include ordinary butter pecan and mint chocolate chip but also bourbon ball, Kentucky coffee, and hot banana, which combines banana and Sav's own spicy piment sauce. Sav's Chill Wagon food truck takes its flavors to venues such as Ashland Jazz on the Lawn, Woodland Art Fair, Crave Lexington, Lakeside Live, and Keeneland. Sav regularly makes contributions to community events and groups and has participated in such events as the Passport to Flavor fund-raiser put on by Kentucky Refugee Ministries.

A newer, smaller restaurant in Lexington that opened in July 2015 is Eiffel's Pizza. Mohamed Diop came from Senegal in 2000 and worked at fast food restaurants and gas stations and drove a taxi before saving enough money to open his own restaurant. On the recommendation of his sister, who is a patent lawyer in France, he studied at a pizza school in southern France for a month and half. He thought French influences might be more popular with American tastes than Senegalese, and his gourmet menu includes tuna, salmon, and shrimp as well as chicken and beef, and fresh arugula, tomatoes, and goat cheese for salads. He bought his oven and mixer in Italy.[11] He also made a tasty Senegalese rice dish for the 2018 Kentucky Refugee Ministries Passport to Flavor event.

Not all businesses survive. Although Kalisimbi Bar and Grill in Louisville's South End closed in 2014, recipes for peas and potatoes and *chipsi mayai* (eggs and potatoes) from Nicolas Kiza, one of the Rwandan co-owners who arrived as refugees, live on in the book *Flavors from*

Home: Refugees in Kentucky Share Their Stories and Comfort Foods. That book also described the Refugee Agricultural Partnership Program (RAPP) in Louisville, a federally funded, grant-based program begun in 2007 and administered by the Kentucky Office for Refugees, a division of Catholic Charities, to empower refugee families through urban agriculture. One of the active farmers and sellers highlighted in the book is Amina Osman, who came from Somalia to the United States with her husband and seven children in 2004. During the growing season Amina takes care of two garden plots, one for commercial sale to several local markets and to local restaurants and one for her family. She grows onions, kale, tomatoes, okra, watermelons, and hot peppers, all of which she grew when she farmed in Somalia. Like fellow Somali refugee Ismail Nur Ali, she wishes she could grow sesame in Kentucky as she did in Somalia. "Working in her garden also helps Amina stay active and eat nutritiously, which is critical due to her diabetes. And on the days she sells her produce to the public she can practice her English."[12]

By 2019 Common Earth Gardens, as the agricultural program in Louisville is now called, was working with 450 refugee families and reporting that they grew food to feed themselves and their families: 495,634 pounds of produce grown annually with a value of $742,000. One of the eleven gardens with which they work is the New Hope International Farm at the Passionist Earth and Spirit Center. Refugee families from Burundi, Democratic Republic of Congo, and Rwanda, collaborators from Common Earth Gardens and the Earth and Spirit Center, plus members of the returned Peace Corps community, gathered on a Saturday in April 2019 to celebrate their farm's accomplishments: fourteen growers providing culturally appropriate, healthy, and affordable produce to over 150 family members and friends, two beehives harvesting 2.5 gallons of honey, produce shared with Camp Nature Odyssey at the Earth and Spirit Center, increase of farmland to one acre, and construction of two high tunnels to extend season production. Victor Eddie, the executive director of New Hope International and himself a refugee and now a licensed mental health counselor, handed out awards to four farmers and talked about future plans, including the two tunnels, where refugee farmers plan to grow vegetables to sell. "We want people in Louisville to buy vegetables from us so we can buy books for our children," he said. "And in our part of Africa we liked to eat goat meat so we want to introduce goats."

Immigrants have made other contributions to their communities. Former ambassador from The Gambia Essa Bokar Sey was on a mayor's task force for a new police chief in Louisville, has worked with the

Office of Globalization on business relations, and has participated with various groups in the city, including marching with the mayor to show Louisville's support for immigrants. He has been a contractor with the US Department of Defense, for example, in fall 2017 working in North Carolina on a special project for the Marines in French. Nkongolo Kalala heads the Mayor's International Affairs Advisory Commission in Lexington, of which Francis Musoni is also a member. In the mid-1990s he organized a major conference on the future of the Democratic Republic of Congo at the University of Kentucky, and in the early 2000s he brought former president of Zambia Kenneth Kaunda to the University of Kentucky campus for speeches to students and the public related to AIDS in Africa. Desmond Brown from Sierra Leone has done research on tourism development in Kentucky, the horse industry, and casino gaming and has been a member of the Lexington Convention and Visitors Bureau. Gashaw Lake from Ethiopia has served on the ACCESS Soup Kitchen and Men's Shelter board of directors in Frankfort for more than twenty years. Under his leadership an annual Thanksgiving Day Walk of Awareness was started as the major fundraiser for the shelter. His students have included many Kentucky government officials, two major generals, and a former prime minister of Thailand. Iddah Otieno chairs the Education Committee for Kentucky Refugee Ministries and serves on the board of directors of the Telford YMCA in Richmond, Kentucky.

Jemima Roberts is an active member of St. Andrews Episcopal Church and a member of the Episcopal Diocese of Lexington's executive council. Bibi Roberts Sr., Jemima's husband, became involved with Lexington's Community Action Council as a volunteer in the Foster Grandparent Program in 2008 and worked in a preschool classroom until he died in early 2013. He shared his agricultural knowledge from his many years in Liberia with the children through a garden where they planted seeds and harvested vegetables to take home to their families. The lead teacher lauded his presence "as a real solid caring grandfather figure to the children. The children talked about how working with Mr. Bibi would make them smart."[13] Kennedy Boateng and his wife opened their home to foster children through an agency. They "fell in love" with two siblings who lived with them from 2013 to 2016 and when the brothers asked if they could continue to live with the Boatengs, they agreed to adopt them.

Tite Niyonizigiye and Kiluba Nkulu are both interpreters who work with Fayette County Schools, often helping parents understand how the schools work. Kiluba explained that he is called to intervene in specific cases ranging from testing and evaluating to connecting schools with families because of the language barrier. Sometimes he goes to a home as an interpreter when there is an extreme case or attends a meeting at school with parents when there are issues with behavior or with academic performance. Parents "are coming into a system that operates by laws and rules and they come from a system that has none of that so it is confusing." Beatrice Mbayo has shared her experience of domestic violence with American women "to help those women to also stand." She frequently speaks about the Congo to groups ranging from community college students to law school students. Beatrice is proud to have been awarded a Kentucky Colonel because of her work.

African immigrants, especially university professors and particularly those in social science and humanities classes, perform a special role in educating students about the history, politics, economics, and literature of the continent of Africa. They have the opportunity to do what Iddah Otieno calls, borrowing from Chinua Achebe, "balanced storytelling" about Africa. "I'm in the classroom. I tell the other side of the story. I change the narrative one student at a time. Teachers are uniquely positioned to do that. My students come in with a mindset of poverty and war. I use a lot of videos. In answer to the question 'Are there schools?' I google Maseno University [in western Kenya], where I got my undergraduate education, and show them pictures." For The African Experience course she teaches at Eastern Kentucky University, Iddah has used as a text *(Re)tracing Africa: A Multidisciplinary Study of African History, Societies, and Cultures,* edited by Salome Nnoromele and Ogechi E. Anyanwu. Supplemental readings have included Chinua Achebe's *Things Fall Apart* and his essay "An Image of Africa: Racism in Conrad's *Heart of Darkness*" as well as Binyavanga Wainaina's satirical "How to Write about Africa." Students also watch Chimamanda Ngozi Adichie's classic TED talk "*The Danger of a Single Story*" and several movies. The final exam asks students to use what they have learned to respond to the mid-twentieth-century charges by Hegel and Trevor-Roper that Africa has no history. Iddah is also faculty advisor to the African Student Associations at both Bluegrass Community and Technical College and Eastern Kentucky University. She has used that platform to educate the campus community about the untold stories of the continent and its people.

Iddah expanded her education about Africa to organizing faculty members from Bluegrass Community and Technical College and elsewhere in Kentucky for ongoing alternate-year summer trips of several weeks to Kenya to "expose my colleagues, get them to step out of their comfort zone, debunk the myths, and impact their worldview." The program is an exchange so faculty from Maseno University have come to BCTC as well. The exchange expanded in summer 2018 to include the United States International University (USIU) in Nairobi. Over the years more than twenty-five faculty and staff have traveled to Kenya, mentored Kenyan faculty on campus, hosted visiting scholars at their homes, attended International Dialogue Series, which focuses on candid conversation about topical world issues, and served on the International Committee. Because participants have come from the Kentucky Community System, the University of Kentucky, Eastern Kentucky University, and the University of Louisville, Iddah's program has enhanced the international dimension within the whole Commonwealth. In the Bluegrass and Kenya, enrichment activities have included visiting families, preparing meals and eating together, community events, educational tours, customized safaris, and other local excursions. These avenues have provided program participants with alternative views about the host culture through firsthand experiences and observation.

Francis Musoni's History of Sub-Saharan Africa from the 1880s course aims to introduce students to African perspectives on some of the major sociopolitical and economic developments that made the continent what it is today. "I introduce myself and talk about Zimbabwe on the first day of every class. And in every class I always have an Africa map quiz." To broaden students' perspectives he also tries not to assign anything written by a non-African. He has assigned such books as A. Adu Boahen's *African Perspectives on Colonialism* and Thomas Sankara's *We Are the Heirs of the World's Revolutions: Speeches from the Burkina Faso Revolution* and Irene Stanunton's *Mothers of the Revolution,* about the war experiences of Zimbabwean women. He has also invited guest speakers to discuss topics such as the concept of a United States of Africa and Africa's engagement with China. His Migrations in History class includes a focus on African migration, covering both African vendors in New York City and border crossing between Zimbabwe and South Africa, his dissertation and book topic. For his fall 2018 Introduction to African Studies class for first-year students, Francis experimented with organizing the large class into small groups that were assigned various topics for presentations, including myths and stereotypes about Africa and Africans, African foods and recipes, blogging Africa in the news, proposals for civic action initiatives, reports on Lexington-based community groups working with Africans or University of Kentucky faculty members working on Africa, and role plays of scenes from the assigned novel *Nervous Conditions* by Zimbabwean

Professor Iddah Otieno in her mother's garden in Kenya. (Photo courtesy of Iddah Otieno.)

author Tsitsi Dangarembga. Another semester he assigned Adichie's *Americanah*.

In his interview, Francis said he would like to help organize programs for the campus and larger community about topics such as the African Union so students and others can "learn about Africa from a different perspective." An example of going beyond the campus to educate the community occurred on May 25, 2018, when he gave a lecture entitled "Being an African in Lexington, Kentucky: Migration, History, and

Art" to open an art exhibit at the Global Lex's International Art Gallery. He concluded by saying that migration is not an event that ends with arrival in a host country but a life-long process of negotiating identity and differences and a transformative experience. And, he pointed out, migration also helps to spread and transform cultures. Certainly artist Kiza Mukandama, originally from Democratic Republic of Congo, who began painting in Cape Town, South Africa, before coming as a refugee to Kentucky, has taken on negotiating difference by painting horses as well as large African animals like elephants. He also paints African women: portraits of a Khoisan woman of South Africa and a multicolored woman titled *Diversity* were on display. Kiptoo Tarus, a sculptor and potter from Kenya who originally came to study at the University of Kentucky and has a studio in Lexington, was also an exhibitor.

Marie-Antoinette Sossou in the University of Kentucky's College of Social Work has brought a global perspective to social work by developing and teaching the undergraduate Global Poverty elective course each semester. It is always full, especially of international studies majors. Each student has to volunteer ten hours at a local agency such as Catholic Action, the Hope Center, or the International Book Project, which "opens their eyes to the community." In class she starts with "poverty in our backyard" and in the US and then moves to poverty globally, showing documentaries at each stage so students hear and see about topics such as child brides and human trafficking. "You see tears falling from their faces." The final project divides students into continents and they pick issues such as women and children, health, and education to research and present to the class. Some students have said, "Everyone at UK ought to take this class." For several years Marie-Antoinette also took students to Ghana for six weeks in the summer, placing them in social welfare agencies, mostly in Accra, and including visits to tourist attractions, too. The students she has taken to Ghana always want to go back. "They like the country."[14]

For a decade University of Kentucky students and faculty have also been introduced to Ghana through Kwaku Addo's two-week program.[15*] Even in 2016, after he had moved to Prairie View University in Texas, he consulted on the University of Kentucky program. Participants spend three days in Accra listening to professors from the University of Legon talk about the role of women in development, the history of modern Ghana, and agriculture systems, followed by visits to an orphanage, the cultural center, and then to Kwaku's home village, where his uncle is chief. One year participants saw his younger brother being enstooled (installed) as chief. His uncle also always hosts

Professor Marie-Antoinette Sossou with University of Kentucky social work students she took on a study abroad trip to Ghana. (Photo courtesy of Marie-Antoinette Sossou.)

a traditional durbar celebration with dancing and drumming. Other activities include a cruise on Lake Volta and visits to the museum of the Ashanti king, the cocoa-growing region, the gold mines of Obuasi, the canopy walkway at Kakum rain forest, and the Elmina and Cape Coast castles. The participants also visit and volunteer at the Kentucky Academy, founded in his wife Esther's home village. A dancing and drumming workshop at University of Legon closes the trip. Asked what the travelers have learned, Kwaku said: "I think they've learned about how Ghanaians are. Ghanaians are the friendliest people on God's earth."

Iddah Otieno summarized the case for the contributions of African immigrants not only to Kentucky but more broadly to the United States. "We need to change the way we view immigrants. Immigrants bring a lot to the US: the culture, the expertise, their willingness to work. They are the hardest workers. We are just human beings. We love our families. We want to give the best to our children. We mean well for the United States of America. We are grateful for the opportunity." Ever the teacher, she concluded, "Africans in Kentucky need to do their part to address the stereotypical and rewrite Africa in history."

A Bishop and a Judge

Two individuals whose contributions transcend national boundaries and who work transnationally are Bishop Armstrong Cheggeh from Kenya and Judge Bankole Thompson from Sierra Leone. Both had careers in their home countries before coming to the United States to live and have continued to make substantial contributions that go beyond both the boundaries of the United States and of their own African countries.

In 1998 Armstrong Cheggeh used what he had learned through his education at Kenyan and American higher-education institutions and through professional work in religious organizations in Kenya to establish his own Fountain of Life Churches International. He began with one congregation in Kenya and by 2017 the church had more than three hundred congregations in Kenya, Uganda, Tanzania, Rwanda, Burundi, Congo, and India. He explained that the structure is based on Assemblies of God theologically, Baptists organizationally, with Sunday school and youth departments, and Anglicans of Kenya hierarchically. Training preachers in a two-year Bible program is a major part of his work, and as the presiding bishop or archbishop he has empowered others to become bishops. Although he lives in Kentucky he goes overseas regularly, in 2017 taking two trips to graduate more than three hundred preachers who will join two hundred already trained. He goes to Africa several times a year for leadership seminars and spends a lot of time fund-raising, often inviting Americans to go with him to "see" and then hopefully support his work. One Kentucky businessman gave him $12,000 to help with a conference for pastors from four countries. "That was a good day for me."

Armstrong explained that coming with his family to Asbury Seminary for his doctorate "made me and my family Kentuckians. My five children have done well." Two sons did master's degrees at the University of Kentucky: one an MBA, one at the Patterson School of Diplomacy. A surprise was that those sons, one who went to Asbury College and one to Berea College, fell in love with white American girls and have been married for eleven and seven years respectively. "They are more American than we expected," he said with good humor. A third son, who is getting a PhD in political science in Dallas, is marrying the daughter of Kenyan immigrants. When people ask, "Where are you from?" Armstrong used to say he was Kenyan but now he says Kentuckian; he sees his accent as just another addition to the various Kentucky accents.

Judge Rosolu John Bankole Thompson was professionally successful in both Sierra Leone and the United States and has had an impact beyond Sierra Leone to West Africa more generally.[16*] In Sierra Leone he was first a state prosecutor and then was seconded to become legal advisor for the Mano River Union of Liberia and Sierra Leone and later Guinea. In 1981 he was appointed a high court judge of the Superior Court of Sierra Leone. During his years as a professor in the US he was the first African to hold the Brennan Endowed Chair of Comparative Constitutional Law at University of Akron and the first African appointed as dean of graduate studies at Eastern Kentucky University. He has also published four scholarly books: *The Constitutional History and Law of Sierra Leone (1961-1995), The Criminal Law of Sierra Leone, American Criminal Procedures,* and *Universal Jurisdiction: The Sierra Leone Profile.* Perhaps most interesting and important, he was appointed by United Nations secretary-general Kofi Annan in 2002 to the Residual Special Court for Sierra Leone, an international war crimes tribunal set up to deal with crimes in connection with Sierra Leone's ten-year war, and he remains a judge of that court. The judges do their work electronically and go to The Hague once every two years for plenary sessions. The mandate for the court was to try all persons who bore responsibility for violations of international humanitarian law, so that included not only groups in Sierra Leone but also President Charles Taylor of Liberia. That court was a hybrid court set up by the United Nations and Sierra Leone. Bankole was the designated judge to study the evidence and decide whether to indict Taylor and issue an arrest warrant. He looked at the law: was it permissible to indict a sitting head of state? Based on the Nuremberg principles, which affirm that being head of state does not exonerate an individual from international crimes, he decided for indictment and in 2012 signed the indictment for Charles Taylor's arrest. In 2012 he also took on another responsibility, becoming a member of the West African Commission on Drug Trafficking and Other Transnational Crimes.

The judge keeps in touch with Sierra Leone by telephone and email and visits fairly frequently. He said that his children have been in and out of Sierra Leone, too, and "have significant contacts with their home country. They seem to like it there. They are very much wedded to their native country." When asked where he is from, he says West Africa but that he is a "citizen of the world."

Do We Live in Between?

The concept of identity appears again and again as African immigrants describe their lives. Although the bishop and the judge may seem to be more active in the transnational social space than some other immigrants, they are not alone in having feet and feelings in two places. Iddah Otieno explained: "Home is here, there, confusing, and uplifting because I get the chance to live in two cultures." Her poem concludes this chapter. It can be seen as her answer to George Ella Lyon's "Where I Am From" poem referenced in chapter 1. After recognizing the importance of family for African immigrants, the next chapter deals in more detail with the question of identity. The following and final chapter looks at the concept of transnationality in the context of the present and wonders about its future.

Borderland

They traverse the borderland,
Voluntary and involuntary sojourners
In search of a new beginning
In the land of milk and honey.

They write letters home,
Nostalgic memoirs of childhood years
Now a distant memory tucked away
In the hurl and twirl of the borderland.

They work the graveyard shift,
Send money and honey home
With hopes of a grand return
To the place they once knew.

They get their degrees
In the trenches of the borderland,
Shuffling and hustling

In the daily routine that is the norm
In the land of opportunity.

They meet and marry,
Raise children and grandchildren
With stories of home that was
Once upon a time.

They toss and turn
In the dark of night,
Stroking their snow white hair
As it dawns on them,
They have been home all along
In the borderland.[17]

5

Family and Identity in the United States

> There is no wealth where there are no children.
>
> —Ghanaian proverb

The African immigrants featured in this book were interviewed as individuals, but they are all part of families. As Kwame Gyekye writes: "One outstanding feature of the communal structure of African society and the ever-present consciousness of ties of kinship is the emphasis on the importance of the family."[1] To deal with individual identity we also have to deal with families. Individuals sometimes came first by themselves to get a university education, for example, but they also often came with spouses and children or spouses followed them and then they had children. Refugees have usually arrived as families. Family reunification has also resulted in extended family members joining original immigrants. For instance, Abraham Sven-Peters brought his mother from Sierra Leone to the US, and Jemima Roberts from Liberia was able to become a citizen because her son became a citizen.

Importantly, opportunity—that often stated reason for coming to the United States in the first place—includes in the minds of African immigrants opportunities for their children. Originally from Democratic Republic of Congo, Kikoko Godfrey wanted to leave the refugee camp in Namibia because "my children have no opportunities." Karin Krain, coming from South Africa to be a pharmacist in Kentucky, was very clear: "Every decision is based on setting our kids up for their future." Judge Bankole Thompson remained in the United States rather than returning to Sierra Leone because of the educational appeal for his children. Bishop Armstrong Cheggeh explained that he stayed in Kentucky rather than returning to Kenya mainly for the family. Said Jose Kazadi, who came to Kentucky from Democratic Republic of Congo via Russia: "Kentucky is a good place to grow up children."

This chapter begins by broadening the story of individual African immigrants to include their lives as parents and adds the voices of some of their children. The first section is entitled "African Immigrant Parents" and the second section "The Next Generation Speaks." Then, in "Where We Are from Now," the chapter takes up the complex question of how African immigrants identify themselves after they have lived in Kentucky for some time. How immigrants talk about their identity often encompasses family and their children as well. As Essa Bokar Sey, the former ambassador from The Gambia explained: "When I am on the media like BBC, I always tell people I am from Louisville, Kentucky. It goes with me everywhere. Kentucky worked with me to mold my child." This chapter comes full circle from the first chapter, which began with the story of Robert Chirwa growing up in a family in Malawi, by concluding with details of the Chirwas' lives in "One African Immigrant Family in 2018."

African Immigrant Parents

Parenting in the shifting terrain of the borderland is one of the greatest challenges facing African immigrant families. There may be differences in family experience depending on whether children are born in the US or in an African country, whether a parent is a college professor with American graduate education or a certified nursing assistant who came to the US as a refugee. Usually, however, balancing between parental control and respecting their children's autonomy is a tightrope that African immigrant parents walk. Raised in authoritarian homes and close-knit family networks where the community was part of the "village" that raised the child, these parents can find it extremely difficult to raise children in the United States, where their authority is quite often questioned.

It is not easy to be an immigrant parent. In fact, one parent exclaimed: "These children are immigrants in *our* lives. We came here alone, then the children came into our lives. They look like us, but their behaviors are totally alien." As Bishop Armstrong Cheggeh cautioned fellow parents at the annual Kenyans in Kentucky (KIK) gathering in December 2016: "This generation lives in their own world. These children are not from Murang'a. They are Americans. They know their rights. You must be careful how you engage them. They live in a society where children and pets have more power than their parents."

Nigerian American anthropologist Emmanuel Babatunde advocates a middle of the road parenting approach: "Blend cultural aspects of the communities of origin and encounter together and incorporate them in the socialization of . . . children born in the land of encounter." He suggests teaching the importance of independence, cooking, thriftiness, and the ability to save for a "rainy day" by deferring instant gratification. He also urges families to nurture new experiences and talents that their ethnic culture may not approve.[2] In *The Scattered Family: Parenting, African Migrants, and Global Inequality,* Cati Coe focuses on what she calls repertoires developed by Ghanaian immigrants in transnational families as they deal with differences between Ghanaian ways and American ways. Her interviews show that immigrant parents are adapting and adopting and adding to their cultural frameworks.[3]

Dating is one thorny issue in the African immigrant home. African children born or raised outside their parents' countries of origin do not view dating in the same way their parents do. As a matter of fact, some of their parents never dated before marriage. Because of this cultural difference, children of African immigrants quite often face resistance from their parents in the area of dating before marriage. Explained Yamukumba, a recent college graduate living on his own: "I have taken the view that it is possible to live with a girl without getting married. This does not make sense to my mom. Sometimes uncomfortable conversations go on in my presence when my mom is trying to arrange a marriage between me and her friend's children. I do understand why it is important to her that the families get involved."[4]

Parental concerns and areas of conflict with younger children include social interaction outside school, dress, and expectations of academic success and specific careers. African parents are often particular about whom their children spend time with outside their home. For example, during events such as sleepovers and birthday celebrations, it is not uncommon for African immigrant parents to demand to meet with the host parent and ask about details such as adult supervision, time limit, and other details. Expectation regarding clothing and general appearance at home or in public is yet another challenging area. Most African parents require their children to be appropriately dressed. Sagging clothes and unkempt hair are not acceptable, even in cases where their children's peers exhibit alternative dress and grooming codes. And in reference to technology, African immigrant parent complaints seem very similar to those of American parents. "These children text each other even in the same room" and "They are either in their rooms flat on their backs with a cell phone in hand or sloughing on a couch, head bowed low, oblivious of their surroundings. It's like I'm raising total strangers in my home."

All African immigrant parents believe that education is important for their children. Parents who come to the United States with academic credentials—for example, professors—are especially likely to expect their children to succeed. Cases of academic drop-outs or stop-outs are rarely tolerated. African immigrant parents also expect their children to seek employment in reputable organizations with decent salaries. Parents push to enroll their children in highly specialized fields such as law, medicine, engineering, and business administration. In fact, a study seeking to understand the academic and occupational pathways for African immigrant children concluded that these children had higher social and economic aspirations compared to their peers with US-born parents.[5] Of course it is also true that well-educated nonimmigrant American parents often have high and specific expectations.

Abraham Sven-Peters talked in his interview about the challenges of bringing up children in the United States, especially keeping them connected with Africa.[6*] Although his older son spent the first five years of his life in Freetown, the capital of Sierra Leone, he is not interested in Africa. He thinks people there live in the forest or the bush. Abraham believes he learned that in school. However, the younger middle school–age son, born in the US, wants to visit both Sierra Leone and Liberia "to see how it looks." Meanwhile, Abraham tells the boys about the early history of Liberia, the connection to Kentucky with nineteenth-century President Russell, who came to Liberia from Kentucky, and the town of Clay-Ashland, named for the Henry Clay estate in Lexington. He wants them to know their family in West Africa but, after suffering from violence and war, Abraham feels blessed to live in Kentucky. He said, "Lexington is a safe and good place to bring up my kids."

The Next Generation Speaks

Eight children of interviewed immigrants talked about how they identify themselves and in what ways they feel connected to the country of their parents, as well their challenges and their dreams.[7] "I was born in Kentucky but my parents are from Kenya. I consider myself a Kenyan American," said Ochieng. His sister Mikal agreed: "I usually say I am Kenyan American. Kenya will always be a special part of our lives. We just happen to have been born here in Richmond, Kentucky." Oraida stressed her Libyan heritage. "I was born in Lexington, Kentucky. When I tell people I am African they get confused because I am white in complexion. I am a Libyan Arab from North Africa. That is how I identify myself." Bangaly said, "I identify myself as both African and American. My mother is American and my dad is from Guinea, West Africa. So in the truest sense of the word, I am African American."

Not being born in the United States may make some difference. Two of the interviewed young people were born in African countries. Nyasha was born in Zimbabwe and came to the US with her parents as an eight-year-old. She said, "I was born in Zimbabwe. I'm Zimbabwean." Yamukumba was born in the Democratic Republic of Congo but when he was eleven years old he escaped with his mother to Zimbabwe, where he became a refugee. He moved to the United States at age fifteen. He explained that he identified as an Emba and an African in America.

Occasional family visits back to Africa, attending African events in the United States, reading African books, wearing African clothes, listening to African music, and for some speaking African languages are keeping African culture alive for the next generation. "Going to Libyan events in Lexington has helped me not to be ashamed of my Libyan heritage," explained Oraida. "The community as a whole is like family. There is always someone to lean on." Said Mikal: "Kenyans in Kentucky still find time to get together. Even if you are not blood related you are still treated like family. Surrounded by people like that is how I have met my African friends. All of my African attire have a special place in my closet."

These young people understand that as, Odhiambo said, "People view Africa negatively." Like their parents, they educate Americans. He pointed out that "Africa has a more family feel to it than the US, where people may not even know their next-door neighbors. Kenya is a beautiful place. I show them pictures. I explain to them that Africa is a lot more than what they see on TV." Mikal explained: "I think people have a totally different view of Africa. They often think of poverty. Whenever I visit Kenya, I enjoy going back to our compound. I love going to Aunt Jane's house and my grandparents'. I have lots of cousins in Kenya. In class we watched a video about how we should be fortunate to go to school here in the US compared to African children. I tell them Kenyan children love going to school. I also did a scrapbook about my visit with pictures I took in Kenya. I feel that it changed their perspective on Africa." Oraida has also tried to respond with education. "People have one image of Africa and they are stuck with it. Of course there are some bad things that have happened in Africa but there are also amazing things like buildings, educated people, doctors, lawyers, and many other professionals. I try my best to create a new image."

Bangaly Savané with his father Mamadou Savané at Sav's Grill and West African Cuisine. (Photo courtesy of Kopana Terry.)

The interviewed young people are also working very hard to live up to the high standards set by their parents. Bangaly, who was working on aviation certification to become a pilot at the time of his interview, pointed out: "Our parents have taught us to be self-reliant. Look at my sister. She is only eighteen and she can balance the books at my mom's jewelry store while I step in for my dad." Bangaly took over for his father at Sav's Grill and West African Cuisine when Sav was badly burned in 2015, and in late 2016 and early 2017 he was in charge of both that establishment and Sav's Chill, the ice cream shop, while his parents were in Guinea and Denmark for several months. "Had I not traveled with my dad and experienced the discomfort most people live with daily in Guinea, I would not have turned out the way I have." Bangaly hopes this "next generation of African immigrant children do not forget where they came from. I hope they are patient and that they are able to educate people, especially in the current political climate. We come from a big continent with a rich history, and there is no reason we should not share that." By 2019 Bangaly was sales associate and ferry pilot at Airmart in Lexington.

Illustrating the point made earlier about high expectations in academics, Odhiambo explained: "Academics come first in my family. I am expected to do well in academics or I'm not allowed to do sports and other things. My dad is the dean of the College of Science at Eastern Kentucky University. I know he had to do well in Kenya and make good grades and want more in order to be what he is today. My mother is a college professor. She wasn't born here. Both my parents had to face the battle of people thinking they were not good enough, but they worked hard and both have their PhDs." Nyasha, a high school sophomore in a magnet math and science program who has already taken the ACT exam, said, "My parents are always pushing me to do better. They motivate me. If I don't meet their expectations, they are always there to comfort me."

Coming to America as a refugee at age fifteen, Yamukumba had a somewhat different source of motivation. "At the time I started going to school in the United States, my mom was not knowledgeable about the school system in America. I had to work on my own, choosing classes, checking my grades, doing my homework, and applying for university. My mom focused on teaching us to know who we are, our family line, and the struggles we have been through. The journey to the United States motivates me to work harder and where I come from determines the choices I make. My mother is my hero." Yamukumba is now the immigrant and refugee enrollment specialist at Bluegrass Community and Technical College.

Of course, there are challenges for African immigrant young people in language, alienation, and discrimination. They are unlikely to be fluent in their parents' native languages. Fueled by the need to excel in school and find employment, the language of choice for most parents and their children is English. Upon relocation fluency in English is often viewed as the path to survival.[8] Some children, especially within the refugee population, even become translators for their parents. The danger in focusing on English at the expense of the native languages is that the children who were brought into the US as foreign-borns lose their native languages (or sometimes become "ashamed" of them), preferring instead to perfect their English-speaking skills as a coping strategy for assimilation into their new environment.[9] Children of African immigrants also sometimes face discrimination, both in school and in the communities where they live. Young people who were not born in the United States noted they were often singled out because of their accents. Some shared stories of struggle mastering the English language for academic success and general survival. Even in cases where English had been mastered, African immigrant students still felt singled out for their accents by both their peers and teachers. Being labeled "that kid who speaks funny" by peers made the early years of schooling difficult for some African immigrant students. Oftentimes these students felt the burden of daily proving themselves worthy of belonging to groups and ended up interacting with students from similar backgrounds. Others felt the burden of representing an entire continent in their classroom discussions, especially when any topic focusing on Africa was discussed. The label of being poor, displaced, and hungry is a load that most African immigrant children carry.[10]

Refugee children with single mothers who have moved homes and schools multiple times and are living in section 8 subsidized apartments face particular challenges. Three seventh-grade boys talked about their experiences.[11] Remy, who arrived in Lexington in 2015 from the UNICEF refugee camp in Tanzania where he was born and whose father is still in Democratic Republic of Congo, was in his fourth school in two years in December 2017. "I love how they treat people here," he said of his new middle school. "The teachers understand me." His favorite subject is math because he thinks it will help him in the future to become an engineer. But math is not easy. When he is done with homework, he studies flash cards. He admires an American man who picks him and his family up to go to services at Christ the King Cathedral. Bienvenue, the youngest of thirteen children, arrived in Atlanta in 2014 from the refugee camp in Rwanda where he was born. He had attended four different schools before his current middle school, but although it was particularly hard to leave friends he made in Atlanta that first year, he also appreciated his current school. "They care about us so much and help us with our work." His favorite classes are social studies, "learning about religions and cultures," and gym. He would like to be an NBA player. Freddy, the second-oldest of six children who came to Chicago in 2013 from Republic of Congo (Brazzaville) via a refugee camp in Malawi, is in his sixth school. He finds presenting a project in front of a class difficult, but the previous year he had enjoyed talking about himself in class and letting fellow students ask him questions, even stereotypical questions like "Did you race with cheetahs?" Freddy likes math because "I am good at solving stuff in my head." He said, "The good thing about the United States is the bunch of opportunities. You can be anything you want if you work hard. You can find a better life and make this place better." Freddy wants to be a NBA basketball player or a doctor or engineer. He is already playing in an amateur basketball league and knows the names of successful University of Kentucky basketball players now in the NBA.

Young people in high school are also thinking about the future. Oraida is interested in getting a law degree "so I can be a voice for the voiceless. I want to be a lawyer so that I can help undocumented students pursue education in the US. I have worked with ESL and Hispanic students [at her high school] and seen firsthand what they go through." As mentioned in an earlier chapter, as a high school senior Oraida was one of the organizers in spring 2017 of a rally to support immigrants in downtown Lexington, and she was a chief organizer of a multicultural fair at Lafayette High School. She began her college education at Bluegrass Community and Technical College in fall 2017 and worked in the Latino Outreach Center there before transferring to Berea College in fall 2018.

Sometimes students' futures involve Africa, becoming a transnational in some sense. Sometimes they are more focused on life in the US. Nyasha said, "I would like to go back to Africa." She wants to excel in school and become a pediatric surgeon. "I do want to have contact with my relatives in Zimbabwe. That is where I am from and that is where I feel I should be. There is a great need there." However, Ochieng, who also wants to be a doctor, said, "I'd love to visit and help but I will always live in the United States." Still, he is choosing a medical career because it will offer him a broader platform to "make a difference in the lives of others, not only in America but also in Africa."

For Cubuka, a young adult Congolese refugee who lost his mother to a house fire in Uganda when he and his six siblings were young and who is now living in Kentucky with his father, a Pentecostal minister, going back home is a life-long dream. "I want to help people to be sufficient on their own, to be able to develop ourselves. I want to go back to Africa and be part of the growth. There is so much work to be done at home. I want to make a difference in the lives of others." Cubuka's brother Pacifica seemed more interested in what he can do in the US when in May 2018 he talked to high school students who had interviewed refugees for a class project.[12] He told them about his memories of living as a refugee, his mother's death, the many interviews with identical questions he underwent before coming to the United States, arriving in Lexington at age thirteen in shocking snow and cold. He described taking a photography class at Tates Creek High School, buying a friend's camera, and after graduation starting his own company producing videos. Pacifica, who also works in Fayette County Schools as a para-educator, said he doesn't consider himself a refugee now. "America is the land of opportunity."

An example of a young person who is already acting transnationally by figuring out how to make a difference back in her home country of Burundi is Aisha, a student at the STEAM Academy in Lexington, whose family arrived as refugees in 2007. She received the 2017 Outstanding Youth in Philanthropy Award from the Bluegrass Chapter and Thoroughbred Collegiate Chapter of the Association of Fundraising Professionals for her BackPack PayBack program. Aisha was nominated by her English teacher, who encouraged her students to find a topic they were passionate about, research it, and try to make an impact. Aisha raised money from supporters at the academy, at a middle school, at the University of Kentucky, and at First Presbyterian Church, which had sponsored her family when they first arrived as refugees, in order to buy backpacks for students at the Muyange School in Burundi, which her cousins attend. In July 2017 she delivered about three hundred backpacks and $1,600 worth of school supplies to the school when she went to Burundi on a family trip. Aisha also spent a day at the school teaching some English and sharing her story of living in the United States.[13] She shared her feelings about that trip: "Seeing and hearing my parents' thoughts on BackPack PayBack and seeing the looks on my aunts, uncles, and cousins' faces the day I was giving out the supplies to the chosen school, it was an amazing feeling knowing that I was setting an example not only for my siblings but for all of my family, classmates, and peers."[14] In March 2018 Aisha held a successful fund-raiser for the continuation of her project.

Taiye Selasi's novel *Ghana Must Go* is a complex story of family, immigration, and love that describes the growing up into adulthood of the children of a doctor originally from Ghana. In Selasi's novel, as in the examples in this chapter, it is clear that second-generation lives are different from those of first-generation immigrants. But to say second-generation immigrants have become Americanized is too simplistic. In a 2015 TED talk that was rebroadcast on National Public Radio in 2018, Taiye Selasi says, "Don't ask where I'm from, ask where I'm a local." She does not want to think of herself as the citizen of a nation or even as a multinational—that is a company. Instead she wants to be considered a human being who is a multi-local, and she proposes a 3-R test of rituals, relationships, and restrictions to determine where one is local. Her examples of rituals include taking off shoes in the house and eating slow-cooked spicy food that her mother brought from Ghana. Relationships are with people who "shape your days, with whom you speak at least once a week." Her restrictions on where you are able to live include racism, civil war, passport, dysfunctional governance, and economic inflation.[15]

Taiye Selasi challenges the question of home and the myth of "returning" by arguing that the immigrant is already home in several local experiences of rituals, relationships, and restrictions. Her ideas seem to fit with the concept of transnationality and perhaps can apply to both first and second generations. In the next section the interviewed first-generation immigrants grapple with the question of where they are from now.

Where We Are from Now

Where African immigrants say they are from now depends on many factors. Whereas chapter 1 dealt with the origins of immigrants, the countries where they were born and lived as children and often as adults, this chapter focuses on what influences how the interviewed African immigrants explain the evolution and complications of their self-identity. Geography, culture, dress, accent, skin color, length of time in the US, and family are some of the areas that matter, to a greater or lesser degree.

Is geography or place a defining feature? How much does a sense of place matter, even for refugees who were very young when they left Burundi or Somalia? Moulaye Indrissa Barry said he loved "Lexington during the summer because it always reminds me where I'm from, the green part of Senegal." Karin Krain likes access to the Gulf Shore beaches because they remind her of the beautiful beaches in Cape Town, South Africa. "I feel like I'm at home." On the other hand, Francis Musoni believes his growing up in a rural village in Zimbabwe and being rooted there in Buhera during his entire childhood and teenage years without access to the outside world is why he is so attached to that village. His mother still lives in the same homestead where he grew up. "That means I still feel a great deal of belonging and attachment to that place and space."

How important is culture? Do immigrants, especially first-generation immigrants, often become cultural hybrids, doing selective borrowing, taking what they see as the best from the birth culture, the culture of parents, of ethnic group, of nation, and combining that with the culture of the new location, of Kentucky, of America? It does seem to make a difference when Americans value and respect who immigrants are and are even willing to learn from them. Ismail Ali wants his daughter to do well in her studies because free education is a "golden opportunity." However, he is also thankful for a mosque where he can pray. Mulbah Zowah told a story: "I brought my traditional background [from Liberia] to the college and they [the nursing class at Berea College] thought it was amazing." He had talked to his mother about "her fifty years as a midwife. She was very hesitant because it is taboo to talk to men about childbirth. Among other things she said she never did a C-section. It doesn't matter how big the child, it is possible to be born through the vagina." For Jacob Guot, a continual question from Americans concerns the Dinka scarification on his forehead. "We are so sorry about your injury," they say. He wants to educate Americans about his culture, both the scarification ceremony and marriage customs. He says, "Instead of reading my head, read my book."[16]

Does dress matter? Many women from African countries, perhaps especially Muslim women and those recently arrived, continue to wear traditional dress every day. One can see a Congolese woman in traditional dress carrying a baby on her back walking in or near the Westminster Village housing compound where more than forty Congolese and Burundian refugee families live in Lexington. Venus Niza from Côte d'Ivoire was surprised to see even older American women wearing shorts. She always wears long skirts herself. Samah Sadouki from Algeria dresses fashionably and conservatively with a long dress and head covering. Both African women and some men sometimes wear African dress for formal and special occasions. Angene and Jack Wilson know well a Liberian immigrant, now a retired professor living in northern Ohio, who came to the United States in the 1960s and who has always worn African dress, including a head tie. While she says the head tie is a convenience so she doesn't have to worry about her hair, African dress does seem to be part of her identity.

Does accent matter? The accent of African and other immigrants is troublesome to some native-born Kentuckians, who at times don't realize they are actually hearing English but spoken with a different accent than they have. Tite Niyonizigiye said, "I am from Burundi but I live here. I am an American citizen but I don't have an American accent so I am from Burundi." Aka Kpla and Kennedy Boateng agree that people ask where they're from because of their accents. Aka says Africa first, then Ivory Coast, and then explains where Ivory Coast is. Kennedy says, "I am an American now. I am originally from Ghana." Jacob Guot, originally from Sudan, was offered help from a speech therapist. He told her: "Be careful not to get rid of my accent, just reduce it in a way to help me communicate." He does not want to lose who he is.

Does skin color matter? Nkongolo Kalala identifies himself as from the Congo, although most Americans assume he is African American until he speaks. Children with whom his lighter-skinned daughter was working were puzzled when she said she was from the Congo. But you are not black, they said. There is an assumption that African equals black. Hamidou Koivogui from Guinea said, "We can never be American. We can have a passport and citizenship and they will call you African man." Khadar Abdullahi from Somalia was more positive. He told the interviewer over the samosas he served his guest, "I am a Kentuckian now." He cheers for the University of Kentucky in sports because his brother went to UK.

Does the length of time one has lived in the United States matter? Mulbah Zowah said, "Being here for ten years and my interaction with different people, I feel integrated in this society. When I went home [to Liberia] in 2011 I felt lost. I have changed a lot. It was hard to accept that this is the country where I grew up and now I look like a stranger." Since 2011 he has returned to Liberia several more times.

What role does family play in one's identity? Sim Oyetunji provides an example. Understandably proud, he brought a large picture of his family with him to his interview. The picture, taken at a family reunion at a daughter's home in Cincinnati, included his seven children (two married to white Americans) and their families. The hosting daughter is a chemical engineer manager at Procter and Gamble. Other daughters are in the fields of computer science, mechanical engineering, accounting, and pharmacy. One son is also a pharmacist, and in 2017 the youngest son had just returned from his national service in Nigeria and was applying to a doctoral program in chemical engineering. Sim is now a US citizen because of his family. Because of his good experience as a student himself, he sent his children to college in the United States. They stayed and eventually persuaded him to join them. Still, he returns to Nigeria every year for a visit.

Being a first-generation immigrant is just plain complex and is to some extent must be worked out individually. Zineeddine Hamoudi explained, "People think you become American 100 percent, which is not true. This will never be the case with any immigrant. I say I am African American and a guy says, 'You don't look like an African American.' So I say I'm Algerian American. I'm trying to become more American in the things I see that are good, like things in the US Constitution." Zineeddine also pointed out that Algeria is a country that allows one to hold dual citizenship.

Gashaw Lake, who finally became a citizen in 2006, perhaps admitting that he would not return to Ethiopia from his "comfortable life and achievement of the American dream," said: "I used to think I'm living in my daughters' country, but now the US is my country. I've been here forty-five years. I love and have a big faith in the American system of democracy. Any willing person can achieve whatever they want to do in their lifetime." His house in Frankfort demonstrates his Ethiopian heritage—the picture of Haile Selassie, the classical Ethiopian music playing, the manuscript of Amharic poetry he is writing—but he also describes himself as an "American product who understands very well the establishment of the government, the Constitution." However, considering the election of Donald Trump as president, he said, "the politics is not as refined as the science and technology." Gashaw wrote and shared the following poem, written in November 2017, illustrating the ambiguity of being an immigrant even after forty-five years.

Mercedes

Nowadays I have been seen driving
A Mercedes downtown.
People gaze at me with puzzled looks—
The Mercedes speaks to them;
I don't know what it evokes.
But still they stare at me as if the car owns me or they see me as driving for someone.
In silence, I watch them passing me
With strange looks and frowning faces.
It is a German-made car
And drives smoothly with grace
And I own it with pride.
Just like I would any other car.
I hope not to hurt people's feelings.
But it is the only means I have for traveling, seeking rural Kentucky's blessing.
So far, the police have not pulled me over.
It is my black Mercedes for retirement.
My car and my time.

Abraham Sven-Peters said that he had been asked why he would live in Kentucky—that's a white man's state. He says no, there are Africans, Asians. He says he is from Liberia, but "I call myself an American citizen. I don't care what you say, your origin and culture will always be there but you have to balance it with American culture. That brings balance to my worldview. I don't feel inferior if someone asks me where I am from. Where I am from is who I am along with being a Kentuckian." Sam Vorkpor is proud of both parts of his life. "I am an American of African descent. I did my schooling in Liberia. I got my medical degree in Liberia."

Venus Niza says, "I am from Ivory Coast in West Africa" but she also said, "I'm not so attached to a culture, a country. I can attach myself to where I am right now but keep what is good for me." Planning to continue studying chemical engineering, she likes science because regardless of language science is the same. A member of an international church, she also considers that everyone is a brother or sister in religion "regardless of where you come from or what language you speak."

Rahel Bosson, who comes from an Ethiopian family but has lived in both Europe and the US much longer than her first seven years in Ethiopia, said in her interview, "I don't have a home. I belong to everywhere but then usually say I'm from Kentucky. It is very hard for me to identify with only one culture. When I hang out around Ethiopians they say you really aren't Ethiopian. When I hang out around Europeans they say you really aren't American." Sylvia Uwamaliya Stainback, like Rahel married to a white American, explained, "I say I was born in Uganda but my parents are from Rwanda. I can't separate the two. There is the Ugandan part of me, the Rwandan part of me, and the American part of me." Jacob Guot says: "I am from South Sudan but I am also American. It's both of me. I have to stand in the middle."

Identity is particularly complicated for people like Shamik Aikat and Boyd Mpho Hayes, introduced in chapter 1. Shamik's answer to where he is from is, "It is a long story": with Indian parents, he grew up in Zambia, went to college in India, then England, then the US, coming to Kentucky as a doctor. Boyd hates the question. Born in South Africa, he grew up in Botswana, Zimbabwe, and Kentucky. He is often mistaken for Latin American or Samoan because of his looks and accent. "It's tough. I am absolutely an American citizen. I love Kentucky but it doesn't tell the whole story. I was born in South Africa. My parents always said I was a global citizen. I am an American citizen but I feel very African." Time spent in South Africa during college and now two years in the Peace Corps in Senegal are shaping his future. Back in Kentucky briefly in March 2018, Boyd talked about his best friend, his Senegalese brother, a farmer who was working with him on a plan for the school club to pick up trash in the village. Boyd was surprised that the people in the village said he was African, perhaps because although he was a white man he spoke Pular, the local language. In contrast, African friends in the US with whom he interacts in online forums considered only black Africans as African. But Boyd used his Pular during his March 2018 visit when he met Senegalese immigrant Mohamed Diop at his Eiffel Pizza restaurant. In fact, as he walked in the restaurant, Mohamed was face-timing with a friend in Senegal and Boyd

Boyd Mpho Hayes meeting Mohamed Diop, owner of Eiffel Pizza in Lexington and originally from Senegal, where Boyd served as a Peace Corps volunteer. (Photo courtesy of Jack Wilson.)

joined their conversation. After completing their Peace Corps service in November 2018, Boyd and his girlfriend planned to fly to Cape Town, then travel in southern Africa visiting friends and return to Botswana and Zimbabwe, where Boyd lived as a child. He was thinking about graduate school, perhaps in political economy, perhaps in the US, perhaps in Canada, perhaps in Cape Town, South Africa.

When asked, Ibrahim Bakoush, who has lived in Kentucky for thirty-five years, says, "I am from Lexington."[17*] He explained, "I have lived here longer than in Benghazi in Libya. But deep down I am from Benghazi." Still, I "sell Lexington and Kentucky a lot," and he concluded, "I value this country in a different way than people who were born here because I have seen both sides. There is nothing wrong with loving two countries." After more than a decade in the US, Karin Krain still says she is from South Africa. Her husband says he is from Kentucky. She recognizes there are insiders and outsiders. "We became part of the outsider community." It helped when she realized that Americans not born in Kentucky were outsiders, too, for instance, individuals who come from elsewhere to work at the state's universities. Americans like Angene and Jack Wilson, who were born elsewhere and have lived elsewhere but have now lived in Kentucky for more than forty years, more than half their lives, are still occasionally told, "Oh, you're from away."

Most of the interviewed African immigrants are thankful to be in the United States. Still, living in the US can continue to be hard. In her 2014 oral history interview social work professor Marie-Antoinette Sossou said, "Maybe fate brought us here. You have to look on the brighter side. As an immigrant I am grateful for the opportunity I've been given. I thank God for bringing me from Keta, Ghana, to a research university in the United States. It has been a heartwarming and gratifying experience regardless of loneliness and isolation. Lexington is a typical traditional city: people are born and bred here, and this is their hometown. People have already established their links so if you are an immigrant integrating into that well-established place you are always at the periphery but never a member. I have met so many wonderful people. I am Catholic, I sing in the choir, but I still feel a stranger even in church. Compared to where I am coming from, it takes a lot of guts to live in a place where you don't really belong." In 2017 and 2018 conversations with Marie-Antoinette, she talked about her current research project interviewing and surveying refugee children aged twelve to seventeen, and given the challenges refugees face, she suggested that two years of aid for refugees in Norway, where she lived earlier in her life, was preferable to the only three months usually offered in the US. Marie-Antoinette looked forward to retirement in a year or two and working with friends to start a new university in Ghana, then going back and forth between Ghana and the United States. And she told about her daughter's wedding at Talon Winery near Lexington to a white American, with an event planned the day before so the Ghanaian and American families could get acquainted.

One African Immigrant Family in 2018

Almost four years after he was the first African immigrant to be interviewed for the African Immigrants in the Bluegrass Oral History Project, Robert Chirwa told a story. He had been thinking about his maternal grandfather, with whom he lived for several years when he was young, and was considering writing a blog post about him. Robert remembered his grandfather as a very strict Christian. The family prayed before every meal and there were daily Bible devotions. His grandfather was also very modern and Westernized. In his house Western medicine was always used. But Robert remembered that once, when he was a small boy, he had been very sick with diarrhea. If you had diarrhea you took Pepto-Bismal. But Robert's diarrhea persisted over several days, and one night he spent more than half the night in the outhouse. The next day his grandfather went into the neighboring forest and came back with some leaves and made a broth for Robert to drink. The diarrhea stopped immediately. Perhaps this story is relevant in thinking about where African immigrants are from. One can embrace, even adopt new ways of doing things, but one also remembers and connects to where one comes from.

Robert and Tambu have become American citizens, as has their younger son, who was born when they were in Malawi between Robert's studies as a master's and then doctoral student in Kentucky. Their older son was born in the US. Both sons have graduated from college—Vanderbilt and Bellarmine—and now have graduate degrees from the University of Kentucky and Louisiana State University. Robert has been promoted to full professor at Bluegrass Community and Technical College. Tambu completed her BA in social work at Morehead State University in December 2018 and is working in Child Protective Services in Louisville. Because of her own experience, she is aware of refugee backgrounds and more conscious, for example, of tension between different ethnic groups in Congo than nonimmigrant Americans. She also understands that family and youth service centers in the schools can be helpful to newly arrived families whose kids need winter jackets because she has been in that situation. Both Tambu and Robert continue to connect with and contribute to Malawi and keep close ties with family. Tambu has taken two nephews born in the United States to visit Malawi and collaborates with her sister Catherine in Blantyre to fund scholarships for girls. Robert welcomes his brother Evans, who has a PhD in civil engineering from the University of Kentucky and is a professor in South Africa, when he comes to the US at least once a year for conferences and to visit Lexington. Catherine and Evans and six other family members came to the US for the Chirwas' younger son's wedding on September 1, 2018.

Professor Robert Chirwa, Tambu Chirwa, and sons Ulalo and Kabelo, 2006. (Photo courtesy of Robert Chirwa.)

Tambu pointed out that the question asked of her has changed over more than twenty years in Lexington. "Where are you from?" has become "Where are you originally from?" She wondered if that is because of the increasing diversity of Lexington or "maybe it is me who has changed." Robert and Tambu are definitely part of the Lexington community. However, Robert still says, "I am from Malawi." His geographic definition of home is his village. One of his brothers once urged him to come back to Malawi where he could become an important man, the CEO of some organization. He could have done that but he made other choices, based in part on educational opportunities for his sons. Perhaps Robert is like his maternal grandfather in embracing change, what some would call modernity, the future. He is, after all, a computer science professor teaching the next generation of Americans. Still, the past and one's roots continue to have a place in the United States, where one has grown.

6

Transnationality in the Present and Future

> The world is like a Mask dancing. You do not see it well if you stand in one place.
>
> —Igbo proverb in Chinua Achebe's *Arrow of God*

In the late teens of the twenty-first century, it seems to many Americans as though things are falling apart and whatever center there was is not holding—not only in terms of immigration but regarding the openness of America to the world in general. We are living in a time when the president of the United States has made vulgar, racist remarks about African nations as sources of immigrants.[1] When the United States has withdrawn from the United Nations Migrant and Refugee Compact and from the United Nations Human Rights Council.[2] When a White House plan for only thirty thousand refugees was announced for 2019, the lowest number since the program began in 1980; fewer than twenty thousand of forty-five thousand allowed for 2018 had arrived by July 31, 2018.[3] When one travel ban has followed another and yet another, succeeded by challenges in the courts up to the Supreme Court, which in June 2018 allowed the president's third iteration of the travel ban to stand.[4] When visas for people in different mixes of majority-Muslim countries have been on hold—from Chad to Yemen.[5] When arguments are being made for focusing on merit-based immigration and eliminating both the Diversity Visa Lottery and family reunification as pathways to US citizenship.[6] When TPS (temporary protected status) and DED (deferred enforced departure) have ended for a number of countries whose citizens were granted that status because of war and violence—the latter was scheduled to end in March 2019 for Liberians who came to the United States more than twenty years ago because of civil war but after protests was extended for another year the day before expiration.[7] When ICE (Immigration and Customs Enforcement) agents are picking up and deporting increasing numbers of the undocumented immigrants; the increase was 42 percent in the first eight months of 2017.[8] When children were separated from their parents at the border with Mexico in summer 2018 as a result of a new zero-tolerance policy and, after an outcry, putting families back together again proved extremely difficult.[9] When numbers of international students coming to the United States are declining partly because of the US political climate, with a 7 percent dip of new international students in fall 2017.[10] When the Commerce Department has announced that it plans to reinstate a citizenship question on the 2020 census form for the first time in seventy years; the question was to come before the Supreme Court in June 2019.[11] When the Trump administration has organized a Citizenship and Immigration Service task force to denaturalize some American citizens, and a former administration official has proposed getting rid of birthright citizenship by executive order.[12] When the Trump administration is considering penalizing legal immigrants for using government benefits such as Medicaid and food stamps if they want to obtain green cards.[13] When less than a week before the 2018 midterm November elections, the president himself proposed ending birthright citizenship and ordered more than five thousand troops to the border with Mexico and pledged to deploy more in response to a caravan of several thousand unarmed men, women, and children fleeing violence in Central America who were still a thousand miles from the US.[14] When the Trump administration launched a "Remain in Mexico" program, under which migrants seeking entry to the US must stay in Mexico while their immigration hearings go on north of the border.[15] When President Trump threatened in early April 2019 to close the southern border and to send migrants to sanctuary cities as he seemed to be preparing to make immigration a centerpiece of his 2020 campaign. And finally when, even with a House of Representatives that gained a Democratic majority in the 2018 election, it continues to be unclear whether DACA young people will be able to continue to dream and whether there will ever be bipartisan, thoughtful, and comprehensive immigration reform.

Still, a Gallup poll conducted June 1–13, 2018, when the House of Representatives was debating immigration reform, showed a record-high 75 percent of Americans, including majorities of all party groups, saying immigration is a good thing for the US, up slightly from 71 percent in 2017. When the question's wording was changed to "legal" immigration, 84 percent agreed.[16] Indeed, the unauthorized immigrant population in the US has fallen since 2007, and the number of illegal migrants apprehended by US Border Patrol on the southern border has dropped each year since 2014, from 555,185 to 341,054 in 2017.[17]

In 2017 there were several local victories related to the intertwined issues of race and immigration in Kentucky and elsewhere. In mid-October 2017 in Lexington the Confederate statues that South African immigrant Shaista Vally spoke against in summer 2017 were moved from in front of the old courthouse, destined for the Lexington Cemetery, where they arrived in July 2018. In November 2017 Liberian immigrant Wilmot Collins was elected mayor of Helena, state capital of Montana. Collins, who came as refugee in the mid-1990s escaping Liberia's civil war, is from far eastern Maryland County in Liberia, the county where Jemima Roberts, whose life story was explored in previous chapters, was born.[18] In addition, some media stories at the beginning of 2018 about the continent of Africa itself were positive. The January 15, 2018, *Time* magazine explained "why the world should celebrate Mohamad Nasir's 5th birthday" as part of a focus on "The Optimists" as a theme with guest editor Bill Gates. Mohamad is an example of Ethiopia's success in reducing its child mortality rates for children under five by two-thirds between 1990 and 2012.[19] Also in January 2018 columnist Nicholas Kristof listed ways the US could learn from African countries, for example, the ease of transferring money by cell phone in Kenya and the drive to eliminate cervical cancer in Rwanda by vaccinating almost all girls for HPV.[20]

However, we wonder how transnationality can work in a nation where in August 2017 in Charlottesville, Virginia, white nationalists marched holding torches while shouting Nazi slogans, or in a world in which graphic posters in Berlin before the German election in October 2017 said, "We prefer bikinis to burqas," and the American president retweeted anti-Muslim videos from the extreme right Britain First group, much to the consternation of our ally Great Britain. How can transnationality work when the African American head of an American Language School in Morocco explained that while she and her Moroccan husband and children lived in the United States at one time, they are now planning to remain in Morocco? In the year after eight years of a black American president with a Muslim father, she did not think the Trump presidency was a good time to bring up her black son with a Muslim father in the United States. Interestingly, in contrast to the United States, Morocco "has bolstered its clout and soft power on the African continent with the adoption of an immigration and asylum policy based on a human rights approach seeking to guarantee to migrants in Morocco access to basic services."[21]

Perhaps ironically, at the same time the president and some Americans are increasingly hostile toward immigrants, there is growing interest by African students now studying in the United States and Europe in returning home because of opportunities in Africa, a brain gain for African countries. It seems likely that African immigrants and students who once might have become immigrants in the United States will see more possibilities to return to Africa for a number of reasons. In fact, a 2017 survey revealed that 70 percent of African MBA students at the ten top US and European schools are planning to go home after graduation to work, and nine of ten African PhD students studying abroad plan to work on the continent. One factor: multinational companies are beginning to replace expatriates with diaspora talent since these "repats" speak the language, blend in, have a sense of responsibility, and see that prosperity in Africa is possible.[22] As well, African nations are working toward no borders by 2063. Already no visas are needed by citizens of the fifteen West African nations that are part of the Economic Community of West African States (ECOWAS) or in the East African Community (EAC) to travel within those countries. On April 2, 2019, The Gambia became the twenty-second country to ratify African Continental Free Trade Area (AFCTA), meeting the minimum threshold for African Union countries to move forward on their vision of the world's largest free movement and single-currency union.[23]

Certainly President Nana Akufo-Addo of Ghana is looking for that brain gain from Africans. In early December 2017 his speech about a Ghana that does not need aid to develop went viral with young Africans on social media. President Akufo-Addo said: "We have to get away from this mindset of dependence. . . . We need to have a mindset that says we can do it . . . and once we have that mindset we'll see there's a liberating factor for ourselves." Using the examples of Ireland and Italy, he pointed out that migration is centuries old and happens because there is not opportunity where people are. Citing the resilience and ingenuity of African young people who were crossing the Sahara and the Mediterranean to get to Europe, he said, "We want those energies working inside our countries. We want young Africans to stay in Africa. Their opportunities are right here, with us."[24]

How does African immigration to America fit into Akufo-Addo's picture of an African future? Will Africans still want to come to the United States for graduate education? Will even a few stay? Or will more try to go back and forth? Is it possible to live six months on one continent and six on the other or some combination that suits the work one is doing? Is loyalty to only one government crucial? Will the number of countries allowing dual citizenship increase? Or will the United States become much more restrictive, not only in who can obtain a visa of any kind but in who can or cannot become a citizen? How do family ties with children, with parents, with the extended family fit into changes in opportunities in both Africa and America and in relation to immigration laws in both African nations and the United States?[25] Finally and much more broadly, what will be the outcome of the trend in the United States and in some other nations in the world to talk about being a nationalist, to privilege identity over democracy, seemingly because of fear of difference and of migration?[26] Kenya-born folk singer J. S. Ondara, who came to the US on a diversity visa in 2013 for the American dream and because he loved Bob Dylan's music, asks that very question in his song "God Bless America": "Will you let me in, or are you at capacity?"[27]

The authors, like all those interviewed as well as those described briefly, relate to the idea of transnationality individually and differently, on a continuum. Francis Musoni would strongly consider going back to Zimbabwe to live and teach at some future time, although he understands that his children may want to visit Zimbabwe but live in America. After publication of his first book on the Zimbabwe–South Africa border, one idea for a future book Musoni has is the story of spirits that memorialize those who have traveled to South Africa to work and died on the highway. He would need to do that research in Zimbabwe. Francis explains that it is easy for him to say, "I am going home after work" in reference to his apartment in Lexington, but he does not say, "I am going home to America" when he is returning from trips outside the United States. When, at the end of a trip to Niger for a conference in 2017, someone asked if he was going back home, he responded, "I wish I could say yes but I am going back to the US." Since he first came to the United States in 2005 he has been back to Zimbabwe eight times, including a year to conduct archival and field research for his doctoral dissertation. He is very comfortable transnationally.

Iddah Otieno is also comfortable transnationally and sees herself eventually retiring in either Kenya or the United States. Meanwhile, she will continue to teach American students about Africa and take educators, administrators, and community leaders to Kenya through the Kenya Exchange Program. She does hope her children will marry spouses who will come to her home with their families for holidays and that she will not die in a home for old people. She sticks with her image of the borderland as the way of life for the first-generation African immigrant. "It is where we work, learn, live, marry, laugh, grieve, play, and raise our children and grandchildren. We traverse these spaces with pride and resolve, creating a beautiful tapestry that makes America what it is—home away from home."

Angene and Jack Wilson will continue to act in the transnational social space, serving on the boards of several nongovernmental organizations headed by a Liberian and a Liberian American they know and interacting with close friends from various African countries while making new African immigrant friends.[28] For them, two African immigrants whom they know well—Bibi Roberts Jr. and Irène Assiba d'Almeida—illustrate opposite ends of a continuum of transnationality.

Angene and Jack and their two young daughters first met Bibi Jr. (they have a picture of him on his tricycle) when they visited Jemima and Bibi Roberts Sr. and their family at their Cuttington College campus home in Liberia in 1972. Bibi Jr. began his studies at Berea College in Kentucky in 1988, a year before the Liberian civil war began. At Berea his best friends included African Americans, and his first wife was an African American whom he married after she graduated. Following his own graduation, Bibi lived with Angene and Jack for a year while he worked at the University of Kentucky hospital and got a master's degree in social work. He then worked for many years as a social worker in Lexington Fayette County's Day Treatment program for troubled youth. In 2010 he moved to Atlanta and was remarried, to a Ghanaian immigrant, adding her three children to his own two daughters. In Georgia he has worked with youth, families, veterans, and individuals with mental health and substance abuse disorders and started his own consulting company called Accelerated Dreams Coaching. He is currently an intake social worker at a hospital, and is very active in All Nations Church, working on a Global Youth Initiative that teaches leadership skills and character building. Very rarely do people ask Bibi where he is from. He recalls a Liberian saying to him, "I don't believe you are Liberian." He convinced her by saying something very Liberian: "Thank you for your children." Bibi has not been back to Liberia since he arrived thirty years ago, and except for a younger sister and her family, he no longer has close connections there. At his fiftieth birthday party in Lexington in March 2019, Bibi ate cassava leaf over rice with hot pepper sauce as well as cake. He also held his two-month-old grandson for the first time. His close Liberian connection in the US is his mother Jemima, and with a cousin he was beginning to plan a big party for her seventy-fith birthday in August 2019.

Angene and Jack welcomed Irène Assiba d'Almeida, who is a recently retired University of Arizona French studies professor, when she first came to the United States in 1980 as a Fulbright foreign curriculum consultant. She shared an office with Angene at the University of Kentucky for a year before going on to earn a doctorate at Emory

University. Irène, who had been teaching in Nigeria and had translated Chinua Achebe's *Arrow of God* into French, was born in Benin and educated in Senegal and Benin. She has been back and forth between Benin and the US regularly over the years. For four months in 2017 she enjoyed living in the house she built for herself in Benin, and she thinks she could make a contribution in that country. "Should I live in Benin permanently?" she wonders. But her daughter, who came with her as a three-year-old to the US, and her young grandson are in New York City. She likes her home in Tucson. She has access to such good health care in the US. "Where is home?" she asks. As Angene and Jack read Irène's poetry, which she has written in French and translated into English, they see someone who connects her two continents and lives transnationally. For instance, her poem "Africa" is one of longing for the beautiful, strong, great, rich, welcoming, honest, pure, alive Africa, which in the last stanza butts up against a depressing image of weakness and misery. And her poem "Atlantic of a Thousand Crossings" makes that ocean a hyphen and a rainbow between the Americas and Africa.[29] In October 2018 she called Angene and Jack and told them that after she voted in the November election, she was flying to Benin to stay for eight months.

The four authors of this book believe that transnationality is a helpful concept to consider in understanding the African immigrant diasporic experience. We offer it as an alternative approach in analyzing the immigrant experience in the United States that goes beyond the ideas of assimilation or integration of immigrants into a salad or stew. Transnationality for African immigrants gets support from African proverbs such as the epigraph of this chapter: "The world is like a Mask dancing. You do not see it well if you stand in one place." Two other African proverbs also offer a world-connected view: "It is only the child who has never traveled away from home who says that only his mother can prepare tasty meals" and "If you look in only one direction, your neck will be stiff."[30] Finally, listen to Chinua Achebe, who concludes his "Africa Is People" essay, mentioned in the preface, with "Africa believes in people, in cooperation with people. . . . Our humanity is contingent on the humanity of our fellows. No person or group can be human alone."[31]

Also relevant to a discussion of transnationality in this time of reinvigorated nationalism is British-born Ghanaian American philosopher Kwame Anthony Appiah's description and defense of cosmopolitanism in his 2019 "The Importance of Elsewhere" essay. He writes: "Cosmopolitanism . . . sees human beings as shaping their lives within nesting memberships: a family, a neighborhood, a plurality of overlapping identity groups, spiraling out to encompass all humanity." He continues,

"Cosmopolitans worthy of the label have rhizomes, spreading horizontally, as well as taproots, delving deep; they are anything but rootless."[32]

We agree that "when people use identity in ways that everyone else is 'the other,' it is helpful to offer up a reminder of the power and richness that can be drawn from the long, slow simmer of a multicultural bouillabaisse."[33] However, including the transnational connections and possibilities, reaching out to the world beyond the United States, can make the stew even richer and more powerful. African immigrants can become part of the "us" that is the United States, even be drawn in as part of bell hooks's Kentucky "culture of belonging."

Acknowledgments

Francis Musoni

I came into this project initially as an interviewee for the African Immigrants in the Bluegrass Oral History Project that Jack and Angene Wilson coordinated for the Louie B. Nunn Center for Oral History at the University of Kentucky. I therefore owe my deepest gratitude to Jack and Angene, not only for inviting me to be a coauthor but also for conducting the bulk of the oral interviews that form the backbone of this book. Many thanks are also due to Iddah Otieno, whose camaraderie made it enjoyable to work on this book. As coauthors, the four of us brainstormed and argued over many aspects of this book, but we did not forget the value and benefits of compromise and collegiality. By the end of the three years it took us to complete the writing process, we had become a family, not just friends. At the lunch meetings we regularly held at Sav's Grill (thanks to the hospitality of its owner, Mamadou Savané) our discussions often strayed way beyond the concerns of this book to various matters of personal interest to each one of us. It was really a pleasure being part of this team.

During the entire time that we worked on this project, I was also writing my single-authored book on the history of illegal migration across the Zimbabwe–South Africa border (now in production at Indiana University Press) while fulfilling my duties at the University of Kentucky, where I am an assistant professor of African history. I was able to perform all these simultaneous tasks only thanks to the support and encouragement of my colleagues in the history department, the African American and Africana Studies Program, and the International Studies Program at the same institution. I want to thank all from the bottom of my heart. Special thanks go to Karen Petrone (chair of the history department), Mark Kornbluh (dean of the College of Arts and Sciences), and Elizabeth Leibach (director of International Student and Scholar Services) for standing with me and my family when the process of changing our immigration statuses became more complicated than I had anticipated.

My contributions to this book also greatly benefited from a directed reading seminar I designed for Dana Lea (former community outreach coordinator at Kentucky Refugee Ministries) when she was a master's student at the University of Kentucky's Patterson School of Diplomacy and International Commerce. In addition to several discussions I had with Dana, my interaction with other staff members of the Lexington office of the Kentucky Refugee Ministries, where I served as a member of the advisory board from March 2013 to December 2017, helped me to develop a broad perspective of the African refugees' experiences in Kentucky. The feedback I received from a presentation entitled "Being an African in Kentucky," which I gave at the Lexington Center for International Engagement (Global Lex) on May 25, 2018, also helped in shaping my understandings of the stories of African immigrants that are contained in this book.

Last, but very importantly, I would like to salute my wife Everjoy and our children Nyasha, Anopa, and Taonashe for their love and support, which made it a joy to come home at the end of each and every day I spent working on *Voices of African Immigrants in Kentucky.*

Iddah Otieno

First and foremost, I would like to recognize Dr. Angene Wilson and her husband Jack Wilson for their dedication to African studies through their work, travels, and residence in to numerous African countries over the years. The idea for this book started with their oral history project at the University of Kentucky focusing on African immigrants in the Bluegrass. Thank you both for your passion. Your friendship and mentorship made all the difference.

I would also like to extend my deepest gratitude to the children of African immigrants who participated in the interviews that informed the chapter on the next generation of African immigrants in Kentucky. The children whose stories are included here gave freely of their time and insight on being raised by African parents in the United States. This book took many years of brainstorming and consultation with different African immigrant groups, agencies, and individuals. Thank you for sharing your stories and welcoming us into your communities.

We are especially indebted to Mamadou Savané, whose West African restaurant located near the University of Kentucky became the meeting place for the four authors. Over the years, we shared food and laughter, and developed a friendship that will last a lifetime. This book has benefited greatly from insightful and candid deliberations and perspectives from the four authors whose expertise in the field of African studies made the writing and review processes a joy.

Last but not least, we are profoundly grateful to our reviewers and the staff of the University Press of Kentucky for their feedback and guidance. And to our families, thank you for your support and encouragement in the journey.

Angene and Jack Wilson

We begin by thanking Doug Boyd and Kopana Terry of the Louie B. Nunn Center for Oral History at the University of Kentucky for facilitating and encouraging our second oral history project, African Immigrants in the Bluegrass. Without interviews with the following individuals, there would be no book: Khadar Abdullahi, Kwaku Addo, Shamik Aikat, Ismail Nur Ali, Ibrahim Bakoush, Moulaye Idrissa Barry, Kennedy Boateng, Rahel Bosson, Desmond Brown, Armstrong Cheggeh, Robert Chirwa, Tambu Chirwa, Kikoko Godfrey, Jacob Guot, Zineeddine Hamoudi, Boyd Mpho Hayes, Princia Itaula-Kifoumba, Nkongolo Kalala, Jose Kazadi, Nkulu Kiluba, Hamidou Koivogui, Aka Kpla, Karin Krein, Gashaw Lake, Fiston Boyita Bo Malinga, Mwana Mbaka, Kaite Beatrice Mbayo, Francis Musoni, Pierre Ngog, Tite Niyonizigiye, Venus Niza, Efosa Austin Osayamwen, Iddah Otieno, Asimiyu Akinade Oyetunji, Jemima Roberts, Samah Sadouki, Mamadou Savané, Essa Bokar Sey, Hussein Sombe, Marie-Antoinette Sossou, Sylvia Uwamaliya Stainback, Abraham Sven-Peters, Bankole Thompson, Abigail Unuakhalu, Bandushubwenge Vanisa, Sam Vorkpor, and Mulbah Zowah.

As well, there would be no book without our more than fifty-year friendship with Jemima and Bibi (now deceased) Roberts, beginning with our two years as Peace Corps volunteer teachers in Liberia from 1962 to 1964where our connection with Africa began, continuing with the thirty-year experience of being "aunt" and "uncle" in the African sense to their whole family, including Bibi Roberts Jr. We particularly appreciate our twenty-first-century friendship with Robert and Tambu Chirwa, including our trip with them to Malawi in 2007 and their willingness to be the first interviewees in 2014. We thank Robert for graciously allowing excerpts from his blog about his father to begin chapter 1. Thank you to Dorothy Davis Martin, our student in Liberia more than fifty years ago, since then our friend, the first African immigrant we knew, and the first reader of the manuscript; to Irène Assiba d'Almeida, who did not read this manuscript but several years ago read, critiqued, and introduced Angene's *Africa on My Mind: Fifty Years of Educating Americans,* and whose friendship and life inspire us; to Nkechi Amadife, whose dissertation about nonreturning Nigerian students planted a seed in Angene's mind about African immigrant issues; to African immigrants and Americans we did not interview as part of the oral history project but who also appear in the book or were helpful in suggesting interviewees—Craig Borie, Gabriel Brown, Mohamed Diop, Keith Gilbertson, Vanessa Grossl, Alice Kamadjou, Elizabeth Kizito, Dana Lea, Gary Leibert, Kiza Mukandama, Adikat Oyetunji, Camellia Rizk, Angela Selby, Kiptoo Tarus, and Shaista Vally. A special thanks to Mamadou Savané, whose Sav's Grill and West African Cuisine was a welcoming home for our regular author lunch meetings.

Especially, and unreservedly, we are grateful for the opportunity to have worked with our coauthors Francis Musoni and Iddah Otieno, who added this project to their very busy academic and family lives. The experience has been a joy. Yes, we became like family.

We also recognize and thank our daughters, son-in-law, and granddaughters as well as our extended family and many friends who have listened to us talk about the African Immigrants in the Bluegrass Oral History Project and the projected book since 2013.

At University Press of Kentucky, we thank Director Leila Salisbury for believing this book was important, Patrick O'Dowd for his unfailing encouragement in shepherding us through the process, Robin DuBlanc for her expert copyediting, and all the people at the press who worked on various aspects of the book's publication.

Appendix

Suggested Oral History Interview Segments for Listening

The following interview segments give readers an opportunity to hear the actual expressive voices of interviewees, to hear their eloquence in talking about specific issues and experiences in detail. Complete interviews with many African immigrants included in this book are available online at the Louie B. Nunn Center for Oral History, University of Kentucky Libraries, under the project title African Immigrants in the Bluegrass. They are indexed in the form of an outline and also searchable by word/topic so an interested individual can listen to a segment or the whole interview. These interviews utilize the innovative OHMS system, which connects a textual search to the corresponding moment in the online audio interview. They can be accessed at https://kentuckyoralhistory.org/catalog/xt7tb27prz26 or at https;//www.kentuckyoralhistory.org.

To access interviews:

- From the following list select the interview you would like to access.
- If the interview is available for searching and listening to online, you are given the choice to select the "Access Interview" or "Play" option. If you are not given this option, the interview is not yet available online.
- The viewer will present, providing a player and a searchable index/transcript if available.
- Press "Play" on the player, perform a search, or simply click on the segment you would like to access.

Here, listed by chapter, are some suggested interview segments that are starred in the text.

Chapter 1, "Origins: Where We Are From"

"Stories of Childhood: Independence"—Armstrong Cheggeh, Kenya
https://kentuckyoralhistory.org/catalog/xt7prr1pk513

"Experience Russia and Creating a Magazine"—Jose Kazadi, Democratic Republic of Congo
https://kentuckyoralhistory.org/catalog/xt7gqn5z8v7z

Chapter 2, "Opportunity: Why and How We Came"

"University"—Gashaw Lake, Ethiopia
https://kentuckyoralhistory.org/catalog/xt79cn6z0605

"Ambassador in US and Afterward"—Essa Bakarr Sey, The Gambia
https://kentuckyoralhistory.org/catalog/xt7gb56d5120

Chapter 3, "Struggles and Successes"

"Coming to the US for College"—Rahel Bosson, Ethiopia
https://kentuckyoralhistory.org/catalog/xt776h4crc1j

"Adaptation to American Culture"—Sylvia Uwamiliya Stainback, Rwanda
https://kentuckyoralhistory.org/catalog/xt7bzk55hm49

"Questions People Ask"—Mulbah Zowah, Liberia
https://kentuckyoralhistory.org/catalog/xt7gqn5z8v6c

"Living in Lexington/First Jobs/Learning English"—Mamadou Savané, Guinea
https://kentuckyoralhistory.org/catalog/xt7gqn5z8v6c

Chapter 4, "Connecting and Contributing to Two Continents"

"Concern about Her Country"—Beatrice Mbayo, Democratic Republic of Congo
https://kentuckyoralhistory.org/catalog/xt70p26q2222

"Family and Study/Service Tour Connections to Ghana"—Kwaku Addo, Ghana
https://kentuckyoralhistory.org/catalog/xt7hqb9v4186

"Special Court"—Bankole Thompson, Sierra Leone
https://kentuckyoralhistory.org/catalog/xt73ff3m0387

Chapter 5, "Family and Identity in the United States"

"Family and Education"—Abraham Sven-Peters, Liberia
https://kentuckyoralhistory.org/catalog/xt776h4crc72

"Why Immigrants Come/Identity"—Ibrahim Bakoush, Libya
https://kentuckyoralhistory.org/catalog/xt7fqz22fr08

Notes

Preface

1. Hans Rosling, Ola Rosling, and Anna Rosling Ronnlund, *Factfulness: Ten Reasons We're Wrong about the World—and Why Things Are Better Than You Think* (New York: Flatiron Books, 2018), 24–33.

2. Angene H. Wilson, "Teaching about Africa: A Review of Middle/Secondary Textbooks and Supplemental Materials," *Social Studies* 86, no. 6 (November–December 1995): 253. Angene heard Ali Mazuri speak at the Nairobi conference in 1994.

3. This idea comes from Bahiyyih Nakhjavani in her novel *Us & Them* (Stanford, CA: Redwood, 2017), 68. The transnational Iranian author uses "we" throughout the novel, seeming to include all Iranians worldwide.

4. Ngugu wa Thiong'o, *Moving the Centre: The Struggle for Cultural Freedoms* (London: James Currey; Nairobi: EAEP; Portsmouth, NH: Heinemann, 1993).

5. The final essay in Chinua Achebe, *The Education of a British-Protected Child* (New York: Knopf, 2009).

6. An excellent example of such a book is Pat Nyhan, *New Mainers: Portraits of Our Immigrant Neighbors* (Gardiner, ME: Tilbury House, 2009). Six of the twenty-five are from African countries, including two from Somalia, two from Nigeria, and one each from Ghana and Sudan.

7. These numbers come from the Migration Policy Institute's analysis of State Immigration Data Profiles (accessed April 14, 2019).

8. For a discussion of earlier relevant African literature, see chapter 3, "Imagined America in African Texts and the Desire to Migrate," in *Across the Atlantic: African Immigrants in the United States Diaspora,* ed. Emmanuel Yewah and 'Dimeji Togunde (Champaign, IL: Common Ground, 2010).

9. Tom Gjelten, *A Nation of Nations: A Great American Immigration Story* (New York: Simon and Schuster, 2015), 943.

Introduction

1. Abdoulaye Kane and Todd H. Leedy, "African Patterns of Migration in a Global Era: New Perspectives," in *African Migrations: Patterns and Perspectives,* ed. Kane and Leedy (Bloomington: Indiana University Press, 2013).

2. Han van Dijk, Dick Foeken, and Kiky van Til, "Population Mobility in Africa: An Overview," in *Mobile Africa: Changing Patterns of Movement in Africa and Beyond,* ed. Mirjam De Bruijn,Rijk A. van Dijk, and Dick Foeken (Leiden: Brill, 2001).

3. For more detailed discussion on this, see Paul Nugent, "Arbitrary Lines and the People's Minds: A Dissenting View on Colonial Boundaries in West Africa," in *African Boundaries: Barriers, Conduits and Opportunities,* ed. Paul Nugent and Anthony Asiwaju (New York: Pinter, 1996); William F. S. Miles, "Postcolonial Borderland Legacies of Anglo-French Partition in West Africa," *African Studies Review* 58, no. 3 (2015): 191–213; Francis Musoni, *Border Jumping and Control in Migration Southern Africa* (Bloomington: Indiana University Press, forthcoming).

4. Jonathan Crush, "Migrations Past: An Historical Overview of Cross-Border Movements in Southern Africa," in *On Borders: Perspectives on International Migration in Southern Africa,* ed. David A. McDonald (New York: Palgrave Macmillan, 2000); David Lucas and Barbara Edgar, "Zimbabwe's Exodus to Australia," *SAMP Policy Brief* 30 (2015), http://imrc.ca/wp-content/uploads/2015/05/PB-30-Zimbabwes-Exodus-to-Australia.pdf (accessed December 12, 2016).

5. Statistics drawn from Migration Policy Institute, "Regions of Birth for Immigrants in the United States, 1960–Present," http://www.migrationpolicy.org/programs/data-hub/us-immigration-trends (accessed April 14, 2019)).

6. Patrick Manning, *The African Diaspora: A History through Culture* (New York: Columbia University Press, 2009).

7. Several writers and filmmakers have examined the story of the so-called Lost Boys of Sudan. See, for example, Jacob Thon Guot, *The Lost Is Found: A "Lost Boy's" Story of Faith, Hope, Charity, and Love* (Oviedo, FL: EA Books, 2017); ~I+Lost Boys of Sudan,+I~ a documentary film about two Lost Boys, Santino Majok Chuor and Peter Nyarol Dut, who came to the United States. Aired on *POV* (2003).

8. See http://www.wrapsnet.org/admissions-and-arrivals/ (accessed August 26, 2018). See also Yearbook of Immigration Statistics, https://www.dhs.gov/immigration-statistics/yearbook (accessed August 26, 2018). For more information on wars and forced displacement in postcolonial Africa, see Elizabeth Schmidt, *Foreign Intervention in Africa from the Cold War to the War on Terror* (New York: Cambridge University Press, 2013); Adekeye Adebajo and Ismail Rashid, eds., *West Africa's Security Challenges: Building Peace in a Troubled Region* (Boulder: Lynne Rienner, 2004); Liisa H. Malkki, *Purity and Exile: Violence, Memory, and National Cosmology among Hutu Refugees in Tanzania* (Chicago: University of Chicago, 1995); Mahmood Mamdani, *When Victims Become Killers: Colonialism, Nativism and the Genocide in Rwanda* (Princeton: Princeton University Press, 2002).

9. Yearbook of Immigration Statistics, https://www.dhs.gov/immigration-statistics/yearbook (accessed August 26, 2018).

10. These statistics are derived from the Migration Policy Institute's analysis of State Immigration Data Profiles. For more information, see https://www.migrationpolicy.org/data/state-profiles/state/demographics/US (accessed August 10, 2018).

11. For more on these statistics, see the United States Department of Health and Human Services' Office of Refugee Resettlement, https://www.acf.hhs.gov/org; the Kentucky Office for Refugees, https://www.kentuckyrefugees.org/; and the Kentucky Refugee Ministries, https://kyrm.org/ (accessed August 27, 2018).

12. www.kentuckyrefugees.org (accessed August 16, 2018) is source for refugee

information and statistics.

13. Fraternel D. Amuri Misako, *The Brain Waste of Foreign-Educated Professionals in the United States: Employment Profiles and Policy Issues versus Community Capitals* (European University Publishing, 2018).

14. For further discussion on this see, Thomas Faist, "Extension *du domaine de la lutte:* International Migration and Security Before and After 11 September 2001," *International Migration Review* 36, no. 1 (2002): 7–14; Robert Pallitto and Josiah Heyman, "Theorizing Cross-Border Mobility: Surveillance, Security and Identity," *Surveillance and Society* 5, no. 3 (2008): 315–33.

15. James Gordon Meek and Brian Ross, "Terrorists Once Used Refugee Program to Settle in US," *ABC News,* November 18, 2015, http://abcnews.go.com/International/terrorists-refugee-program-settle-us/story?id=35252500 (accessed September 14, 2016).

16. Polly Mosendz, "In Light of Paris Attacks, 26 GOP Governors, One Democrat to Refuse Syrian Refugees," *Newsweek,* November 16, 2015, https://www.newsweek.com/after-paris-attacks-26-republican-governors-one-democrat-refuse-syrian-394859 (accessed August 2, 2016).

17. See https://www.congress.gov/bill/114th-congress/house-bill/4038; and http://clerk.house.gov/evs/2015/r011643.xml (accessed September 15, 2016).

18. Dan M. Rose and Ron Vissing, "US Should Put Moratorium on Immigration," http://www.kentucky.com/opinion/op-ed/article45549861.html (accessed October 10, 2016).

19. Americans First, "Refugee Resettlement Program Facts Updated," http://americansfirst.org/2016/08/1256/ (accessed October 10, 2016).

20. Ibid.

21. Nina Glick Schiller and Georges Eugene Fouron, *Georges Woke Up Laughing: Long-Distance Nationalism and the Search for Home* (Durham: Duke University Press, 2001), 344. See also Nina Glick Schiller, "Transmigrants and Nation-State: Something Old and Something New in the US Immigrant Experience," in *The Handbook of International Migration: The American Experience,* ed. Charles Hirschman et al. (New York: Russell Sage Foundation, 1999).

22. Stephen Castles, "Towards a Sociology of Forced Migration and Social Transformation," Sociology 37, no. 1 (2003): 20.

23. Thomas Faist, Margit Fauser, and Eveline Reisenauer, *Transnational Migration* (Cambridge: Polity, 2013).

24. See, for example, Dunbar Moodie with Viviave Ndatshe, *Going for Gold: Men, Mines, and Migration* (Berkeley: University of California Press, 1994); Peter Alexander, "Oscillating Migrants, 'Detribalized Families' and Militancy: Mozambicans on Witbank Collieries, 1918–1927," *Journal of Southern African Studies* 27, no. 3 (2001): 505–25.

25. Caroline Brettell, *Anthropology and Migration: Essays on Transnationalism, Ethnicity, and Identity* (New York: Altamira, 2003).

26. See Friends of the Congo, http://www.friendsofthecongo.org (accessed January 3, 2017).

27. For similar works, see Yewah and Togunde, *Across the Atlantic;* Paul Stoller,

Jaguar: A Story of Africans in America (Chicago: University of Chicago Press, 1999); Paul Stoller, *Money Has No Smell: The Africanization of New York City* (Chicago: University of Chicago Press, 2010); John A. Arthur, *African Diaspora Identities: Negotiating Culture in Transnational Migration* (Lanham, MD: Lexington Books, 2010).

28. Cati Coe, *The Scattered Family: Parenting, African Migrants, and Global Inequality* (Chicago: University of Chicago Press, 2014); Sandra Grady, *Impoverished Adolescence: Somali Bantu Teenage Refugees in America* (Madison: University of Wisconsin Press, 2015); JoAnn D'Alisera, *An Imagined Geography: Sierra Leonean Muslims in America* (Philadelphia: University of Pennsylvania Press, 2004).

29. *WEKU Eastern Standard,* June 15, 2018, quoted by Tom Martin in the program *Returnees to Kentucky.*

30. bell hooks, *Belonging: A Culture of Place* (New York: Routledge, 2009), 23.

31. Frank X Walker, *Affrilachia* (Lexington, KY: Old Cove, 2000). 93, 97 (the poems "Affrilachia" and "Kentucke").

32. Bobbie Ann Mason, *Clear Springs* (New York: Random House, 1999), 13.

33. This is found in various lists of his quotations, without specific attribution.

1. Origins

1. The main character in Chimamanda Ngozi Adichie's novel *Americanah,* Ifemelu, "discovers" she is black when she migrates from Nigeria to the US. In a *Washington Post* interview in 2006, Adichie stated that she actually realized she was African when she moved to the US, noting that whenever Africa came up in her college classes, everyone turned to her, whether the country was Namibia or Egypt.

2. The source for Robert's story about his father is http://tropicalsayge.blogspot.com/2016/12/once-teacher-always-teacher.html/.

3. Information about the history of African countries, particularly independence history, can be found in many books. We recommend Kevin Shillington, *History of Africa,* 3rd ed. (New York: Palgrave Macmillan, 2012); Frederick Cooper, *Africa since 1940: The Past of the Present* (Cambridge: Cambridge University Press, 2002); and Toyin Falola, ed., *Africa,* vol. 4, *The End of Colonial Rule, Nationalism and Decolonization* (Durham: Carolina Academic Press, 2002).

4. The description of Sim Oyetunji's memories of Nigeria's independence came in a follow-up conversation recorded on the Wilson's personal recorder and is not available in the Nunn Center collection.

5. * Listen to Armstrong Cheggeh talking in his oral history interview in the segment "Stories of Childhood" about memories of Kenyan independence.

6. Read Hisham Matar, *The Return: Fathers, Sons and the Land in Between* (New York: Random House, 2016) for what has been described as a brilliant portrait of a nation (Libya) and a people on the cusp of change, a disquieting depiction of the brutal legacy of absolute power, and a universal tale of loss and love and of one family's life.

7. David Van Reybrouck, *Congo: The Epic History of a People* (New York:

Harper Collins, 2010), 266.

8. Satoshi Sugiyama, "Doors for Refugees Close as Displaced Population Soars, U. N. Says." *New York Times,* June 19, 2018.

9. For an in-depth story of Dadaab focused on individuals, read Ben Rawlence, *City of Thorns: Nine Lives in the World's Largest Refugee Camp* (New York: Picador, 2016).

10. This sentence comes from Beatrice's interview on episode 10 of *Bluegrass Refugee Voices* on Lexington's Community Radio, WXLU 93.9, November 7, 2016.

11. * Listen to Jose Kazadi talking in his oral history interview in the segment "Russia and Creating a Magazine."

12. "Louisville Catholic Teacher Resigns amid Ebola Crisis," *Louisville Courier-Journal,* November 3, 2014; Rosling, Rosling, and Rosling Ronnlund, *Factfulness,* uses the illustration of Ebola to make the same point in their chapter on "the generalization instinct."

13. Keith Gilbertson, ed., *Slowly Is the Journey: Stories from Bluegrass Community and Technical College ESL Students* (Bloomington, IN: AuthorHouse 2016), 65.

14. Bell I. Wiley, ed., *Slaves No More: Letters from Liberia, 1833–1869* (Lexington: University Press of Kentucky, 1980). More recent books about Liberia include Helene Cooper's *The House at Sugar Beach: In Search of a Lost African Childhood* (New York: Simon and Schuster, 2008) and *Madame President: The Extraordinary Journey of Ellen Johnson Sirleaf* (New York: Simon and Schuster, 2017). Excellent sources on the role of women in ending the civil war are Leymah Gbowee, *Mighty Be Our Powers: How Sisterhood, Prayer, and Sex Changed a Nation at War* (New York: Beast Books, 2011); and the documentary film *Pray the Devil Back to Hell.* One history of Liberia, especially the Americo-Liberians, is James Ciment, *Another America: The Story of Liberia and the Former Slaves Who Ruled It* (New York: Hill and Wang, 2013). Wayetu Moore's *She Who Would Be King: A Novel* (Minneapolis: Graywolf, 1918) reimagines through history and magical realism the beginnings of Liberia. To understand the related civil war in neighboring Sierra Leone, read Ishmael Beah, *A Long Way Gone: Memoirs of a Boy Soldier* (New York: Farrar, Straus and Giroux, 2007); and the novel *The Memory of Love* by Aminatta Forna (New York: Grove, 2010).

15. Some of Jemima Roberts's memories of living on the Cuttington College campus come from a 2010 interview on the Wilsons' personal recorder. That interview was done for the Roberts' children.

16. See George Ella Lyon's Writer & Teacher website, www.georgeellalyon.com and "I Am from Project—A River of Voices" at Iamfromproject.com. The project "is a way to celebrate diversity at a time when our country is divided by hatred and fear. We want to be heard, not herded; we want to speak, not be spoken at or for; we want to break through stereotypes, profiling, and dismissal to be listened to in our full humanity." The website includes suggestion and resources for teaching, organizing, and writing on the theme of "Where I'm From."

2. Opportunity

1. www.britannica.com.

2. Kwame Nkrumah, *Ghana: The Autobiography of Kwame Nkrumah* (Edinburgh: Thomas Nelson and Sons, 1959), 20–39.

3. Obituary, *Patriotic Vanguard,* Sierra Leone News Portal, August 27, 2010.

4. For more details, see Tom Schachtman, *Airlift to America: How Barack Obama Sr., John F. Kennedy, Tom Mboya, and 800 East African Students Changed Their World and Ours* (St. Martin's Press, 2009). Individual students came from other countries as well during the 1960s. Two students whom Angene and Jack Wilson taught in Liberia between 1962 and 1964 had graduated from small colleges in Ohio and Pennsylvania by 1967 and other students they taught also came for higher education and subsequently stayed in the US.

5. N. T. Chideya, *American Scholarship Programmes for African Students, 1959–1975.* (Zambezi, 1981. Accessed through Michigan State Libraries.)

6. The oldest daughter of the Oyetunji family, Jelilat Oyetunji, is pictured and profiled in Nyhan, *New Mainers.* She graduated from the University of Southern Maine in computer science in 2002.

7. The International Book Project (IBP) was begun as an NGO in 1966 by Harriet Van Meter, who had learned of the need for books when she visited India. In 2016 IBP shipped more than four hundred thousand books requested by partners in sixty-one countries. In that year Guatemala, India, Kosovo, Papua New Guinea, and Zimbabwe were top receiving countries.

8. Ron Pelfrey interview, October 4, 2005, Returned Peace Corps Volunteers Oral History Project, Kentucky Digital Library.

9. Nkechi Amadife, "The Non-returning Nigerian Students: Socio-historical Cultural Perspective and Adaptation" (PhD diss., University of Kentucky, 2006), 38, 149.

10. Emails from Mosoka Fallah: "First Quarter Newsletter of Refuge Place International Maternal Child Health NGO," August 7, 2018, and "Appointment as Part-Time Lecturer at Harvard Medical School," July 9, 2018.

11. Jie Zong and Jeanne Batalova, *Sub-Saharan African Immigrants in the United States,* Migration Policy Institute, May 3, 2017. Breaking down by country, Nigerians and South Africans were the most highly educated, with 57 percent holding at least a bachelor's degree, followed by Kenyans (44 percent), Ghanaians (40 percent), Liberians (32 percent), and Ethiopians (29 percent). Somalis had the lowest attainment with 11 percent. Note that North African countries are not included in this report.

12. Interview with Camellia Rizk, October 8, 2016. There is an interview with Rizk archived at the Nunn Center for Oral History, but the interviewer asked him only about his career in Lexington.

13. Email from Edward Kifer, June 24, 2017.

14. * Listen to Gashaw Lake in his oral history interview in the segment "University Education: Coming to America."

15. Iddah Otieno's dissertation was published as a book in 2018.

16. When Angene Wilson was a Senior Fulbright Scholar at the University of Winneba in Ghana in 1997, she was surprised that some of her students, all experienced teachers in the diploma program, and even several professors had applied or planned to apply for diversity visas. One of her former students called her from New York City after he arrived to say that he was working in security and had found it very difficult to meet certification requirements for teaching, as she had warned. But the dream of opportunity was strong.

17. In Imbolo Mbue, *Behold the Dreamers* (New York: Random House, 2016), the author describes a family who cannot stay legally in New York City and must return to Cameroon. In the last chapter, the wife and mother, Neni, lists advantages of returning but laments for her children: "They would lose the opportunity to grow up in a magnificent land of uninhibited dreamers. They would lose the chance to be awed and inspired by amazing things happening in the country, incredible inventions and accomplishments by men and women who look like them. They would be deprived of freedoms, rights, and privileges that Cameroon could not give its children. They would lose unquantifiable benefits by leaving New York City, because while there existed great towns and cities all over the world, there was a certain kind of pleasure, a certain type of adventurous and audacious childhood that only New York City could offer a child" (161–62).

18. For the idea of American marriages falling apart, see the short stories "Imitation" and "The Arrangers of Marriage," in Chimamanda Ngozi Adichie, *The Thing Around Your Neck* (New York: Knopf, 2009).

19. Interview with Alice on *Bluegrass Refugee Voices,* episode 18, Lexington Community Radio, 93.9FM WLXU, March 28, 2017.

20. To consider how the refugee crisis affects individuals in Europe, read the novel (translated from German) *Go, Went, Gone,* by Jenny Erpenbeck (New York: New Directions, 2017), which tells the story of a German professor in Berlin meeting and learning from African migrants.

21. Read Jacob's autobiography for more details about his years in Ethiopia and Kenya. Guot, *The Lost Is Found,* 34–35.

22. Ibid., 38–39.

23. Gilbertson, *Slowly Is the Journey,* 30. Kaite Beatrice Mbayo is the lead author in this book.

24. * Listen to Essa Bokar Sey in his oral history interview in the segment "Ambassador in the US and Afterward."

25. One famous alumnus of Berea College is Tijan Sallah, originally from The Gambia, who graduated in 1982 and went on to get a PhD in economics at Virginia Polytechnic Institute and became a World Bank sector manager. He is also a renowned poet.

26. Merlene Davis, "In Liberia They Lived on the Run," *Lexington Herald Leader,* August 24, 2003.

27. Mohsin Hamid, *Exit West* (New York: Riverhead Books, 2017).

28. *Brief but Spectacular, PBS NewsHour,* May 11, 2017.

3. Struggles and Successes

1. Gilbertson, *Slowly Is the Journey,* 90–91.

2. NoVio et Bulawayo, *We Need New Names* (New York: Little Brown, 2013), 195.

3. Viet Thanh Nguyen, *Nothing Ever Dies: Vietnam and the Memory of War* (Cambridge, MA: Harvard University Press, 2016), 198.

4. Craig Storti, *Figuring Foreigners Out: A Practical Guide* (Yarmouth, ME: Intercultural, 1999). Storti describes four building blocks of culture: concept of self—individualist and collectivist; person versus societal responsibility—universalist and particularist; concept of time—monochronic and polychronic; and locus of control—internal and external. He also describes differences in communication styles: degree of directness, role of context, and importance of face, and deals with nonverbal communication differences, too. Angene Wilson used *Figuring Foreigners Out* for a number of years in the required course she taught for University of Kentucky students planning to student teach overseas and has also used exercises from the book in general cross-cultural training in professional development workshops for groups such as social workers.

5. Desmond Tutu, *The Words of Desmond Tutu,* selected by Naomi Tutu (New York: Newmarket, 1989).

6. Kwame Gyekye, *African Cultural Values* (Accra, Ghana: Sankofa, 1996), 37, 48, in chapter "Communal and Individualistic Values."

7. * Listen to Rahel Bosson in her oral history interview in the segment "Coming to the US for College."

8. * Listen to Sylvia Uwamaliya Stainback in her oral history interview in segment "Adaptation to American Culture."

9. Marie-Antoinette Sossou and Chiston A. Adedoyin, "A Qualitative Study of Problems and Parental Challenges of African Refugee Parents in the USA," *Professional Development: The International Journal of Continuing Social Work Education* 15, no. 2 (2012): 41–54.

10. Allyson Ferry, "Modified Vulnerability: The Efficacy of Refugee Resettlement" (MA thesis, Brandeis University, 2017).

11. Angene Wilson listened to these women on February 5, 2017, at a meeting to discuss possibly starting English classes at the Westminster Village complex.

12. * Listen to Mulbah Zowah talk in his oral history interview about questions Americans ask in the segment "Questions People Ask about Liberia."

13. Michael Eric Dyson, *Tears We Cannot Stop: A Sermon to White America* (New York: St. Martin's, 2017), 209. See also research by Nigerian American anthropologist John Ogbu, who contrasted and studied voluntary (immigrant) and involuntary (caste-like) minorities' school performance, in articles such as John U. Ogbu and Herbert D. Simons, "Voluntary and Involuntary Minorities: A Cultural-Ecological Theory of School Performance with Some Implications for Education" *Anthropology and Education Quarterly* 29 (1998). A critique of Ogbu can be found in Kevin Michael Foster, "Coming to Terms: A Discussion of John Ogbu's

Cultural-Ecological Theory of Minority Academic Achievement," *Intercultural Education* 12, no. 4 (December 2004).

14. Randy J. Sparks, *Where the Negroes Are Master: An African Port in the Era of the Slave Trade* (Cambridge, MA: Harvard University Press, 2014). When Angene taught at University of Winneba in Ghana in 1997, a Ghanaian friend who had taught in Atlanta, Georgia, before returning to Ghana told her that some students in Atlanta had accused her of selling their ancestors. Although that friend lived in Cape Coast, she had never been to Cape Coast Castle, which is a must-see place for African American and many white American visitors to Ghana.

15. Yaa Gyasi, *Homegoing* (New York: Knopf, 2016), 269, 73, 282.

16. James T. Campbell. *Middle Passages: African American Journeys to Africa, 1787–2005* (New York: Penguin Books, 2006); Maya Angelou, *All God's Children Need Traveling Shoes* (New York: Random House, 1986).

17. Ta-Neshi Coates, *Between the World and Me* (New York: Spiegel and Grau, 2015). See also Ta-Neshi Coates, *We Were Eight Years in Power: An American Tragedy* (New York: One World, 2017) for consideration of how President Barack Obama fits into a consideration of who is African American.

18. Lynsey Chutel, "Whose Wakanda Is It anyway? A Black Panther Lawsuit Is Testing the Cultural Exchange between Africans and African-Americans." *Quartz Africa,* May 30, 2018.

19. Gjelten, *A Nation of Nations,* 121.

20. Jane Madembo "The History of Racism I Didn't Want to Share," *New York Times,* April 7, 2017.

21. Nancy Gibbs, "First. One Giant Leap for Womankind." *Time,* September 18, 2017, 74.

22. Chimamanda Ngozi Adichie, *Americanah* (New York: Knopf, 2013).

23. Chimamanda Ngozi Adichie, "Our Africa Lenses," *Washington Post,* November 13, 2006, http://www.washingtonpost.com/wp-dyn/content/article/2006/11/12/AR2006111200943.html (accessed December 29, 2016).

24. Angene and Jack Wilson heard Shaista Vally speak at the Lexington-Fayette County Urban Council meeting on August 18, 2017, talked with her at length on August 22, and she emailed us a copy of her speech on August 23, 2017.

25. Lora Smith and Tunde Wey, "Dinner in Appalachia: Finding Common Ground in Trump Country," *Food for Thought* (NPR), January 7, 2017.

26. Interview by Angene Wilson with Craig Borie, November 28, 2017.

27. Newcomer Academy PowerPoint presentation by Lisa Hillenbrand and Michael D. Daily, Fayette Country Public Schools and discussion at meeting of Mayor's International Affairs Advisory Commission meeting on February 14, 2018.

28. See Warren County Schools website, http://www.warrencountyschools.org/.

29. Kristen H. Perry and Susan Cantrell, "Supporting Language Development and Enhancing Relationships between School and Home" (presentation at World Refugee Day Summit, Lexington, June 21, 2018).

30. Interview by Angene Wilson with Gabriel Brown, November 29, 2017.

31. Emmanuel Babatunde, "The Recent African Immigrant (RAI) as the Radical

Other," in Yewah and Togunde, *Across the Atlantic*, 68–69, 70. Note that Babatunde gives weight to African culture for African immigrants' success rather than their voluntary minority status in American education.

32. Unrecorded interview by Angene Wilson on the day Adikat's husband, Sim Oyetunji, was interviewed by Jack Wilson.

33. Annetta Miller, *African Wisdom for Life* (compiled as a daily calendar) (Nairobi, Kenya: Pauline, 2005).

34. Mary Pipher, *The Middle of Everywhere: The World's Refugees Come to Our Town* (New York: Harcourt, 2002), 285.

35. L. Robert Kohls, *Survival Kit for Overseas Living: For Americans Planning to Live and Work Abroad* (Yarmouth, ME: Intercultural, 2001). This is another book Angene Wilson has used in cross-cultural classes and training, including for university study abroad students and high school exchange students.

36. Angela Duckworth, *The Key to Success? Grit*, April 2013, www.ted.com.

37. Gilbertson, *Slowly Is the Journey*, 1.

38. Ibid., 28, 49.

39. * Listen to Mamadou Savané talk in his oral history interview in segment "Living in Lexington/First Jobs/Learning English."

4. Connecting and Contributing to Two Continents

1. UNCTAD (United Nations Conference on Trade and Development), *Economic Development in Africa Report 2018: Migration for Structural Transformation*, chapter 5, "Migration and Structural Transformation: The Long-Term View," 3, *https://unctad.org/en/PublicationsLibrary/aidcafrica2018.en.pd (accessed August 29, 2018)*.

2. "Manhattan Transfer," *Quartz Africa Weekly Brief*, March 4, 2018.

3. * Listen to Beatrice Mbayo talk in her oral history interview in the segment "Concern about Her Country."

4. Laura Dawahare, "'Mah Krow' to Beloved Couple, Founders of Ghana's Kentucky Academy," Uknow.uky.edu, November 20, 2013.

5. Guot, *The Lost Is Found*, 137.

6. www.africasunrise.org.

7. Beatrice Mbayo, interview on *Bluegrass Refugee Voices*, Lexington Community Radio, episode 20, November 7, 2016.

8. In 2014 Sub-Saharan African immigrants in Kentucky paid $19.5 million in state and local taxes, according to New American Economy, *Contributions of New Americans in Kentucky*, August 2016, 4.

9. "Foreign-born workers in 2016 make up 5% of all entrepreneurs in the state, despite accounting for 3.6% of Kentucky's population. Their firms generated $315.0 million in business income in 2014. Kentucky firms with at least one immigrant owner also provided jobs to roughly 35,000 Americans in 2007" (ibid., 2). Also see New American Economy, *From Struggle to Resilience: The Economic Impact of Refugees in America*, June 2017.

10. Steve Kaufman, "One Smart Cookie," *Tops Louisville,* February 2017, 72–77; and Kizito Bakery website.

11. Mohamad Diop, interview with Vanessa Grossl, Lexington, Kentucky, February 25, 2018, for Savor: An Immigrant Entrepreneur Oral History, Louie B. Nunn Center for Oral History. Also visits by Angene and Jack Wilson.

12. Aimee Zaring, *Flavors from Home: Refugees in Kentucky Share Their Stories and Comfort Foods* (Lexington: University Press of Kentucky, 2015), 88–91, 97.

13. Kathy Hughes, "Sowing Seeds for a Future," *Community Action Council 2012 Annual Report* (Lexington, KY, 2012), 4.

14. See the following articles for more about these two courses: Marie-Antoinette Sossou, "Teaching Global Poverty in Social Work: A Building Block for Cultural Awareness," *Journal of Global Social Work Practice* 4, no. 1 (May–June 2011); and Marie-Antoinette Sossou and Nicole Dubus, "International Social Work Field Placement or Volunteer Tourism? Developing an Asset-Based Justice-Learning Field Experience," *Journal of Learning Design* 6, no. 1 (2013).

15. * Listen to Kwaku Addo talk in his oral history interview in the segment "Family and Study/Service Tour Connections to Ghana."

16. * Listen to Bankole Thompson talk in his oral history interview in the segment "Special Court for Sierra Leone."

17. Iddah Otieno, "Borderland," in *An Anthology of Short Stories and Poems from East Africa,* ed. Iddah A. Otieno (Austin, TX: Sentia, 2014), 213–15.

5. Family and Identity in the United States

1. Gyekye, *African Cultural Values,* 75. The proverb in the epigraph is from his chapter "The Family."

2. Babatunde, "The Recent Immigrant (RAI) as the Radical Other," 66.

3. Coe, *The Scattered Family,* introduction, especially 14–29. Coe deals particularly with the phenomenon of parents, often mothers, working in the US while their children are sent back to Ghana or remain in Ghana. Her explanation of distributed parenting and fosterage as accepted historical practices in Ghana applies, for instance, to Jemima Roberts, growing up in Liberia, who went to live with her aunt and uncle as a child. She also looks at how US immigration law separates families, the issues of work and child care in the US, and children's expectations of care. She interviewed caregivers and children in Ghana as well as parents in the US.

4. To protect the privacy of the children interviewed, only first names are used.

5. Vivian Tseng, "Unpacking Immigration in Youths' Academic and Occupational Pathways," *Child Development* 77, no. 5 (2006): 1434.

6. * Listen to Abraham Sven-Peters talk in his oral history interview in the segment "Family and Education."

7. Iddah Otieno did these interviews. They are not online or archived.

8. For the story of one year with a class of students in a beginner English-language acquisition class, read Helen Thorpe, *The Newcomers: Finding Refuge, Friendship, and Hope in an American Classroom* (New York: Scribner, 2017). The

students she describes in detail illustrate issues affecting the pace of language learning for the newcomers: language proximity, interruption of schooling, education of parents, trauma, and motivation. *The Girl Who Smiled Beads: A Story of War and What Comes After* by Clemantine Wamariya and Elizabeth Weil is an extraordinary memoir by a young woman who was displaced in the Rwandan conflict and migrated through seven African countries as a child before coming to the United States.

9. For an in-depth look at the role of education and language among African immigrants, see Nicholas Tarlebbea, "An Ethnographic Study on the Role of Education and Language among African Immigrants as They Struggle to Integrate and Succeed in the United States," *Journal of Alternative Perspectives in the Social Sciences* 2 (2010): 854–968.

10. See Samson Omotosho, *Being an African Student: Stories of Opportunity and Determination* (Lanham, MD: University Press of America, 2005). See also Carol Schmid, "Education Achievement, Language-Minority Students, and the New Second Generation," *Sociology of Education* 74 (2001): 72.

11. Angene Wilson did these interviews at school with parent permission. They are not online or archived. The interest in athletics and dreams of being a professional athlete are echoed in the first-person accounts by African immigrant young people in middle and high school in Ken Mujkanovic's *Voices of Bowling Green: Tales of Young Visionaries,* which was self-published by a eighteen-year-old Bosnian American immigrant in 2016 "for my city, Bowling Green, Kentucky." Sixth-grader Augustin and ninth-grader Nibby, who lived in Tanzania before coming to the United States, dream of being NFL players. Ninth-grader Tegra, who was born in Congo, wants to play basketball for the University of Louisville.

12. Angene Wilson was a visitor in the class to which Pacifica spoke.

13. "Education Notes," *Lexington Herald Leader,* November 21, 2017.

14. Email from Aisha, January 31, 2018.

15. Taiye Selasi, *Don't Ask Where I'm from, Ask Me Where I'm a Local,* TED talk, 2015, at www.ted.com (accessed June 15, 2018).

16. Guot, *The Lost Is Found,* chapter 2, "Ritual Scarification," and chapter 17, "Dinka Marriage Customs."

17. * Listen to Ibrahim Bakoush talk in his oral history interview in the segment "Why Immigrants Come/Identity."

6. Transnationality in the Present and Future

1. Lisa Desjardins, "Did Trump Say S***hole? Who Said What about What Trump Said?" *PBS NewsHour,* January 15, 2018.

2. Rick Gladstone, "U. S. Quits Migration Pact, Saying It Infringes on Sovereignty," *New York Times,* December 3, 2017; Megan Specia, "U. N. Agrees on Migration Pact, but U. S. Is Conspicuously Absent," *New York Times,* July 13, 2018; Carol Morello, "U. S. Withdraws from U. N. Human Rights Council over Perceived Bias against Israel," *Washington Post,* June 19, 2018.

3. Lesley Wroughtman, "U. S. to Sharply Limit Refugee Flows to 30,000 in

2019," Reuters, September 17, 2018. See Department of State Office of Admissions, Refugee Processing Center, "Refugee Admission by Region, 1975 through 31 July 2018," which lists 84,994 total refugees admitted in 2016, 53,716 admitted in 2017, and 18,214 admitted by July 31, 2018. Figures for African refugees are 31,624 in 2016, 20,232 in 2017, and 8,061 by July 31, 2018.

4. Mary Louise Kelly, "Looking Back at The Timeline of President Trump's Travel Ban," *All Things Considered* (NPR), June 26, 2018.

5. Visas for citizens of Chad were allowed two weeks before commencement at the University of Kentucky in early May 2018 so the mother of a graduating senior from Chad giving the student speech at one of the commencement ceremonies was able to come. See also Abigail Hauslohner, "Coveted Exemptions from Trump's Travel Ban Remain Elusive for Citizens of Muslim-Majority Countries," *Washington Post,* May 22, 2018.

6. For example, Peter H. Schuck, "Why the 'Diversity Lottery' Needs to End," *New York Times,* November 2, 2017; and Aline Barros, "Merit-Based versus Family-Based Immigration Explained," *VOA,* October 11, 2017.

7. Ilona Bray, "Trump Administration to Extend Liberian DED One Year Before Terminating It," Nolo.com, March 27, 2018 (accessed August 30, 2018). Liberians who were first granted temporary protected status (TPS) because of the civil war have been holding deferred enforced departure (DED), a similar status, since 2007. The main difference is that the DED decision comes directly from the US president as a foreign relations consideration, rather than from the US Department of Homeland Security. President Obama extended DED through March 31, 2018. President Trump announced that he would end DED for Liberians on March 31, 2019, and then extended it until 2020 the day before that deadline.

8. Franklin Foer, "How ICE Went Rogue: Inside America's Unfolding Immigration Crisis." *Atlantic,* September 2018, 60.

9. Among other sources, Angelo Fichera, "Fact Check: What's Really Going on with Immigrant Children Being Detained at the Border?" *USA Today,* June 19, 2018.

10. Stacy Teicher Khadaroo, "Why Some International Students Now Raise Questions about US Study," *Monitor Daily,* July 2, 2018. A February 2017 survey showed interest in coming to the US decreased for one-third of 2,104 prospective international students surveyed. The reasons, listed in order of importance, were: concern about the US presidential administration, worry about travel restrictions, worry about expense, prejudice and/or discrimination against people from my country, US people less welcoming.

11. DiVera Cohn, "What to Know about the Citizenship Question the Census Bureau Is Planning to Ask in 2020," Pew Research Center, March 30, 2018.

12. Michael Anton, "Citizenship Shouldn't Be a Birthright," *Washington Post,* July 18, 2018.

13. Joel Rose, "Trump Administration Moves to Penalize Immigrants for Using Government Benefits." *All Things Considered* (NPR), August 20, 2018.

14. Caitlin Dickerson and Miriam Jordan, "For Many American Families, Abolishing Birthright Citizenship Is 'Unthinkable,'" *New York Times,* October 30, 2018;

and Helene Cooper and Thomas Gibbons-Neff, "They're Trained for War: Now American Troops Are Headed to the U. S. Border," *New York Times,* October 30, 2018.

15. "'Remain in Mexico' Policy for Migrants Creating Ambiguity, Fear?" *Roll Call,* April 5, 2019.

16. Megan Brown, "Record-High 75% of Americans Say Immigration Is a Good Thing." news.gallup.com, June 21, 2018.

17. Peter Ford and Henry Gass, "Migration Roils Global Politics Even as It Ebbs," *Christian Science Monitor,* October 24, 2018.

18. "Ex-Liberian Refugee Eager to Serve Montana Capital That Elected Him Mayor," *VOA News,* November 14, 2017. Collins and his wife fled Liberia in Ghana in the early 1990s when the Liberian civil war began. His wife, who was pregnant with their first child and who had been a high school foreign exchange student in Helena, contacted her host family and was able to get a college scholarship and thus a visa. More than two and a half years later, Wilmot was able to come to the US as a refugee. He began work as a janitor at an elementary school and went on to get undergraduate and graduate degrees, serve in the US Army, and become a US citizen. He is a child protection specialist with Montana's Department of Health and Human Services. In the accompanying video on *VOA News,* Wilmot said: "This country provided us a second chance at life. If I can just give back half of what this community has given me, my life will be complete. I will be thankful." See also Christa Case Bryant, "How a Refugee Turned Mayor Seeks to Transcend the Politics of Divisiveness," *Christian Science Monitor,* December, 28 2018.

19. "Why the World Should Celebrate Mohamad Nasir's 5th Birthday," *Time,* January 15, 2018, 18.

20. Nicholas Kristof, "What We Can Learn from 'S-hole Countries,'" *New York Times,* January 17, 2018.

21. Angene and Jack Wilson met the head of the American Language School in Morocco in October 2017. They heard British geographer Michael Collyer give the talk "Migrant Subjectivities and Crisis Narratives in the Euro-Med Region" at the Tangier American Legation Institute for Moroccan Studies on October 9, 2017. The quotation is from "New Migration Policy Strengthens Morocco's Soft Power in Africa," *North Africa Post,* December 23, 2017.

22. Chidimna Irene Nwoye, "African Countries Are Seeing a Brain Gain as Young Elites Give Up on the West," *Quartz Africa,* November 24, 2017.

23. See Nick Routley, "This Is Africa's Ambitious Free Trade Plan, Mapped," www.weforum.org, April 9, 2019, for a map, chart, and explanation of the patchwork problem, especially with Nigeria's lack of commitment.

24. "Ghana's President Is a Viral Hit After Saying Africa Needs to End Its Aid Dependency," *Quartz Africa,* December 10, 2017. Relevant to the migration of young Africans to Europe are the points made in Hein de Haas, "Situation Analysis: Patterns, Levels and Trends of African migration," draft report from African Regional Consultative Meeting on the Global Compact on Safe, Orderly and Regular Migration (Addis Ababa: United Nations Economic Commission for Africa, October 26 and 27, 2017) (accessed in *AfricaFocus Bulletin,* August 27, 2018). The

idea "of a rapidly increasing 'migration crisis' driven by a growing number of young men and women desperately trying to enter Europe denies the basic facts that the vast majority of Africans move within the continent, Africa is the least migratory region in the world, most Africans move for reasons of work, study and family, and most Africans living abroad are not from the poorest sections of their societies of origin." See also Josephine Appiah-Nyamekye Sanny, Carolyn Logan, and E. Gyimah-Boadi, "In Search of Opportunity: Young and Educated Africans Most Likely to Consider Moving Abroad," *Afrobarometer Dispatch,* March 25, 2019.

25. See Coe, *The Scattered Family,* especially chapter 3, "International Migration and Fosterage: How US Immigration Law Separates Families."

26. Max Fisher, "Israel Picks Identity over Democracy: More Nations May Follow. *New York Times,* July 22, 2018.

27. This is the first line of the last song on J. S. Ondara's *Tales of America* album, which was released in early 2019.

28. Faist, Fauser, and Reisenauer, suggest in *Transnational Migration,* 105, that nonmigrants can be transnational too.

29. Irène Assiba d'Almeida, ed. *A Rain of Words: A Bilingual Anthology of Women's Poetry in Francophone Africa* (Charlottesville: University of Virginia Press, 2009), 79, 81, 83, 85.

30. Irène Assiba d'Almeida, "The Meaning and Status of International Studies in West African Schools," *Theory into Practice* 21, no. 3 (Summer 1982): 194.

31. Achebe, *The Education of a British-Protected Child,* 166.

32. Kwame Anthony Appiah, "The Importance of Elsewhere: In Defense of Cosmopolitanism," *Foreign Affairs,* March–April 2019, 20–26. See also his *Cosmopolitanism: Ethics in a World of Strangers* (New York: Norton, 2006) and *The Lies That Blind: Rethinking Identity* (New York: Norton, 2018). The latter deals with creed, country, color, class, and culture.

33. Clayton Collins, *Christian Science Monitor,* November 20, 2017.

Bibliography

Achebe, Chinua. *The Education of a British-Protected Child.* New York: Knopf, 2009.

Adebajo, Adekeye, and Ismail Rashid, eds. *West Africa's Security Challenges: Building Peace in a Troubled Region.* Boulder: Lynne Rienner, 2004.

Adichie, Chimamanda Ngozi. *Americanah.* New York: Knopf, 2013.

———. "Our Africa Lenses." *Washington Post,* November 13, 2006. http://www.washingtonpost.com/wp-dyn/content/article/2006/11/12/AR2006111200943.html (accessed December 29, 2016).

———. *The Thing around Your Neck.* New York: Knopf, 2009.

Alexander, Peter. "Oscillating Migrants, 'Detribalized Families' and Militancy: Mozambicans on Witbank Collieries, 1918–1927." *Journal of Southern African Studies* 27, no. 3 (2001).

Amadife, Nkechi. "The Non-returning Nigerian Students: Socio-historical Cultural Perspective and Adaptation." PhD diss., University of Kentucky, 2006.

Angelou, Maya. *All God's Children Need Traveling Shoes.* New York: Random House, 1986.

Appiah, Kwame Anthony. *Cosmopolitanism: Ethics in a World of Strangers.* New York: Norton, 2006.

———. "The Importance of Elsewhere: In Defense of Cosmopolitanism," *Foreign Affairs*, March–April 2019, 20–26.

———. *The Lies That Bind: Rethinking Identity*. New York: Norton, 2018.

Arthur, John A. *African Diaspora Identities: Negotiating Culture in Transnational Migration.* Lanham, MD: Lexington Books, 2010.

Asiedu, Kwasi Gyamfi. "A Speech by Ghana's President Calling for Africa to End Its Dependency on the West Is a Viral Hit." *Quartz Africa*, December 4, 2017. https://qz.com/africa/114.

Babatunde, Emmanuel D. "The Recent Immigrant (RAI) as the Radical Other." In *Across the Atlantic: African Immigrants in the United States Diaspora,* edited by Emmanuel Yeweh and 'Dimeji Togunde. Champaign, IL: Common Ground, 2010.

Beah, Ishmael. *A Long Way Gone: Memoirs of a Boy Soldier.* New York: Farrar, Straus and Giroux, 2007.

Betts, Alexander. *Survival Migration: Failed Governance and the Crisis of Displacement.* Ithaca: Cornell University Press, 2013.

Brettell, Caroline. *Anthropology and Migration: Essays on Transnationalism, Ethnicity, and Identity.* New York: Altamira, 2003.

Bulawayo, NoViolet. *We Need New Names.* New York: Little, Brown, 2013.

Campbell, James T. *Middle Passages: African American Journeys to Africa, 1787–2005.* New York: Penguin Books, 2006.

Capps, Randy, Kristen McCabe, and Michael Fix. "Diverse Streams: Black African Migration to the United States." A Project for the Migration Policy Institute's National Center on Immigrant Integration Policy, April 2012. https:www.migrationpolicy.org/sites/default/files/pulbications/CBI-AfricanMigration.pdf.

Castles, Stephen. "Towards a Sociology of Forced Migration and Social Transformation." *Sociology* 37, no. 1 (2003).

Chatty, Dan, and Marcus Colchester, eds. *Conservation and Mobile Indigenous Peoples: Displacement, Forced Settlement and Sustainable Development.* New York: Berghahn Books, 2002.

Ciment, James. *Another America: The Story of Liberia and the Former Slaves Who Ruled It.* New York: Hill and Wang, 2013.

Coates, Ta-Neshi. *Between the World and Me.* New York: Spiegel and Grau, 2015.

———. *We Were Eight Years in Power: An American Tragedy.* New York: One World, 2017.

Coe, Cati. *The Scattered Family: Parenting, African Migrants, and Global Inequality.* Chicago: University of Chicago Press, 2014.

Cohen, Roberta, and Francis Deng. *Masses in Flight: The Global Crisis of Internal Displacement.* Washington, DC: Brookings Institution, 1998.

Cooper, Frederick. *Africa since 1940: The Past of the Present.* Cambridge: Cambridge University Press, 2002.

Cooper, Helene. *The House at Sugar Beach: In Search of a Lost African Childhood.* New York: Simon and Schuster, 2008.

———. *Madame President: The Extraordinary Journey of Ellen Johnson Sirleaf.* New York, Simon and Schuster, 2017.

Cooper, Helene, and Thomas Gibbons-Neff. "They're Trained for War: Now American Troops Are Headed to the U.S. Border." *New York Times,* October 30, 2018.

Crush, Jonathan. "Migrations Past: An Historical Overview of Cross-Border Movements in Southern Africa." In *On Borders: Perspectives on International Migration in Southern Africa,* edited by David A. McDonald. New York: Palgrave Macmillan, 2000.

D'Alisera, JoAnn. *An Imagined Geography: Sierra Leonean Muslims in America.* Philadelphia: University of Pennsylvania Press, 2004.

d'Almeida, Irène Assiba. "The Meaning and Status of International Studies in West African Schools." *Theory into Practice* 21, no. 3 (Summer 1982).

———, ed. *A Rain of Words: A Bilingual Anthology of Women's Poetry in Francophone Africa.* Charlottesville: University of Virginia Press, 2009.

Davis, Merlene. "In Liberia They Lived on the Run." *Lexington Herald Leader,* August 24, 2003.

de Haas, Hein, "Situation Analysis: Patterns, Levels and Trends of African Migration." Draft report from African Regional Consultative Meeting on the Global Compact on Safe, Orderly and Regular Migration. Addis Ababa: United Nations Economic Commission for Africa, October 26 and 27, 2017. https://uneca.org/

sites/default/files/uploaded-documents/Social Development/Global-Compact -2017 /drivers-of-migration-in-Africa (accessed August 27, 2018).

Desjardins, Lisa. "Did Trump Say S***hole? Who Said What about What Trump Said?" *PBS NewsHour,* January 15, 2018.

Dickerson, Caitlin, and Miriam Jordan. "For Many American Families, Abolishing Birthright Citizenship Is 'Unthinkable.'" *New York Times,* October 30, 2018.

Dyson, Michael Eric. *Tears We Cannot Stop: A Sermon to White America.* New York: St. Martin's, 2017.

Erpenbeck, Jenny. *Go, Went, Gone.* New York: New Directions, 2017.

Faist, Thomas. "Extension *du domaine de la lutte:* International Migration and Security Before and After 11 September 2001." *International Migration Review* 36, no. 1 (2002).

Faist, Thomas, Margit Fauser, and Eveline Reisenauer. *Transnational Migration.* Cambridge: Polity, 2013.

Falola, Toyin, ed. *Africa.* Vol. 4, *The End of Colonial Rule, Nationalism and Decolonization.* Durham: Carolina Academic Press, 2002.

Fichera, Angelo. "Fact Check: What's Really Going on with Immigrant Children Being Detained at the Border? " *USA Today,* June 19, 2018. https:www.factcheck.org/2018/06/qa-on-border-detention-of-children (accessed August 30, 2018).

Foer, Franklin. "How ICE Went Rogue: Inside America's Unfolding Immigration Crisis." *Atlantic,* September 2018.

Forna, Aminatta. *The Memory of Love.* New York: Grove, 2010.

Foster, Kevin Michael. "Coming to Terms: A Discussion of John Ogbu's Cultural-Ecological Theory of Minority Academic Achievement." *Intercultural Education* 12, no. 4 (December 2004).

Friends of the Congo. http://www.friendsofthecongo.org (accessed January 3, 2017).

Gbowee, Leymah. *Mighty Be Our Powers: How Sisterhood, Prayer, and Sex Changed a Nation at War.* New York: Beast Books, 2011.

Gibbs, Nancy. "First. One Giant Leap for Womankind." *Time,* September 18, 2017.

Gibson, Campbell, and Kay Jung. "Historical Census Statistics on the Foreign-Born Population of the United States: 1850 to 2000." US Census Bureau working paper no. 81, February 2006.

Gilbertson, Keith, ed. *Slowly Is the Journey: Stories from Bluegrass Community and Technical College ESL Students.* Bloomington, IN: Authorhouse, 2016.

Gjelten, Tom. *A Nation of Nations: A Great American Immigration Story.* New York: Simon and Schuster, 2015.

Gladstone, Rick. "U.S. Quits Migration Pact, Saying It Infringes on Sovereignty." *New York Times,* December 3, 2017.

Grady, Sandra. *Impoverished Adolescence: Somali Bantu Teenage Refugees in America.* Madison University of Wisconsin Press, 2015.

Guot, Jacob Thon. *The Lost Is Found: A "Lost Boy's" Story of Faith, Hope, Charity, and Love.* Oviedo, FL: EA Books, 2017.

Gyasi, Yaa. *Homegoing.* New York: Knopf, 2016.

Gyekye, Kwame. *African Cultural Values.* Accra, Ghana: Sankofa, 1996.

Hamid, Mohsin. *Exit West.* New York: Riverhead Books, 2017.

Heisler, Barbara S. "The Sociology of Immigration: From Assimilation to Segmented Integration, from the American Experience to the Global Arena." In *Migration Theory: Talking across Disciplines,* edited by Caroline B. Brettell and James F. Hollifield. New York: Routledge, 2000.

hooks, bell. *Belonging: A Culture of Place.* New York: Routledge, 2009.

Hughes, Kathy. "Sowing Seeds for a Future." *Community Action Council 2012 Annual Report.* Lexington, KY, 2012.

Indra, Doreen, ed. *Engendering Forced Migration: Theory and Practice.* New York: Berghahn Books, 1999.

Jones, Reece. *Violent Borders: Refugees and the Right to Move.* London: Verso, 2016.

Kane, Abdoulaye, and Todd H. Leedy. "African Patterns of Migration in a Global Era: New Perspectives." In *African Migrations: Patterns and Perspectives,* edited by Abdoulaye Kane and Todd H. Leedy. Bloomington: Indiana University Press, 2013.

Kaufman, Steve. "One Smart Cookie." *Tops Louisville,* February 2017.

Khadaroo, Stacy Teicher. "Why Some International Students Now Raise Questions about US Study." *Monitor Daily,* July 2, 2018. https://wwwcsmonitor.com.../2018/...International-students-to-US-Do-you-really-want.

Kohls, L. Robert. *Survival Kit for Overseas Living: For Americans Planning to Live and Work Abroad.* Yarmouth, ME: Intercultural, 2001.

Kuhlman, Tom. "The Economic Integration of Refugees in Developing Countries: A Research Model." *Journal of Refugee Studies* 4, no. 1 (1991).

"Louisville Catholic Teacher Resigns amid Ebola Crisis." *Louisville Courier-Journal,* November 3, 2014.

Lucas, David, and Barbara Edgar. "Zimbabwe's Exodus to Australia," *SAMP Policy Brief* 30 (2015). http://imrc.ca/wp-content/uploads/2015/05/PB-30-Zimbabwes-Exodus-to-Australia.pdf (accessed December 12, 2016).

Madembo, Jane. "The History of Racism I Didn't Want to Share." *New York Times,* April 7, 2017.

Malkki, Liisa H. *Purity and Exile: Violence, Memory, and National Cosmology among Hutu Refugees in Tanzania.* Chicago: University of Chicago, 1995.

Mamdani, Mahmood. *When Victims Become Killers: Colonialism, Nativism and the Genocide in Rwanda.* Princeton: Princeton University Press, 2002.

Mandela, Nelson, and Mandla Langa. *Dare Not Linger: The Presidential Years.* New York: Farrar, Straus and Giroux, 2017.

Manning, Patrick. *The African Diaspora: A History through Culture.* New York: Columbia University Press, 2009.

Mason, Bobbie Ann. *Clear Springs.* New York: Random House, 1999.

Matar, Hisham. *The Return: Fathers, Sons and the Land in Between.* New York: Random House, 2016.

Mbue, Imbolo. *Behold the Dreamers.* New York: Random House, 2016.

Meek, James Gordon, and Brian Ross. "Terrorists Once Used Refugee Program to Settle in US." *ABC News,* November 18, 2015. http://abcnews.

go.com/International/terrorists-refugee-program-settle-us/story?id=35252500 (accessed September 14, 2016).

Migration Policy Institute. "Regions of Birth for Immigrants in the United States, 1960–Present." https://www.migrationpolicy.org/data/state-profiles/state/demographics/US (accessed August 10, 2018).

Miles, William F. S. "Postcolonial Borderland Legacies of Anglo-French Partition in West Africa." *African Studies Review* 58, no. 3 (2015): 191–213.

Miller, Annetta. *African Wisdom for Life.* Nairobi, Kenya: Pauline, 2005.

Misako, Fraternel D. Amuri. *The Brain Waste of Foreign-Educated Professionals in the United States: Employment Profiles and Policy Issues versus Community Capitals* (European University Publishing, 2018).

Moodie, Dunbar, with Viviave Ndatshe. *Going for Gold: Men, Mines, and Migration.* Berkeley: University of California Press, 1994.

Morello, Carol. "U.S. Withdraws from U.N. Human Rights Council over Perceived Bias against Israel." *Washington Post,* June 19, 2018.

Mosendz, Polly. "In Light of Paris Attacks, 26 GOP Governors, One Democrat to Refuse Syrian Refugees." *Newsweek,* November 16, 2015. https://www.newsweek.com/after-paris-attacks-26-republican-governors-one-democrat-refuse-syrian-394859 (accessed August 2, 2016).

Mujkanovic, Ken. *Voices of Bowling Green: Tales of Young Visionaries.* Self-published, 2016.

Musoni, Francis. *Border Jumping and Coltrol in Migration Southern Africa.* Bloomington: Indiana University Press, forthcoming.

Nakhjavani, Bahiyyih. *Us & Them.* Stanford, CA: Redwood, 2017.

New American Economy. *From Struggle to Resilience: The Economic Impact of Refugees in America,* June 2017. www.newamericaneconomy.org;wp-content/uploads-2017/NAE_Refugees_V5.pdf (accessed August 29, 2018).

Nguyen, Viet Thanh. *Nothing Ever Dies: Vietnam and the Memory of War.* Cambridge, MA: Harvard University Press, 2016.

Nkrumah, Kwame. *Ghana: The Autobiography of Kwame Nkrumah.* Edinburgh: Thomas Nelson and Sons, 1959.

Nugent, Paul. "Arbitrary Lines and the People's Minds: A Dissenting View on Colonial Boundaries in West Africa." In *African Boundaries: Barriers, Conduits and Opportunities,* edited by Paul Nugent and Anthony Asiwaju. New York: Pinter, 1996.

Nwoye, Chidinma Irene. "African Countries Are Seeing a Brain Gain as Young Elites Give Up on the West." *Quartz Africa,* November 24, 2017. https://qz.com/africa/112.

Nyhan, Pat. *New Mainers: Portraits of Our Immigrant Neighbors.* Gardiner, ME: Tilbury House, 2009.

Ogbu, John U., and Herbert D. Simons. "Voluntary and Involuntary Minorities: A Cultural-Ecological Theory of School Performance with Some Implications for Education." *Anthropology and Education Quarterly* 29 (1998).

Omotosho, Samson. *Being an African Student: Stories of Opportunity and Determination.* Lanham, MD: University Press of America, 2005.

Otieno, Iddah Aoko. *Kenyan Public Universities in the Age of Internationalization: Challenges and Prospects.* Lanham, MD: Lexington Books, 2018.

Pallitto, Robert, and Josiah Heyman. "Theorizing Cross-Border Mobility: Surveillance, Security and Identity." *Surveillance and Society* 5, no. 3 (2008).

Peil, Margaret. "Host Reactions: Aliens in Ghana." In *Strangers in African Societies,* edited by William A. Shack, and Elliot P. Skinner. Berkeley: University of California Press, 1979.

Pelfrey, Ron. Interview, October 4, 2005. Returned Peace Corps Volunteers Oral History Project. Kentucky Digital Library, Nunn Center for Oral History, University of Kentucky, Lexington.

Pipher, Mary. *The Middle of Everywhere: The World's Refugees Come to Our Town.* New York: Harcourt, 2002.

Rawlence, Ben. *City of Thorns: Nine Lives in the World's Largest Refugee Camp.* New York: Picador, 2016.

Rose, Dan M., and Ron Vissing. "US Should Put Moratorium on Immigration." http://www.kentucky.com/opinion/op-ed/article45549861.html (accessed October 10, 2016).

Rose, Joel. "Trump Administration Moves to Penalize Immigrants for Using Government Benefits." *All Things Considered* (NPR), August 20, 2018.

Rosling, Hans, Ola Rosling, and Anna Rosling Ronnlund. *Factfulness: Ten Reasons We're Wrong about the World—and Why Things Are Better Than You Think.* New York: Flatiron Books, 2018.

Sanny, Josephine Appiah-Nyamekye, Carolyn Logan, and E. Gyimah-Boadi, "In Search of Opportunity: Young and Educated Africans Most Likely to Consider Moving Abroad." *Afrobarometer Dispatch,* March 25, 2019. http://tinyurl-com/53nunrZ.

Schachtman, Tom. *Airlift to America: How Barack Obama Sr., John F. Kennedy, Tom Mboya, and 800 East African Students Changed Their World and Ours.* New York: St. Martin's, 2009.

Schiller, Nina Glick. "Transmigrants and Nation-State: Something Old and Something New in the US Immigrant Experience." In *The Handbook of International Migration: The American Experience,* edited by Charles Hirschman et al. New York: Russell Sage Foundation, 1999.

Schiller, Nina Glick, and Georges Eugene Fouron. *Georges Woke Up Laughing: Long-Distance Nationalism and the Search for Home.* Durham: Duke University Press, 2001.

Schmid, Carol. "Education Achievement, Language-Minority Students, and the New Second Generation." *Sociology of Education* 74 (2001).

Schmidt, Elizabeth. *Foreign Intervention in Africa from the Cold War to the War on Terror.* New York: Cambridge University Press, 2013.

Schultheis, Michael J. "Refugees in Africa: The Geopolitics of Forced Displacement." *African Studies Review* 32, no. 1 (1989).

Selasi, Taiye. *Don't Ask Where I'm from, Ask Me Where I'm a Local.* TED talk, 2015. https"/www.ted.com talks taiye_selasi.

———. *Ghana Must Go.* New York: Penguin, 2013.

Shillington, Kevin. *History of Africa.* 3rd ed. New York: Palgrave Macmillan, 2012.

Smith, Lora, and Tunde Wey. "Dinner in Appalachia: Finding Common Ground in Trump Country." *Food for Thought* (NPR), January 7, 2017.

Sossou, Marie-Antoinette. "Teaching Global Poverty in Social Work: A Building Block for Cultural Awareness." *Journal of Global Social Work Practice* 4, no. 1 (May–June 2011).

Sossou, Marie-Antoinette, and Chiston A. Adedoyin. "A Qualitative Study of Problems and Parental Challenges of African Refugee Parents in the USA." *Professional Development: The International Journal of Continuing Social Work Education* 15, no. 2 (2012).

Sossou, Marie-Antoinette, and Nicole Dubus. "International Social Work Field Placement or Volunteer Tourism? Developing an Asset-Based Justice-Learning Field Experience." *Journal of Learning Design* 6, no. 1 (2013).

Sparks, Randy J. *Where the Negroes Are Master: An African Port in the Era of the Slave Trade.* Cambridge, MA: Harvard University Press, 2014.

Spears, Valerie Honeycutt. "Academy for Immigrant, Refugee Students Planned for Fayette." *Lexington Herald Leader,* June 19, 2017.

Specia, Megan. "U.N. Agrees on Migration Pact, but U.S. Is Conspicuously Absent." *New York Times,* July 13, 2018.

Stoller, Paul. *Jaguar: A Story of Africans in America.* Chicago: University of Chicago Press, 1999.

———. *Money Has No Smell: The Africanization of New York City.* Chicago: University of Chicago Press, 2002.

Storti, Craig. *Figuring Foreigners Out: A Practical Guide.* Yarmouth, ME: Intercultural, 1999.

Tarlebbea, Nicholas. "An Ethnographic Study on the Role of Education and Language among African Immigrants as They Struggle to Integrate and Succeed in the United States." *Journal of Alternative Perspectives in the Social Sciences* 2 (2010).

Thompson, Paul. *The Voice of the Past: Oral History.* New York: Oxford University Press, 2000.

Thorpe, Helen. *The Newcomers: Finding Refuge, Friendship, and Hope in an American Classroom.* New York: Scribner, 2017.

Tseng, Vivian. "Unpacking Immigration in Youths' Academic and Occupational Pathways." *Child Development* 77, no. 5 (2006).

Tutu, Desmond. *The Words of Desmond Tutu.* Selected by Naomi Tutu. New York: Newmarket, 1989.

UNCTAD (United Nations Conference on Trade and Development). *Economic Development in Africa Report 2018: Migration for Structural Transformation.* https://unctad.org/en/PublicationsLibrary/aidcafrica2018.en.pd. (accessed August 29, 2018).

UNHCR (United Nations High Commissioner for Refugees). *Convention and Protocol Relating to the Status of Refugees,* 1951. http://www.unhcr.org/3b66c2aa10.html (accessed November 27, 2016).

van Dijk, Han, Dick Foeken, and Kiky van Til. "Population Mobility in Africa:

An Overview." In *Mobile Africa: Changing Patterns of Movement in Africa and Beyond,* edited by Mirjam De Bruijn, Rijk A. van Dijk, and Dick Foeken. Leiden: Brill, 2001.

Van Reybrouck, David. *Congo: The Epic History of a People.* New York: Harper Collins, 2010.

Walker, Frank X. *Affrilachia.* Lexington, KY: Old Crow, 2000.

wa Thiong'o, Ngugi. *Moving the Centre: The Struggle for Cultural Freedoms.* London: James Currey; Nairobi: EAEP; Portsmouth, NH: Heinemann, 1993.

———. *Wizard of the Crow.* New York: Pantheon Books, 2006.

White, Gregory. *Climate Change and Migration: Security and Borders in a Warming World.* Oxford: Oxford University Press, 2011.

Wiley, Bell I., ed. *Slaves No More: Letters from Liberia, 1833–1869.* Lexington: University Press of Kentucky, 1980.

Wilson, Angene H. *Africa On My Mind: Educating Americans for Fifty Years; Living Peace Corps' Third Goal.* Oakland, CA: Peace Corps Writers, 2013.

———. "Teaching about Africa: A Review of Middle/Secondary Textbooks and Supplemental Materials." *Social Studies* 86, no. 6 (November–December 1995).

"Why Nations Need a Mass Awakening to Mass Killings." *Christian Science Monitor,* November 27, 2017.

Yewah, Emmanuel, and 'Dimeji Togunde, eds. *Across the Atlantic: African Immigrants in the United States Diaspora.* Champaign, IL: Common Ground, 2010.

Zaring, Aimee. *Flavors from Home: Refugees in Kentucky Share Their Stories and Comfort Foods.* Lexington: University Press of Kentucky, 2015.

Zolberg, Aristide R. *A Nation by Design: Immigration Policy in the Fashioning of America.* New York: Russell Sage Foundation, 2006.

Zong, Jie, and Jeanne Batalova. *Sub-Saharan African Immigrants in the United States.* Migration Policy Institute, May 3, 2017.

Index

Kentucky Remembered: An Oral History Series

James C. Klotter,
Terry L. Birdwhistell,
and
Douglas A. Boyd,
Series Editors

Books in the Series

Conversations with Kentucky Writers
edited by L. Elisabeth Beattie

Conversations with Kentucky Writers II
edited by L. Elisabeth Beattie

Barry Bingham
Barry Bingham

Crawfish Bottom: Recovering a Lost Kentucky Community
Douglas A. Boyd

This Is Home Now: Kentucky's Holocaust Survivors Speak
Arwen Donahue and Rebecca Gayle Howell

Burley: Kentucky Tobacco in a New Century
Ann K. Ferrell

Freedom on the Border: An Oral History of the Civil Rights Movement in Kentucky
Catherine Fosl and Tracy E. K'Meyer

Arab and Jewish Women in Kentucky: Stories of Accommodation and Audacity
Nora Rose Moosnick

Voices of African Imigrants in Kentucky: Migration, Identity, and Transnationality
Francis Musoni, Iddah Otieno, Angene Wilson, and Jack Wilson

Bert Combs the Politician
George W. Robinson

Tobacco Culture: Farming Kentucky's Burley Belt
John van Willigen and Susan C. Eastwood

Food and Everyday Life on Kentucky Family Farms, 1920–1950
John van Willigen and Anne van Willigen

Voices from the Peace Corps: Fifty Years of Kentucky Volunteers
Angene Wilson and Jack Wilson